MONTREAL
The New Cité

Also by Gerald Clark

Impatient Giant: Red China Today
The Coming Explosion in Latin America
Canada: The Uneasy Neighbour

MONTREAL
The New Cité

Gerald Clark

McClelland and Stewart

The Canadian Publishers
McClelland and Stewart Limited
25 Hollinger Road
Toronto, M4B 3G2

Canadian Cataloguing in Publication Data
Clark, Gerald, 1918-
   Montreal : the new cité

ISBN 0-7710-2116-X

1. Montréal (Quebec) – Description.
2. Montréal (Quebec). I. Title: Montreal : the new cité.

FC2947.3.C52   971.4′28104   C82-094509-9
F1054.5.M84C52

Printed and bound in Canada

In memory of Ruthie

Contents

Preface

This is a report on Montreal today: political, social, cultural, economic. Montreal is not a decaying city. It is a reshaped city: a reflection of the Province of Quebec, dominated by a fresh wave of French rather than English Canadians. This is a substantial development that should be regarded in an affirmative sense. Regardless of the doubts of many English-speaking residents, the quality of Montreal is positive and on the ascendancy. The attitude of the francophone majority towards the anglophone minority is supportive – provided the anglophones accept new dimensions of life. Even such a contentious measure as Bill 101, setting out rules of language, can be looked on as a challenging evolution that removes much of the emotional appeal of separatism.

I am a Montrealer, born and educated here. I have, however, the advantage of a newspaper career that took me abroad for many years into almost every country of the world. Therefore I approach my own city with some kind of objectivity, as though it were a foreign city. I cannot make an easy villain of the governing Parti Québécois; and despite the party's renewed cry for sovereignty, I believe that any public enthusiasm for the pursuit of Quebec independence is on the decline. As for Montreal's future, the reader will have to decide for himself or herself whether I am excessively optimistic.

Included in my research were more than 200 interviews, with politicians such as Premier René Lévesque and Mayor Jean Drapeau; celebrity sports figures like Maurice "Rocket" Richard and Ken Dryden; stars of the cultural scene, among them Yvon Deschamps and Mordecai Richler; and business leaders represented by Paul Desmarais, Charles Bronfman, and Rowland C. Frazee. Mrs. Claude Ryan and Gabrielle Roy are here, but the men and women whom I do not name deserve an apology. If they remain unidentified, their information and thoughts helped substantially. Obviously, I alone am responsible for the book's theme and conclusions.

Perversity from the Start

There they lay at anchor, the *Netuno*, the *Marina del Cantone*, the *Jalamurugan* – not quite as romantic as the nineteenth century brigantines and barques whose places they took, but very important. The *Netuno*, a Brazilian motor vessel on the run between Montreal and Recife, was loading containers and general cargo. The *Marina del Cantone*, Italian, on her first visit here, was picking up flour for Cuba, while the *Jalamurugan*, a 10,000-ton freighter of the Scindia Steam Navigation Company of India, was hauling containers for stops at many other ports. In the old days – even as recently as twenty or twenty-five years ago – ships from India were commanded by British officers while the crews were native. But now the entire complement was Indian. Much had changed, in the world and in Montreal. Only twenty-four ocean-going ships were in harbour on this fine July day of 1981, compared with something like forty-nine large sailing and twenty-one ocean steamers 100 years ago. Included then among the Allan Line ships under steam (and even these relied on a great deal of auxiliary sail), was the magnificent liner *Parisian*. The *Parisian*, built by a Montreal family for the lucrative trade between Britain and North America, was the wonder of the time, with the pillars in the elegant saloon decorated in leather.

Alas, on this July day in 1981, not a single passenger ship was docked at any berth, nor was any liner worthy of note due in for the year, unless one counted the occasional cruise ship. Nor were hordes of seamen making their way across Common Street to Joe Beef's tavern, where, in previous times, they were assailed not only by the aroma of beer but the smell of live buffalo. Joe, an immigrant from County Cavan, Ireland, had kept an animal – rather tame, but a buffalo nonetheless – down the stairs, in the cellar. The tavern still

11

functions as a restaurant and bar, though Joe himself departed the world on June 15, 1889. The street is now called Rue de la Commune and the owner is named Luc Drouin. He depends for patronage on secretaries and salesmen and the residents of Old Montreal, the recaptured and charming quarter of which Joe Beef's is part.

Luc Drouin, thirty-five, is not even a professional restaurateur. He fell into it, in 1978, from his construction business, because the previous owner couldn't pay for renovations and repairs he had ordered on the three storey stone building. But one should not grieve if the sailors and stevedores are not there in large numbers. Drouin says the business potential is good. He shut it down in 1982 while working on a scheme to re-open as a combined brasserie and Joe Beef Museum. There is plenty of memorabilia around, including an ad that says, "Two-eyed beefsteak with tripes, 5 cents." Even more to the point, Luc Drouin, while hanging on to the acquisition which he loves, intends also to return to the construction trade – such is the up-surge in building and restoration, not only in Old Montreal but in the rest of the city. As for the absence of sailors and stevedores from the premises, even that, curiously, is a sign of prosperity in the port of Montreal. The old ships, which used to shelter at the bottom of Rue St. François-Xavier or Rue St. Sulpice, are now scattered along the fourteen-mile stretch of the harbour, with most of them concentrated in the east end, several miles from Joe Beef's. The pattern of shipping has changed drastically, with fewer vessels and men required to do a more massive job than in the past.

Montreal began its rise as a major seaport and city because of a revolution in technology and fuel. Its current revival – and it is a major one – can be attributed to another revolution in technology and fuel. The first burst forward came in 1809, when John Molson, a Montreal brewer, built a steamship, *Accommodation*, only two years after Robert Fulton, the American inventor, designed his successful steamboat. Until 1809, Quebec City was the important port, for it was too hazardous for sailing vessels to come all the way upriver through the strong St. Mary's current on the approaches to Montreal. *Accommodation*, powered not by wind but by a wood-fired boiler, easily made the run. Within two decades steam tugs regularly hauled sailing ships past St. Mary's current, causing Quebec City's decline and setting up Montreal as the principal port of entry to Canada and the gateway to commerce with the interior of the continent. Montreal still suffered a handicap, winter, which meant that it could function only eight or nine months of the year. More grievously, it was again bypassed in the 1960's, after the opening of the St. Lawrence Seaway, when vessels went straight to Toronto, Chicago, or Milwaukee on the Great Lakes.

Many people still think the port is closed in the winter. But, with better navigational devices, improvement in the channel, and construction of an ice boom, it became operational the year round in 1963, when seven Norwegian ships sailed up the river in dead of winter as pioneers. What is also hardly recognized is that a technological breakthrough, comparable to that represented by *Accommodation*, has taken place. It is called "containerization," the method of packing cargo in boxes. Instead of ships requiring a fortnight to load or unload, as in the old conventional way, huge cranes lift or lower the boxes to handle a vessel's capacity in two or three days.

The revolution in Montreal began in 1968, when the first container service was set up by Manchester Liners Limited. That year, 3 per cent of cargo was carried in boxes; now it is at least 75 per cent, making Montreal once again the busiest and most profitable port in the country. Indeed, in 1980 and 1981 it had to turn away business – two million tonnes of loose dry bulk (chemicals or gravel or limestone) – because of a lack of storage space. Much of the waterfront is a ribbon, in places no wider than 100 metres. Three levels of government – municipal, federal, and provincial – are trying to work out a program for expansion of facilities. The upsurge in traffic was created not only by the development of the container, but, as in the time of *Accommodation*, by fuel, in this instance oil. Thirty per cent of US exports originate in the midwest, with Chicago the hub. After the 1973 Arab-Israeli war, when fuel costs escalated, shippers took a closer look at Montreal, which, thanks to its position inland on the St. Lawrence River, is 315 miles nearer Liverpool than is New York. Exporters, aiming for Liverpool or Le Havre or Rotterdam, found it cheaper to move goods to Montreal by rail, for trans-shipment by sea, than through New York.

Higher tolls, and the crew wages which must be paid during the slow process of passage through locks, also reduce competition from the St. Lawrence Seaway. In addition, proper management plus labour peace and security have altered the face of a harbour once moribund. "It doesn't matter what your fuel advantage is," says Nicholas Beshwaty, the port's general manager. "If you have poor labour relations and pilferage, the rest means nothing. Ours is a fragile industry." Beshwaty, who has worked for the federal port authority for thirty-seven of his sixty-one years, knows whereof he speaks. His memory takes him back to the time when murder on the waterfront was not uncommon. As recently as 1973, insurance companies placed an extra premium on shipments through Montreal. But now a large police force, made up partly of former Royal Canadian Mounted Police officers, has stimulated the publication *Ports of the World*, a guide for brokers, to comment on the high standards and conclude that "pilferage is not a problem." Perhaps even more dramatic is the establishment of labour peace on a waterfront that was notorious for strikes. In 1973, when police issued twenty tickets because longshoremen were parked illegally, the port emptied in twenty minutes. Today dockers still get tickets for unlawful parking, but they don't walk out. Because of a contract that will guarantee tranquillity at least until 1984 (paying longshoremen $31,000 a year), and because of containerization, employers hire half as many as in past years.

Montreal is the only port in the world where stevedores are called in by computer as needed, in contrast to the old days when they reported to a common hiring hall on the chance that work was available. If a man is allergic to flour, the computer knows it and automatically switches him to other cargo. The port is a city within a city, with 10,000 people – longshoremen, railwaymen, truckers – working there. But one would hardly suspect it. Vessels are so widely dispersed, with far fewer than a mere generation ago, that a casual visitor comes away with the erroneous impression that business is slack. A ship like the *Jalamurugan*, which holds 1,000 containers, does what ten vessels used to do, even if crew members don't make it to Joe Beef's. The confluence of favourable factors enabled the port of Montreal to thrive in 1981, reaching a record profit of $18.6 million and handling twenty-five million tonnes of freight. "We've never been so enthusiastic about the future," says Beshwaty.

Montreal is a French-Canadian city. English-speaking Canadians continue to occupy a vital place, but they no longer dominate it. If that sounds like a truism, it is only one of many simple facts that must be absorbed before an individual can begin to understand the profound changes that have taken place in the last two decades. Montreal is not a dying city; it is, instead, a changing city. It has

14

always been a changing city, inhabited by a people who come close to anarchy at times and show a strong streak of independence or non-conformity at all times. They can elect as prime minister of the country a fervent federalist such as Pierre Elliott Trudeau; as premier of the province an ardent separatist, René Lévesque; and, most archly of all, a mayor like Jean Drapeau. Drapeau goes his own way, running the City Council and the city itself with mild authoritarianism – because that's the way Montrealers want their city to be run. And that's the way it started out, a kind of city-state, or colony within a colony. Whatever the purists among historians say about the definition, the fact is that when the founder of Montreal, Paul de Chomedey, Sieur de Maisonneuve, arrived in 1642, he was his own man. There may have been, in theory, a French overseer in Quebec City, but as far as Maisonneuve and his band of zealots – forty men, four women, and a few children – were concerned, they were answerable only to two authorities: God, and, in Paris, La Société des messieurs et dames de Notre-Dame de Montréal, (the Society of Gentlemen and Ladies of Notre-Dame of Montreal), who paid out 600,000 livres for the conversion to Christianity of the Indians, "les sauvages," of New France.

Maisonneuve called it "Ville Marie," after the Virgin Mary. But almost from the start his disciples insisted on referring to it as "le Montréal," so that it could have equal status with what others, up in Quebec, were calling "le Canada." They were a fairly homogeneous and dedicated group, under Maisonneuve, but even he had occasional trouble with them. When the first horses arrived, the colonists insisted on racing after church; and if the service lasted too long, they walked out early so the competition could commence. The clergy complained. Graeme Decarie, professor of history at Concordia University, suspects that what really bothered the priests was not so much disrespect for religion – all the colonists were believers – but rather the impression that the colonists were not keeping their place in the social order; that is, the lower classes were a threat to the higher classes. But Decarie, who is forty-nine, and can trace his ancestry back to the seven members of the Descarry family when the first census was taken in 1666 (Montreal had a population of 627), is a bit of an iconoclast in the eyes of historians who stick to conventional political and economic interpretation. Decarie (the "Graeme" arises from Scottish infiltration), leans more heavily towards social evolution, and in 1980 was co-founder of the Centre for the Study of

Anglophones, to offset the stereotypes which depict all English Montrealers as capitalists or oppressors.

Of course there were no English among the Maisonneuve group, just the French mystics who exhibited their self-reliant streak right from the start and made Montreal the nearest thing to a Venice or Florence before the Renaissance; or, perhaps, a member of the Hanseatic League, especially Hamburg, whose unrestrained inhabitants flourished in the fifteenth century. The fact is that Maisonneuve, as governor of the seigniory and island of Montreal, was accountable, in his own mind, only to the Society of Montreal in Paris. Indeed, when a fresh governor general of New France, Pierre Voyer, Vicomte d'Argenson, landed in Quebec on July 11, 1658, Maisonneuve deliberately ignored him, neglecting even the normal courtesy of acknowledging his arrival. D'Argenson, frustrated, wrote Paris: "I must tell you about Montreal, a place that makes so much noise and amounts to so little." Three years later another governor, Baron d'Avaugour, replaced d'Argenson and also promptly encountered resistance. Wanting to reorganize the fur trade and improve the colony's finances, he proposed the establishment of a public warehouse in Ville Marie, for which fees, naturally, would be paid. Montrealers, under Maisonneuve's inspiration, took this as a threat to their own autonomy and demonstrated angrily. D'Avaugour, in turn, called it sedition and sent off two officers of justice from Quebec to take proper action. But they drowned near Trois-Rivières.

The condition of confusion – or one might say wilfulness – ended with the departure of Maisonneuve for France in 1665. This also marked a finish to a particularly heroic period in the city's history, but not to its record of perversity. When Louis de Buade, Compte de Frontenac, the swashbuckling governor of New France in the 1670's, tried to conscript Montreal civilians to use their canoes to help soldiers in war against the Indians, they resisted – even if it meant a protester was thrown in jail. But one should not assume that such bloody-mindedness was confined to francophones. (For purposes of simplicity, the designation "francophones" will be henceforth employed to describe all those whose mother tongue is French; the rest, even if of Italian or Greek descent, will be referred to as "anglophones.") In the 1840's Montreal merchants decided they faced a better future with the US than with Britain, and set out to prove it by signing an annexation manifesto, having first joined a mob in burning down the House of Parliament in Montreal. Prominent

16

among the insurrectionists was an anglophone, John Molson II, son of the brewer.

Montreal may be a unique city, pioneered by zealots, but the mercantile element was never far behind. Jean-Claude Robert, a professor of history at the Université du Québec à Montréal, says sardonically, "It was probably a merchant who held the cross for Maisonneuve when he landed."

The merchants who fled Montreal in the 1970's, particularly after the Parti Québécois came to power, were not the first to set off a wave of panic or be a part of it. Throughout its history Montreal has undergone fluctuations in its fortunes, exemplified by the social and economic stresses that accompanied the wave of sick and impoverished Irish immigrants in the 1840's, or by the disruptions that went alongside industrialization in the 1870's and the Depression of the 1930's. But these were the types of crises common to the world at large. According to Professor Robert there is no historic parallel with the recent decline in commerce and the flight of capital. "This is our first exposure to being hurt alone," he says. But, as a staunch francophone, aged thirty-nine, he makes a telling point: "What we are experiencing now is a realistic approach to adjustment and to change. We are not sitting back and feeling sorry for ourselves." On the contrary, one can easily argue that the mood of the Montrealer (and this is not confined exclusively to francophones), is one of cheer and optimism, backed by statistics that indicate that Quebec's economic growth rate is higher than Ontario's. Moreover, an endangered species has been saved: the sidewalk superintendent. A building boom since 1980 has brought back the huge cranes that marked Montreal's skyline in the intoxicating days of Expo 67 and the Olympics of 1976. Men and women stare through portholes in fences that encase excavation sites, almost in awe, as though trying to remember that those workers in yellow hard hats can construct life before them.

That is a physical reaction, and substantial, but most important of all is the psychological uplift that compensates for any sense of hurting alone. There is self-confidence, there is pride, there is dignity, and for much of the credit one must look, ironically, to the Parti Québécois, which, softening its drive for secession, has given francophones something they required more than formal independence:

the assurance that they are truly "maître chez nous" ("masters in our own house"), a slogan promoted by the Liberal government in the 1960's. This is best illustrated by use of language. Bill 101, the law introduced in 1977 establishing French firmly and officially as paramount, had a curious and probably quite unexpected effect. Despite some pettiness and negative features, it defused separatism. It removed from extremists their strongest emotional weapon, the appeal to the francophone's need for cultural and linguistic security.

One might speculate that in more evil times, or certainly under sinister men, such a clearcut decision would never have been made. In Hitler's Germany, a Dr. Goebbels, with a cunning perception of propaganda, would have kept alive such a highly charged issue as language. But virtually overnight, with the legislation, French-Canadian grievance, so visible in the past, vanished. Clerks in department stores no longer resented or refused talking English to anglophone customers. Of equal importance, many anglophones, if they did not already possess a working knowledge of French, made an effort to learn enough to prove they were trying. If there is not yet complete acceptance, especially among older anglophones, at least one no longer hears the facetious yet racist comment of a generation ago: "If God had meant me to be bilingual he would have made me a French Canadian." Actually, Bill 101 can be reduced to simple dimensions: first, French Canadians felt their language and culture should be protected by law; second, the provincial government had the power to do it; third, it did it – and it happened to be a Parti Québécois government.

The most important turning point, however, undoubtedly was the referendum of May 20, 1980. The Parti Québécois had been in office three and a half years, but 60 per cent of Quebecers, in response to the referendum's question, refused to give the government a mandate even to discuss with Ottawa any process of "sovereignty-association" (a euphemism for secession). Again, practically overnight, the effect was striking. Anglophones, if not entirely reassured, felt more secure than they had in many years. Francophones said in effect, "Okay, that's settled. Now let's get on with the job of building the economy and better harmony between the two main communities."

Only an unrealistic observer would pretend that René Lévesque and other *péquistes*, (supporters of the Parti Québécois), have abandoned their ambition of one day establishing an independent Quebec. But in real political terms, having gained power because of the ineptitude of the previous Liberal government, and having discovered the limit to which the electorate would permit them to go in quest of a breakup of Canada, Lévesque and his closest associates have pushed sovereignty-association into the background. The re-election of the Parti Québécois on April 13, 1981 – a re-election made possible by the support of many of the same people who voted *Non* in the referendum – created barely a ripple of unease. Anglophones who had decided to remain in Quebec after friends departed in 1976, continued to stay. There was no repetition of the flight of individuals or capital or head offices. What did emerge was the reminder that Montreal, along with the rest of the province, was a French haven, reflected in the need of businesses to communicate with government agencies – and even, in theory, with one another – in French, except in instances of international companies. Names over store fronts were changed to emphasize the new francization drive. "Bob's Restaurant" became "Restaurant Bob," and "Yellow Shoes," a chain of shops, was turned into "Chaussures Yellow." Trivia was such that for a while debate ensued over whether illuminated signs at the Olympic Stadium promoting the sale of smoked meat sandwiches would have to be amended to "viande fumée;" the compromise was "le smoked meat." Hamburger, however, translated into "hambourgeois."

Sometimes the expense incurred was small, sometimes it became major because of the wrangling with the government agencies that supervise control over the use of French. A supermarket chain piled up a thick file of correspondence over one word: quality. Bananas had affixed to them the label "Del Monte quality." The word was in tiny letters, taking up less than one-eighth of an inch, but a bureaucratic warning said it must be spelled "qualité." The president of the company wrote to L'Office de la langue française and the Surveillance Commission to point out that the bananas originated outside Canada – in fact were trans-shipped from Chicago – and when Del Monte planted its label it had no way of knowing where an order would be destined. In response came a letter threatening a fine. The supermarket chain, wanting to avoid any publicity, managed to get Del Monte to drop the word "quality." Henceforth even Americans would see on their bananas simply "Del Monte," because of a

Quebec functionary's insistence on adherence to the law. But one can rationalize that it is a small price to pay for the kind of peace and tranquillity that now prevail.

Pierre Gascon, a magazine publisher and member of a close family of fourteen sisters and brothers (including Jean Gascon, the distinguished theatre director), says that as recently as two or three years ago when the clan, nephews and nieces among them and numbering at least 100, got together for a festival, there was discomfort among the older men and women. The *péquiste* attitude of the eighteen- and nineteen-year-olds was strident. Today? He answers, not entirely sadly nor entirely with relief: "They are a bore." That is, the current generation of eighteen- and nineteen-year-olds, only a couple of years younger than their brothers and sisters, talk, not of politics but of careers, anticipating buying their first car and enjoying a life of material comforts. "In that sense," says Gascon, "they are no different from other North Americans."

Montreal has always been a city described by words like "grandeur" or "fantastique" from the earliest days of commercial shipping, when it competed effectively against New York – to which it looked for stimulation or comparison rather than to London or Paris. Years before the birth of a Montrealer named Jean Drapeau, who had fancy notions of building a world exhibition or attracting the Olympics (at enormous cost), other citizens emerged regularly with schemes that were wild but exhilarating. In 1902 a periodical, *l'Album universel*, held a contest to see who could come up with ideas in harmony with the twentieth century. A man named Arsène Lavallée, who sat on the City Council, believed that all the villages on the island should be annexed by the city of Montreal (Mayor Drapeau in 1982 would have liked the same), and connected by a divided highway running the entire length of thirty-five miles. When one considers that in 1902 there were precisely two automobiles in Montreal, it was indeed visionary.

Another man decided that what the city's centrepiece, Mount Royal, needed was a lake – not, dully and logically atop the park, but *under* it. This would enable swimmers to enjoy the romantic sight of stalactites overhead while sheltered in a grotto-like atmosphere. The mayor at the time, an unimaginative Anglo-Saxon, James Cochrane (this was during the period when the chief magistrate's office alter-

20

nated between a francophone and an anglophone), was not amused. He said the city budget would not permit such extravagance. But railwaymen, in private enterprise, did manage a decade later to carve a tunnel through Mount Royal in order to compete with rivals who had easier entry into the city.

The public perception of a Drapeau of flamboyance or fantasy or extravagance depends on one's own values. But perception is difficult to alter, as the Chambre de Commerce learned in a study conducted in the mid-1970's. The examination was designed to indicate how English Montrealers and French Montrealers regarded Toronto and Montreal in terms of quality of life, culture, and safety. The overall view of Montreal by both groups was generally positive. But when it came to quality of life, francophones were inclined to see Toronto as more densely populated than Montreal. According to Statistics Canada, anglophones were right in viewing it as less densely populated. Anglophones perceived Montreal as a more violent city than Toronto. Yet Statistics Canada figures for 1969 to 1973 set the number of murders and cases of involuntary homicide per 100,000 as roughly the same for both cities. Anglophones believed there were fewer rapes in Toronto than Montreal. But, again according to Statistics Canada, in the period under scrutiny there were proportionately fewer rapes in Montreal than Toronto. Finally, Montreal did maintain its image, among francophone respondents, as a city of amusement and recreation. For anglophones, Toronto had the edge.

Ironically, another survey, conducted more recently by Air Canada, showed that Toronto businessmen travelling on Rapidair, the hourly service between the two main cities, tended to plan it so they could spend the night in Montreal. Montreal businessmen, however, worked it so they could get back home the same day. The obvious interpretation was that Montreal was still the fun city.

There is nothing new about the movement of finance or people away from Montreal. The Montreal Stock Exchange, founded in 1874, was the first in Canada and it remained dominant until just after the Second World War. By 1946, the Toronto Stock Exchange began to pull ahead, partly because of the starchy attitude of members of the Montreal board and the Quebec securities commission. The opening of mines in Ontario and the development of oil resources in Alberta meant the massive selling of penny stocks. But Montreal was aloof towards listing such stocks, and Toronto volunteered a more enterprising approach. The stock exchange there stayed ahead by offering better service all around. One should note that this was long before there was any uncertainty about Quebec's political status; on the contrary, it was during the authoritarian period of Premier Maurice Duplessis, the friend of capitalists, whether American, English-Canadian, or French-Canadian, and the foe of trade unions. Montreal and the Province of Quebec were the safest places in the world.

Equally, any exodus of anglophones in recent years should be considered in the context of their perennial mobility, especially of the élite: the executives, the heads of corporations. McGill University statistics indicate that long before 1976 – always, in fact, since any records were kept by the Graduates' Society in the last century – 70 per cent of alumni have moved away within a decade of graduation. A difference, of course, is that any replenishment of the departed Montrealers is no longer met by an influx from provinces such as Nova Scotia and New Brunswick. Nonetheless, the anglophone community of Greater Montreal, at 750,000 (of a total population of 2.8 million), remains healthy, and some English Canadians do come in from other provinces. Prominent among them is James W. Burns, president of Great-West Life Assurance Company, whom Paul Desmarais, the leading francophone industrialist, asked in 1979 to assume the presidency of Power Corporation.

Burns, a handsome, lean Winnipegger, six feet two inches tall, and now fifty-two, recalls that any hesitation on his part was not due to a lack of knowledge of French; he had learned, from experience with the Montreal end of his insurance business, that francophones were "open-minded, lively, and sensitive to what's going on around them." What did make him pause, however, was his previous contact with English Montrealers, "the Wasps," whom he found "very provincial, narrow-minded, and small-eyed." It is, to phrase it mildly, a neat, and not unrealistic, switch from the usual cliché that elevates the anglophone and denigrates the francophone. Most of the English-speaking friends Burns has acquired since his residence in Montreal have been Americans in charge of US subsidiaries. Philosophically, he says, "When you're a newcomer anywhere, you tend to gravitate towards other people who haven't roots." But basically it is because he finds the Americans more sophisticated and ready to accept change than many English Montrealers. The francophones?

He predicts: "They'll eat the English alive. They're more worldly and they work harder. They're coming to the fore very fast, and once they take off, it'll be like a rocket."

Even if the notion of today's Montreal functioning like a city-state seems strained, it is a fact that half of Quebec's population and 60 per cent of its industry are located in and around the city, and so is virtually all of the province's important cultural life. This gives Montreal a punch, of which all mayors in recent generations have been aware. They are often more dynamic and powerful than the premiers with whom they deal. In any case there is a mentality of a city-state constantly lurking and ready to emerge. Before the referendum, some francophones, as well as anglophones, told René Lévesque: "If you separate, why shouldn't we secede? Montreal will go its own way." It was far from a new thought. A McGill Red and White Revue in the mid-1950's featured a song titled, "Nothing Succeeds Like Secession." In the first verse Canada secedes from the Commonwealth; in the second, Quebec secedes from Canada; in the third, Montreal secedes from Quebec; in the fourth, Westmount secedes from Montreal; and in the final verse, Upper Westmount secedes from Westmount.

Senator H. Carl Goldenberg – no man in Canada has a more intimate knowledge of politics than he – recalls once sitting in the suite of Mayor Camillien Houde in the Mount Royal Hotel and listening to a belligerent mayoral statement. Houde, a bombastic type, entered history as the mayor who was interned for urging young men to refuse to register during the Second World War; and he reappeared later to be elected with a greater majority than ever. At one point in his career he competed against Maurice Duplessis for leadership of the Quebec Conservative Party. Duplessis outmanoeuvred him. Houde was so incensed that, as Goldenberg remembers it, he vowed revenge on Duplessis, saying he would declare Montreal a separate province.

There will be frequent references in this book to Bill 101. The importance of its nature and what it did for the francophone psyche cannot be overemphasized. André Raynauld, who was a Liberal member of the Quebec National Assembly before returning to the

Université de Montréal as professor of economics, says quietly, as though a deep secret inside him has been revealed, that within every French Canadian there lives a reason for supporting the fundamentals of Bill 101, even if he deplores some negative features. Raynauld illustrates with a personal example. While he was deputy, (for Outremont), he had to sign a lease for rental of his constituency office. The timing turned out to be ironic because it was during the debate on Bill 101, in which Raynauld was one of the more determined critics. The lease was in English. Raynauld, who is fluently bilingual, said to the landlord: "I am the buyer and you are the seller, and you want to impose on me an English lease?" The landlord quickly grasped the principle that infuriated Raynauld and said he would get it drawn up in French. He did – and soon afterwards Raynauld received a bill from the landlord's lawyer for $150 for translation. He refused to pay, and, with charity, defines the landlord's act as "stupidity, not arrogance." Now, in a province in which 80 per cent of the inhabitants regard French as their mother tongue, leases, contracts, and other legal documents are written automatically in French; by prior agreement between the parties concerned they can appear in English. Raynauld says, "I didn't need Bill 101, but a lot of people did because they were facing this kind of situation – with a landlord or employer – all the time."

The language legislation creates some curious situations. In a company whose head office is in Montreal, but which has branches scattered across the country, the secretary of the president must be French-speaking or bilingual, because she is identified as working in Quebec. The president himself is exempt from this requirement because he is categorized as an executive in a national or multinational head office. Internal memos related to Quebec operations, as distinct from national or multinational functions, must be written in French. There are incongruities in large corporations of an anglophone son sending his father a memo in French. Sometimes L'Office de la langue française demands that when a store holds a sale it calls it "solde," which it regards as better French than "vente." But in practice the system is not necessarily niggardly or pervasive. Some engineers from France happened to visit the plant of Pratt & Whitney Aircraft of Canada Limited on the same day that a team from L'Office was in conference with company representatives who were laying out documentation to prove that the cost of translations into French would be prohibitive. In the aerospace industry, manuals and technical data, around the world, are in English. The visitors from France told L'Office officials: "You'd better back off." They did. Thus, while workers in the plant can comfortably communicate in French, the manuals remain in English.

But language is not the big complaint of the national or international corporations with head offices in Montreal. This they have quickly learned to live with; in fact many, such as Alcan, the biggest multinational of all, made the adjustment several years before the Parti Québécois was even in existence. The main grumble is about the rate of personal taxation which makes it difficult to recruit middle or upper executives. Even though Ontario's budget of 1981 narrowed the gap, the disadvantage remained; a married man with two children earning $35,000 a year in Montreal, paid $3,000 more in income tax than his counterpart in Toronto. The president and chief executive officer of Bell Canada, A. Jean de Grandpré, recounts the dilemma when the Quebec tax law was introduced in 1978. Bell employs five executive vice-presidents; three in Quebec, two in Ontario. De Grandpré had to approve a $33,000 increase for each of his Quebec seniors so they could net $10,000 and meet prior commitments, such as mortgages or private schooling, and remain on the same level as their Ontario peers. Later, Bell, to counter what De Grandpré calls "a punitive tax law," took other measures, including the transfer of some executives to the Ottawa-Hull region, where they can reside in the capital and pay the Ontario rate.

De Grandpré, like Pierre Elliott Trudeau, is a member of the old francophone élite of Montreal. In fact, de Grandpré, tall, lean, and baldish, was president in 1937 of the students' society at College Jean de Brébeuf while Trudeau was vice-president. A gold medallist in law at McGill University, he, along with other leading businessmen, both anglophone and francophone, attended hearings in Quebec City to present a brief against Bill 101. A Parti Québécois spokesman bitingly asked him: "How can anyone of your noble blood feel the aspirations of ordinary people?" De Grandpré pointed out that his ancestral family name was Taillot. But there were so many Taillots in the old days, all farmers, that to distinguish one from the other, those with large holdings labelled themselves "de Grandpré" (meaning the Taillot of the big field or meadow).

But he was really infuriated when Camille Laurin, the father of the bill, called him "un inféodé," roughly "a vassal," of the English. That night de Grandpré sat down and wrote Laurin a long letter in which he pointed out that his great-grandfather, on his mother's side, was François Thomas Chevalier de Lorimier, one of the followers of Louis-Joseph Papineau in the 1837 rebellion against the British. The insurrection was easily put down, and Papineau fled to the US, leaving de Lorimier among the dozen of "les patriotes" to be hanged. "Where," de Grandpré asked Laurin, "was your great-grandfather at the time?" After finishing the letter, de Grandpré cooled off and decided against sending it, on the grounds that it would only inflame Laurin and do more harm than good.

Today's Missionaries

André Raynauld, at the age of fifty-four, is one of Canada's outstanding economists. Before his brief flirtation with politics, he served for five years as chairman of the Economic Council of Canada and achieved an international reputation. In 1970, Raynauld completed an elaborate study for the federal Department of Regional Economic Expansion, setting out guidelines for the development of Quebec, with much of the emphasis on Montreal. The basics of that report of more than a decade ago are unchanged. In sum, in 1970 – long before government by the Parti Québécois and the consequent departure of some head offices and industries – Raynauld noted that Montreal was losing ground to Toronto, and if it wanted to stay alive the answer was straightforward: *external* forces must not be allowed to diminish.

That is, the future, like the past, depends on Montreal's ability to remain globally minded. "If you think of an international role instead of domestic," says Raynauld, "the loss may not be as serious as we feared originally. A lot of head offices have moved to serve the *Canadian* market; that has made sense because the west is developing rapidly. But *international* operations are still largely quartered in Montreal. Montreal is still Canada's main window on the rest of the world." To Raynauld it is no surprise that 42 per cent of the Export Development Corporation's financial investments are related to Montreal-based companies, much more than to Toronto companies. This apart, the three largest employers in Canada – Canadian Pacific, Canadian National, and Bell Canada – retain their headquarters in Montreal, even if some divisions are situated elsewhere. It is noteworthy that all are in communications and transportation, along with Air Canada, which has also clung to Montreal, part of Raynauld's window on the world.

Accurate figures on the actual shift from Montreal are difficult to obtain. It is known that in 1950 about 27 per cent of head offices in Canada were located in Montreal, 19 per cent in Toronto. In 1961 the cities were equal. But a decade later Toronto was ahead by 10 per cent. Since then various estimates have come into conflict with one another. Quebec government figures are ridiculously low; those by despondent individuals usually too high. Members of both the Chambre de Commerce and Board of Trade regard as the most reliable a survey made by Reed Scowen, a Liberal deputy in the Quebec National Assembly who has his MBA from Harvard and an administrative background from Ottawa. Scowen, fifty-one, took a simple and direct path. He engaged as his pollsters three prominent retired businessmen who could get through to presidents of corporations they knew personally. They asked three questions: Have you moved? Do you intend to move? What, if any, departments have moved or intend to move? From January 1976 to January 1981 the total was 150 companies affected, completely or in part, with a loss to Montreal of 11,000 positions. Scowen does not minimize the significance of "positions lost." When the Bank of Montreal transferred its Master Charge operation to Toronto, only twelve persons moved there; but since then 420 have been hired in Toronto to deal with expanded needs. Nonetheless, Scowen says, "It's bad, but I don't think it's the end of Montreal. The city is destined to become an international centre."

The picture now becomes possibly something like this: Toronto geared more and more to a North American economy, while Montreal's strength lies in an international role, in such service areas as engineering or food merchandising (as represented by Provigo, a unique francophone firm that has spread across Canada and into the US). Simultaneously, high technology, as demonstrated in the aviation industry, has grown impressively in Montreal. And since manufacturing, never a strong point in the Canadian economy, employs less than one quarter of the labour force, the wave of the future might well lie precisely in those fields: service and high technology. There are some who see Montreal's potential also in relation to global agencies, since it already serves as headquarters for the International Civil Aviation Organization, a branch of the United Nations, and for the International Air Transport Association, composed of 111 airlines from ninety countries. Indeed, Carl E. Beigie, president of the C.D. Howe Institute, a non-profit, non-political body that conducts research and commentary on Canadian economic issues, visualizes even wresting the United Nations itself from New York.

Beigie, a forty-two-year-old native of Cleveland who has lived in Montreal since 1971, says he has long believed in the Island of Montreal as an international centre for head offices of multinationals of all types, commercial or governmental. Its attributes include location and bilingualism, safety for the residents (unlike New York), and a kind of intellectual tranquillity (unlike Toronto). "Montreal is like a demilitarized zone," he says, "the only place in Canada where I feel I can stand above the chaos that is going on, where you can put things in perspective. You can't stand above this chaos in Toronto; the attitude there is too narrow." What Beigie advocates is akin to a West Berlin status. Quebec, he argues, is really two provinces: the Island of Montreal and the rest, which is pastoral. Thus the concept of city-state rises again, and Beigie has visions that it could become "the first twenty-first century city in North America," geared to a world-wide outlook in service and leaving it to Toronto to deal in matters such as finance and manufacturing.

The occupant of another think tank, Marie-Josée Drouin, executive director of the Hudson Institute of Canada, also contemplates an international position for Montreal. But she adds a caveat – that what is still lacking is the political will on three levels of government: municipal, provincial, and federal. She notes that when Mayor Drapeau talks of Montreal he does so in terms of "grandeur," such as the Olympics, but not in relation to the kind of economy that will make up the future. (The mayor, as will be gathered in a later chapter, often does have business on his mind.) Mainly, however, Mlle Drouin speaks about the need for decision – and this has to emanate basically from Ottawa – regarding the fields in which various cities and regions in Canada should specialize. For instance, should Mirabel, the controversial Montreal airport for overseas flights, be classified as a duty-free area? If the aerospace industry is to continue to flourish, should more be done to consolidate Montreal as a focal point of expertise? If so, it means making it attractive enough, in terms of favourable taxation, to draw engineers from around the world.

Half of the Canadian output of aircraft bodies and engines is concentrated in the Montreal area, due largely to the accomplishment of two firms: Canadair Limited, and Pratt & Whitney. Canadair now employs 7,000, but there was a point in 1975 when its payroll included only 1,400, and the parent company, the US-owned General Dynamics, was going to close it down. The Canadian government bought it, leaving its directors free to pursue three options, keeping in mind that there were no military contracts or other orders on hand. It could dismantle the buildings and plough the land; it could turn the huge complex into a machine shop; or it could go out and find a basis for continuing in business. Canadair conducted a market survey and determined that the future for executive jets was enormous. It also engaged in a unique experiment by inviting 200 potential customers to suggest what they would like incorporated into such an airplane.

What emerged was the Challenger, drawing on the Lear jet as a nucleus but with a much wider fuselage that demanded virtually a totally new design. With 200 planes on order, at more than $8 million each, production by mid-1982 reached seven a month, one of the biggest successes in the history of Canadian aviation manufacturing. Parallel achievement was experienced by Canadian engineers at Pratt & Whitney, an offspring of United Technologies Corporation of the US, who designed, developed, and produced a small gas-turbine engine that brought in sales of $700 million in 1981. Despite setbacks generally in the aeronautics industry in 1982, the projection for 1985 is $1 billion. Pratt & Whitney, with its 6,800 employees, is now the leader of the world in its field, the engine going into aircraft ranging from the six-passenger Piper Cheyenne to the DeHavilland Dash-7 and the Sikorsky S-587 helicopter.

The future may indeed be bright, linking the present generation of knowledge with likely developments. Harry Halton, sixty, executive vice-president of Canadair and engineering mastermind behind the Challenger, visualizes aircraft, as well as other forms of locomotion, operating on liquid hydrogen within the next ten to fifteen years. It was liquid hydrogen that fed the US moon rockets. Liquid hydrogen is light, providing one third more energy per pound than fossil fuel. And, extracted from water, it exists in unlimited supply. Science fiction? Halton shakes his head vigorously and says, "It's just a matter of time before hydrogen does become the standard fuel, because it's the only real alternative to oil."

He is not alone in this belief. There are some convincing studies, not only about hydrogen's potential but about how it may be connected with Mirabel. Two agencies on the outskirts of Montreal, Noranda Research Centre at Pointe Claire and Hydro-Québec's research institute at Varennes, are working in collaboration, able now to isolate the hydrogen, while Pica Mirabel, a crown corporation, is busy promoting the airport as a logical site to start world aviation on the fuel. Noranda entered the field because of its proficiency in the electro-chemistry used in the refining of copper. Hydro-Québec's interest comes from its control over the power required to draw the hydrogen from water. The combination of the two – plentiful power and an abundance of water – gives the province an advantage over most places in the world. Other countries are in the race, but the Noranda Research Centre, which employs 150 scientists and assistants, is perhaps two years ahead of any competitor.

In any event, Noranda's plan is to build the first demonstration plant somewhere in Quebec, with construction scheduled to start by 1985. Mirabel is a possible site, according to Eric M. Jones, a leader in the project. "Mirabel was built for the future," he says. "It was never meant only for the present, and liquid hydrogen is the fuel of the future." Jacques Rostenne, executive vice-president of Pica Mirabel, envisages the airport as "the hydrogen gateway to North America." Planes from overseas would touch down there, fill up on the hydrogen and transfer passengers to aircraft using conventional fuel; this would go on for several years until other airports could afford to put up plants to produce hydrogen or install facilities for its storage. Existing planes can be adapted to take this new energy source, with Lockheed of California pioneering and planning test runs between Los Angeles and Mirabel.

Whatever the outcome of such broad expectations, Claude Taylor, president and chief executive officer of Air Canada, gets down to specifics when he talks of Dorval, Montreal's first airport. He describes Air Canada now as standing on three legs. Western Canada is a high growth area for passengers and freight. Toronto, the second leg, remains strong. About the third, Montreal, he says: "The question is whether it can find its rightful role in order to keep pace with Toronto's and the west's base." The challenge is to take advantage of the city's international orientation. Air Canada already does maintenance work in Montreal for several other companies, ranging from Air Florida to Saudi Arabian Airlines. It trains pilots for El Al, the Israeli airline, and Japan Air Lines. This is a relatively new development, with Air Canada aggressively promoting its continued growth. As Taylor assesses it, if Mirabel becomes the main airport, Dorval would be a logical training school for the world. "The flavour of two languages, biculturalism, and proximity to Europe give us a natural advantage," he says.

Curiously, while much of the progress is in communications and transportation, traditional industries, such as clothing manufacturing, are also benefiting from new technology. Montreal remains the apparel centre of Canada, with the combined clothing and textile trade the biggest employer. While some factories still rely on antiquated production methods, others are completely up to date. Dominion Textile, Incorporated, one of the largest companies of its kind in the world with sales of $800 million a year, utilizes hundreds of Swiss-made looms that cost $70,000 to $80,000 apiece. No longer can a men's suit manufacturer expect to remain competitive, and hope to export to the US, unless he invests in the latest equipment. The Peerless Clothing Manufacturing Company, in the north end of Montreal, looks more like a plant engaged in turning out fine precision electronics than jackets and trousers. Absent are the rows of sewing machines one associates with yesterday's garment factories. These are replaced by "engineering work stations" in which operators, well spaced from their nearest neighbours, load panels of pants into four different machines representing an outlay of $65,000.

Work for the 500 employees depends largely on the pattern established by computers. After human designers have decided on the original styling, and cut one size, the computers then take over, adjusting to every other size and to every order placed by a retailer. Yet skill of the individual is still essential, with ten separate operations involved in a collar alone. Alvin Segal, the forty-nine-year-old president of Peerless, points out that while buttons are sewn automatically, it takes a highly qualified operator, trained three months, just to load a machine. Segal confesses that he, along with many other major manufacturers, thought seriously of pulling out after the 1976 Parti Québécois triumph. "But where," he asks, "would you find 500 skilled people?" He feels more comfortable now: "As long as working conditions don't deteriorate and the social climate remains reasonable, without too many governmental rules and regulations, the future will be bright."

One of the myths entertained by English Canadians is that French

Canadians are disinclined to leave home. They stay close to Quebec, the impression has it, because they feel secure there. Yet there are contradictions. From the earliest days, missionaries set out from Montreal to spread the gospel, whether it was among the Hurons of Georgian Bay or the Quechua of Peru. One needs only to glance through *Le Canada français missionaire,* a formidable work by the early twentieth-century historian, Canon Lionel Groulx, to sample the enormous range of field work from Addis Ababa to Zambia. The modern-day counterparts of the missionaries are the French-Canadian engineers who have taken their skills to South America, Africa, and the Middle East, in the process consolidating in Montreal the headquarters for two of the ten largest engineering firms in the world, Lavalin Incorporated, and the SNC Group. Lavalin employs a staff of 5,000, SNC 3,800 – spread across Canada and into thirty other countries. Each had its start in a distinctly Quebec situation. The provincial government, which hired few engineers of its own, was in no position to develop hydro power or a network of roads without calling upon outside consultants.

Indeed, Lavalin, founded in 1937, originally did all its business in Quebec. It began to move outside the province only in 1972 (now it has large operations based in Toronto, Calgary, and Halifax), and abroad only in 1978. This adds up to a remarkable success story. One wall in the board room of Marcel Dufour, president of Lavalin International, is covered by a map spotted with dozens of big blue dots designating projects underway. These include the construction of a town in Nigeria for 50,000 inhabitants, a liquefied natural gas plant in Algeria, and a power transmission line in Cameroon. Dufour, burly, bluff, and grey-haired, was born in Murray Bay in 1925 and took his degree in civil engineering at Ecole Polytechnique in Montreal before going on to Harvard for graduate work. Montreal, rather than any other city in Canada, he claims, was the logical place for the germination of engineering companies that compete directly with the biggest and best in the US, West Germany, Britain, France, and Japan. "We have two languages," he says. "It would help if we had a third, Spanish."

Dufour speaks with a kind of nonchalance, just as the church pioneers must have done when they set out in rivalry with other religious orders. But there is more. There is also an advantage directly attributable to international politics. Canada suffers from no imperialist tradition. Thus in former colonies of Britain or

France – or in other countries that decry American tactics – the prejudice may veer in Canada's favour. Arabs, for instance, can take advantage of North American technology without buying it from the US or the UK. The SNC Group in particular benefited from entry into the Middle East back in 1959, when it won its first foreign contract to join a consortium in constructing an airport in Abu Dhabi, on the Persian Gulf. Since then it has gone on to major engineering ventures in Algeria, Morocco, and Tunisia. Of SNC's annual revenues of more than $200 million, about one quarter comes from Arab sources. The Group's largest contract in 1981 was in Saudi Arabia for electrification of an entire province. The hundreds of SNC employees assigned to Saudi Arabia are schooled in advance to be aware that the Saudis are buying skills, not values. That is, the Canadians are expected to conform to local standards and avoid attempting to impose any of their own. It may be abhorrent for a Canadian to know that the Saudis still cut off the hand of a thief; but to Saudis the Canadian custom of pushing the elderly into institutions, instead of caring for them at home, is barbaric. A Canadian woman learns to wear an ankle-length dress to market, and even in compounds for foreigners there is deference to Moslem custom. Mixed swimming, for instance, is not permitted.

To Camille A. Dagenais, chairman of SNC, the challenge of overseas work was essential for the Group's expansion. There is an ironic, yet not unfamiliar, touch in his statement: "The way to national identity was first through international recognition." Thus an organization had to make its mark globally before it was accepted as important in other parts of Canada. Today the SNC Group, which embraces forty companies in various categories of construction and engineering management across the country, has also reached into the US to control firms in New York, Atlanta, Chattanooga, Oklahoma City, and Tulsa. Dagenais, who is sixty-one, echoes Lavalin's Dufour when he says that an enterprise like SNC could not have been created anywhere else in Canada but in Montreal. "We're multicultural," he says. The fact is that SNC has won handsome contracts in French-speaking Africa because its engineers know the language without facing the colonial disadvantage of peers from France.

Interestingly enough, the reason for the head start enjoyed by Lavalin and SNC – the inability of the provincial government to muster its own engineers – no longer applies. The state-owned Hydro-Québec now maintains a world-wide reputation for its own expertise in high technology. Hydro-Québec International, a self-contained subsidiary, exports knowledge, especially in the field of high-transmission lines, and has been engaged to handle needs of Venezuela, Haiti, Tunisia, and Argentina. China sent thirty of its leading engineers to spend six months in a study session at the $16 billion James Bay power project and at Hydro-Québec's research institute at Varennes, thirty kilometres southeast of Montreal. The staff of 600 includes specialists from twenty-six countries, attracted by the institute's pioneering in fields ranging from high-voltage transmission to new-type electrolysis for liquid hydrogen. Apart from the polyglot makeup of the personnel, the institute can count on hand at any given moment trainees from such countries as Algeria, Brazil, Mexico, Egypt, Japan, Argentina, and Zaire. Bill 101 is waived here. Work and study are conducted in English as well as in French, with English, the international language of engineering, uppermost.

What does the blend of the two cultures do? The interplay between the so-called Anglo-Saxon mind and the Gallic mind makes for some stimulating results. In general, engineers are engineers, with the same techniques and mental processes operating regardless of ethnic backgrounds. But something of a Gallic touch or flair complements the stolidity of the anglophone. Both Pierre Ranger and Frank H. Sutcliffe are heads of Lavalin divisions. Sutcliffe, fifty, who worked for engineering firms in Toronto and elsewhere before joining Lavalin in 1970, says that even the style of life is different. For instance, the president of Lavalin "would fire you if you didn't entertain a potential client at the Beaver Club for lunch every day." The restaurant, in the Queen Elizabeth Hotel, is famous for its good food and high prices, and equally renowned for the deals that are consummated at midday. It may require a two-hour effort on Sutcliffe's part, but he is prepared for it; even if it means staying in the office, usually until 6:30 or 7:00 P.M., to catch up with an accumulation of work. He can sum up the variance by continuing the lunch analogy: when he visits his office in Toronto, a noon meal usually consists of a sandwich, with everyone departing for home by 5:00 P.M.

But Sutcliffe goes more deeply into the comparison by recounting the reaction of an Ontario government official whom he drove through the outskirts of Montreal. The Ontarian remarked on the sculptured indentations that characterize concrete overpasses on the Trans-Canada Highway. "What are they supposed to be there for?" he asked. Sutcliffe told him that they were just decorative. "What a waste of money," said the visitor. Actually, as Sutcliffe points out, such embellishments are not costly, "and a lot of countries we deal with in French-speaking Africa or Latin America are receptive to the extra little touches." Sutcliffe, who grew up in a francophone neighbourhood in Montreal, regards himself as an intermediary "between the way someone from Toronto thinks and the way a French Canadian thinks." Broadly, in Toronto people tend to plan ahead on how many engineers and draftsmen will be required at every precise period of an assignment; in that sense a project is highly charted and computerized. The tendency in Montreal is to plan the manning less and to improvise more. If an urgent demand arises, the response is immediate: men will be pulled off other jobs, and then others found to replace them if necessary. "It's a bit like a juggler's act, but much more flexible and pragmatic than the other approach," Sutcliffe says.

Pierre Ranger, who is forty, has been with Lavalin ever since he graduated in civil engineering in 1966. While admitting there might be a difference between an anglophone and a francophone, he doesn't go as far as Sutcliffe. Rather, he says, "In the engineering business two plus two always equals four. We work with the same tools." But he does concede that the anglophone leans more towards precise instructions: "He needs a clear-cut mandate, A-B-C-D. For francophones, A and B would be enough." Moreover, he also agrees that aesthetics enter into francophone mentality perhaps more than into anglophone mentality. If you're involved in a $100 million project, why not throw in another $100,000 to make it more beautiful? In asking the question, he also answers it by saying, "It's a fractional cost." Ranger, who is in charge of the construction of a new Alcan smelter at Grande Baie, Quebec, points to the tall smokestacks which are coming out in orange and white stripes instead of the less expensive – and less attractive – all-white or all-orange. "Alcan will probably operate the smelter for fifty years," Ranger says, "so why not do it right?"

In general, Ranger is an example of the francophone engineer who has emerged in the national and international scene. He says simply, "We have to be better to get the job." If one looks back only ten or fifteen years, he observes, it is striking how many of the tasks offered to francophone firms were from government or Hydro-Québec; few were forthcoming from the private sector. Work on pulp and paper mills, components in Quebec's largest industry, was virtually restricted to such anglophone companies as Montreal Engineering, which even today ranks among the leading consultants in the world. The change now is that Ranger, apart from his Alcan assignment, is in command of a $25 million addition to a Kruger paper mill. "The big clients today don't ask if you're English or French or Chinese," he says. "And decorating a smokestack is secondary. What a client wants to know is availability – if you have the people and capacity to do the job." Ranger is buoyant, not only about the prospects for Montreal engineering companies but for the city itself. "It's going to boom."

The boom is already present in at least one area, the construction of plants and offices and apartment buildings. If the engineers are busy abroad, the local developers and builders and architects have also been engaged in activity that was almost forgotten in the immediate years following the election of a Parti Québécois government. The return of confidence that the province will not break away from Canada manifests itself in statistics alone. The cumulative value of building contracts awarded in Greater Montreal for 1981 reached $1.7 billion, an increase of 43 per cent over 1980. This included one of the most intriguing phenomena of all: the surge towards condominiums. Montreal was about the last major city in North America to find attraction in condominiums, partly because the majority of people were habitually inclined to rent rather than buy their residence. More recently, when separatism appeared to be a growing possibility, investors kept away. But now the independence movement has been put into perspective. Simultaneously, the high rate of inflation has impelled former renters to find a haven for their savings. Stated simply, people are more afraid of inflation than of separation. In some instances, they are fearful of political unrest overseas, for many of the investors in condominiums are Arabs or Italians or others who still live in their own countries but prefer another sanctuary for their money.

Even more striking is the reversal of attitude of Canadian companies towards Montreal. Where, in earlier years, there was unease and a departure of head offices, by 1981 some firms felt they should not only maintain a presence in Quebec but enlarge it. Insurance companies in particular have taken advantage of the pool of bilingual experts by expanding translation services in Montreal. The Toronto-based Confederation Life, which utilized only 25,000 square feet in a building next to the Quatre Saisons Hotel, switched to 70,000 square feet in a new twin-tower glass complex on De Maisonneuve Boulevard, shared by such occupants as the Banque Nationale de Paris, which makes its main Canadian home there. Nearby, the head office of The Mercantile Bank of Canada is also rising, on a site that faces the campus of McGill University. Four old greystone town houses and McGill's Strathcona Hall form the nucleus – part of a widespread effort to protect the special character of Sherbrooke Street.

There are several major developers in Montreal, but a special breed consists of the real estate brokers in their thirties or early forties who put together packages. The Mercantile Bank deal was the creation of Philip M. O'Brien, forty-one, president of the Devencore Group of Companies, who, after serving as vice-president of Trizec Corporation, the real estate giant, set up his own one-man operation in 1972. His staff now consists of fifty, an expansion attributable to his own acumen and imagination, or, as he prefers to put it, "guts and naivety." It was that combination that enabled him to obtain McGill and city approval for the Sherbrooke Street project on which he deposited $70,000 in seed money the day before the 1980 referendum. A developer said he would invest $5 million, provided O'Brien found a tenant with another $5 million. The Mercantile Bank, looking for space, came up with that amount, plus a loan of $40 million. So the plan was underway, and other customers began to arrive.

The Victorian town houses, dismantled stone by stone and reassembled, form separate addresses to the twenty-four storey tower in back of them. "We're regluing the facade to the tower," says O'Brien. More fundamentally, he adds: "It works because we're selling nostalgia." That sentiment for the past means the preservation of marvellous oak and mahogany staircases and woodwork. Montreal's future? O'Brien is convinced it is a healthy one, not only because of the arrival of such newcomers as foreign banks, but because of the fresh generation of young companies that is emerging. "These are the companies that will occupy the new buildings," he says. "The people who are making it are the owner-entrepreneurs, most of them francophones, in their thirties and forties. So if you have fifty starting at once, as you have now, a lot of human energy will grow up in the next ten years."

Another specialist in office leasing who shares this optimism, Stephen Leopold, thirty, began his business in 1977, a few months after the Parti Québécois came to power. Sturdy and handsome, he communicates confidence in himself and the city, as well as a sense of obligation to remain within the community instead of departing, as many of his contemporaries have done. His French is fluent, better than that of his father and late grandfather. He says, "I asked myself a question: What prevents me doing at least as well as my father and grandfather?" Since his grandfather, Samuel Leopold, became a millionaire manufacturing women's hats, and his father, Irwin Leopold, is the owner of Ruby Foo's, the largest and most successful restaurant in Canada, it was a fairly mighty challenge. But Stephen Leopold met it because of a sharp awareness of where Montreal was heading. In 1977 he anticipated a shortage of space, despite the withdrawal of some head offices. He began to put together packages, and the facts emerged to bear out his forecast. By 1981, more office footage was in use in Montreal than before the Parti Québécois victory. Virtually no space was available, contrasted with a vacancy rate of 6.5 per cent in Edmonton and 4 per cent in Toronto. The current building activity, Leopold anticipates, will continue at least until 1984. "It's because of the realization that, with or without the Parti Québécois, people have to clothe themselves, they have to eat, and they have to buy financial services such as insurance." His skill at forecasting, based on a perception of reality rather than emotionalism, was confirmed after the re-election of the Parti Québécois in 1981, when no slowdown in construction took place.

Direct beneficiaries of the upsurge are the architects, many of whom suffered in the slack years after 1976. Max Roth, who graduated in 1937, during the Depression when jobs were scarce, found himself, forty years later, hunting for work after having built up a business in which he employed twenty-five other architects. That operation ceased, and Roth had to compromise by becoming a developer of low-priced suburban housing. By 1981, however, he was back full time, designing loftier structures – including several $500,000 private homes – and engaged in such pleasures as restoring a limestone house on Mountain Street used as a refuge by Jefferson

Davis, president of the Confederate States of America, after the American Civil War.

Raymond Affleck, a man with an ebullient spirit, also remained in Montreal while others left, his name having been associated with such substantial undertakings as Place Ville Marie in Montreal and the National Arts Centre in Ottawa. "I felt a bit stubborn," he says. "I always had faith in Montreal and I couldn't believe that a city that had so much going for it would fall into decline. I was also interested in the post-industrial society – the service fields and communications – and that's what we're into in Montreal." The faith proved justified. Affleck, at the age of fifty-nine, has experienced a remarkable comeback. Thirty architects are kept busy, making his company, Arcop Associates, one of the biggest in Montreal. Much of his work, as Roth's, is in partial restoration: for example, the entry through old buildings on Sherbrooke Street into new Alcan quarters. Montreal boasts a large inventory of what can be preserved. "The challenge," says Affleck, "is in integrating the old with the new."

Anglophone firms tend to receive contracts to do office buildings, while francophone architects have traditionally been engaged more in government work, though the lines now are less rigid than in the past. The partnership of Jodoin, Lamarre, Pratte & Associés provides an index to the variety of tasks currently absorbing francophones: the recycling of Morrice Hall at McGill University, built in 1881 as a meeting place for students of the Presbyterian College and destined to become a library for Islamic studies; the design of a plant for General Electric at Bromont, Quebec, that will produce components for aircraft engines; and the styling of a condominium in downtown Montreal. Denis Lamarre, forty-eight, a senior partner, concurs with Affleck's view about the importance of utilizing old structures – in other words, urban renewal. "For the last three years," he says, "we've oriented our practice mostly to recycling building. I believe it'll be the strongest market for the next decade."

Whether or not the trend will be towards reconstruction of the old or concentration on the modern, architecture is a barometer of good and bad times. There are now more architects in practice in Montreal than ever before. In 1970, the Order of Architects claimed 600 members in the Montreal area; a decade later, the figure was 1,100.

Yvette and Louky

She is an extraordinarily handsome, indeed beautiful, woman – with grey-white hair, a modulated voice, and a warm laugh. She is utterly appealing; frank, forthright, sensitive, elegant, the answer to the charge that her husband, Claude Ryan, leader of the Liberal Party of Quebec, is demagogic and dismissive of strength around him. It is apparent from the story of their meeting, their courtship, their common interests, and from the way Madeleine Ryan refers to him, that this is a rare and inspiring marriage.

One talks easily with her about the role women have filled in Quebec and Montreal history: how they became fur trappers when their husbands died, how they ran the first hospitals and schools. To her, a stirring example is Marguerite Bourgeoys, who arrived in the second pioneer party of Montreal, in 1653, a thirty three-year-old school teacher who was to become the founder of La Congrégation de Notre Dame, one of the great orders of nuns. About Marguerite Bourgeoys, Mme Ryan says: "She listened to the men, to all the advice they thought they could give. And then she made her own decisions."

That might even be her own story – and that of the women of Quebec. She is a feminist, but very, very moderately so. She is not a Louky Bersianik, whose brilliance and unorthodox writing have placed her among the foremost militant feminists of the world. Nor is she a Rita Dionne-Marsolais, a thirty-five-year-old Montreal executive whose recommendations involve millions of dollars, and who has established a network of kindred female managers to ensure that deals that normally go to men are not denied to women.

"I prefer to work in mixed groups of men and women," says Mme Ryan, "but I can understand how women do feel easier with other women. We share the same interests, working at home and experiencing only occasional activity through our husbands. It was a surprise to me during the referendum campaign to see how women liked to be together. It began with big rallies, attended by men and women, and after that the women began to ask for at least one meeting for themselves." In Victoriaville, for instance, 1,000 women appeared, including some from Arthabaska, a separate town whose main street happens to run through Victoriaville. Then the women of Arthabaska demanded their own time in their own place. The men said the idea was absurd because the women would all be at home with their families on that day – Mother's Day, Sunday, May 11, nine days before the referendum. But 400 thronged a restaurant, listened to Mme Ryan, the principal speaker, and then had thoughts of their own to express. Out of those statements emerged some of the most revealing vignettes of true Québécoise values.

The cause, of course, was Yvette, the symbol of the disparagement heaped on Mme Ryan and other women who shared her standards. Yvette, the central character of a primary school textbook still in use in 1980, as it had been for many years, was the stereotype of the good little girl who did everything that was expected of women. She knew how to wield a broom, wash the dishes, assist her mother, and please everyone. Her brother, Guy, had only to be good in sports, to study, and to prepare for a career. Ironically, the education ministry under the government of the Parti Québécois had ignored recommendations from the Quebec Council on the Status of Women, which spoke for Mme Ryan, among others, when it advocated the withdrawal of these antiquated textbooks. Mme Ryan was particularly bothered by the freedom of choice that was offered the male. So was Lise Payette, a Parti Québécois cabinet minister and former television star who, presumably unaware that her own colleagues had hesitated to act on Yvette, spoke to a *Oui* rally in Montreal and said: "If you vote *Non*, the way Ryan wants you to, there will be many Yvettes in the province because Ryan married one." Mme Payette compounded this by adding that Ryan was unable to marry any other type, that Ryan was the kind of man she hated.

There were many elements in the pronouncement. On the political side, Liberals perceived that it was a Parti Québécois device to use women to push separatism, the message being that if you liberated Quebec you liberated women at the same time. If that was the intention, it misfired. As Madeleine Ryan assessed it: "There were worse names to be called than Yvette. For me a name changes nothing; I am the same person. What shocked me was the reference to someone 'hating' my husband."

Madeleine was born in St. Isidore, a small village thirty kilometres south of Lévis, in 1925. Her father owned a general store and sold farm equipment. She did voluntary work for Jeunesse Agricole Catholique, a youth division of L'Action Catholique, the lay organization dedicated to demonstrating how religion could enter into and improve everyday life. The work took her to Quebec City where, in 1953, she met Claude, who was the salaried national secretary of L'Action Catholique. Five years later, when she became the sole paid staff member of the youth movement in Montreal, she and Claude were married.

The decision reached by both was that since they were relatively old (she was thirty-two, Claude thirty-three), the priority would be for her to concentrate on homemaking while losing no time to raise a family. She bore five children in seven and a half years. "It was so new for me, this experience," she recalls. "I had been independent." But Ryan, still deeply involved in Catholic Action, deliberately brought home projects he could discuss and share with her. "I was pushed by Claude to work in education and religion even when I had three children in diapers." It was voluntary, not full time work, but that is her point: "There are not many women who are really Yvettes. Trying to please someone else is not a bad thing, in my estimation. It still leaves you space to be yourself." She is strong in the belief that women as volunteers can be very important: in libraries, in benevolent societies. "There are always new areas to pioneer," she says.

At the start of the referendum campaign the *Non* organizers, representing five political parties, told her only to accompany her husband to rallies. At the end, she was speaking alongside him or on her own. After Lise Payette made her Yvette impeachment, the spontaneous reaction was unprecedented. The first person to seize on it was a lifelong Liberal, Mme Andrée Richard of Quebec City. An interior decorator ("inventive" is the way Mme Ryan describes her), Mme Richard, along with many others, had thought the Liberals were late in moving to rebut the massive *Oui* drive of the Parti Québécois. She recognized a good media attraction when she saw one, organized a Sunday "brunch des Yvettes," and, as an old friend, phoned to ask if Madeleine would come. The answer was yes. They expected at most a couple of hundred women; 1,400 arrived and six big salons of the Château Frontenac Hotel had to be conscripted.

What was the main lesson Mme Ryan learned from the Yvette experience? "It was the way women everywhere came out to say why they would vote *Non*. They were not used to making political speeches. Their argument was not political. It emerged much more out of their daily lives." In Sept-Îles, the local *Non* committee rented hotel space for 400; 1,000 showed up and another hall across the street had to be rented. Later in Montreal, the Forum was filled with 14,000. What was clear – in the rural districts or the cities – was that women did not regard the Payette onslaught as simply an attack on Mme Ryan alone. In Montmorency a woman stood up and said: "I am from a big family – you know, the sort when you decide to take a bath you find everyone has been ahead of you and there is no more hot water. When you decide to go to sleep your brother decides to turn up the volume on his record player. Finally I said to my father, 'I am twenty-one. I earn my own living. I want to live alone.' My father said, 'You are indeed an adult, so I cannot prevent you from going. But before you decide I would like you to consider both sides of the issue.'" The woman paused while her audience awaited the climax of her story. "I will vote *Non* in the referendum because my father taught me to see two sides to every question. René Lévesque tries to tell me there is only his side."

The wording of the referendum question was ambiguous and to many people deceptive. In another town, Berthier, a woman rose and said that when you live in a large family you learn many tricks of behaviour: "My mother liked to read, but with a large family to look after there was not much time for it. When she did take the time she became so immersed in reading that she shooed away the children. But I discovered early on that when I wanted something, the best time was to ask for it when my mother or father was preoccupied. Once my sister and I made a test. My mother was reading and we walked over to her and said, 'Do you permit us to go out and drown ourselves?' 'Yes,' replied my mother, 'but don't be too long.'" The Berthier woman concluded: "I hope people will pay attention and not be tricked into a *Oui* by the question of the Parti Québécois."

In a more whimsical incident, a resident of Granby recounted how her five-year-old son asked how she would vote. She told him, "*Non*. And you? How will you vote?" "The same," he said. "Why?" asked his mother. "Because," he said, "I want to keep Canada in Quebec."

The Ryans live in a lower duplex on St. Joseph Boulevard, just inside the boundary of Outremont. The home is simple but warmly furnished, with a green oriental carpet in the living room to go alongside a couple of minor Quebec-scene paintings and a major collection of classical records. Madeleine Ryan, obviously still sensitive to "Yvette," makes a point of mentioning that as a former member of the Superior Council on Education, she remains active on the committee for adult education and is also involved in a variety of church organizations. A company of women meet every month in her home to discuss the latest books and magazine articles they have read on women's affairs. She accepts invitations to speak to the Women's Canadian Club, the Council of Jewish Women, and other groups. During the 1981 election campaign she moved into the hustings. Lise Payette was not there; she had quit politics because the Parti Québécois had dropped its theme of sovereignty and she felt she must be free to pursue it on her own.

Did Mme Ryan ever thank Lise Payette for unwittingly setting forth the "Yvette movement"? "No," she says with a light laugh. "I've never had the occasion to meet her." But clearly she is not implying that she would consider thanking Mme Payette, even if they did meet. "I don't believe that what she did would have been enough if the women had not already been thinking of *Non*. We made no converts at those meetings. It was just an occasion for women to speak out. Yvette is not a conservative woman unable to open her mind. I am a Yvette because I do what little Yvette does – and I do more."

They always did more, the women of Montreal, with a spirit that occasionally took an illegal direction. The most successful smuggling ring in the early days was conducted by women – three sisters named Marguerite, Magdelaine, and Marie Anne Desauniers – who employed Indian squaws and their braves to transport contraband to and from Albany. They carried on their lucrative trade from 1727 to 1752, moving out deerskin, muskrat, and beaver pelts which the English wanted, and bringing back luxury goods in demand by the French: silver forks and knives, pipes, London-made boots, fine woollens, chocolate, and white sugar. The Desauniers sisters owned a splendid home in Montreal, but for business reasons preferred to live with their couriers in the nearby Iroquois village of Caughnawaga. The French authorities tumbled to the racket, but, since they were at war with the English, and the Indians came back with information and support as well as illicit imports, they did nothing. Finally, the new governor, the Marquis de Duquesne, concluded that the clandestine export of beaver pelts – maybe as much as two thirds of the entire catch – was depriving France of needed tax revenue. He dislodged the Demoiselles Desauniers from Caughnawaga. A quarter century enterprise thus collapsed.

But women still asserted themselves, especially when the war brought shortages. Beef was replaced by a ration of horsemeat, and housewives gathered in protest outside the governor's residence. He shouted from a window that he would imprison them. They stayed. Then he declared he would order half of them hanged. Since there is no record of any execution, it is assumed the women dispersed.

The fact is that it is a myth that women of Montreal, having first arrived as zealots under a mandate from a religious order, were a submissive lot. On the contrary, they held a higher status than contemporaries in New England. From the earliest moment in Montreal, women controlled what in effect was a ministry of education and a ministry of social affairs (agencies which did not come into formal existence until 300 years later). Marguerite Bourgeoys did the teaching and Jeanne Mance, who landed even ahead of her, in 1642, did the healing by establishing the first hospital. A text, written by a visitor from France, made an awed reference: "The Canadian woman is very intelligent; she is better educated than the man."

Certainly her function was multifold: running a family or a family store when the husband was away fur-trapping, and inheriting, under old French law, half his possessions when he died. Thus women who owned property enjoyed the same right to vote as male property owners. In an election in 1832, of sixty-four women who voted in the "West" riding of Montreal (now part of Old Montreal), thirty-eight supported the Tory party and twenty-six the Patriote camp of Louis-Joseph Papineau, the brilliant and erratic reformer. Papineau, annoyed at such conservatism, introduced a bill in Parliament in Montreal, which deprived women of the vote in 1834. It was not to return to them, at least provincially, for a century – that is, not until 1940. In the meanwhile, male religious orders became dominant, making it difficult for women to compete even in teaching and placing the emphasis on values expected of them as "épouse, vierge, et mère." (Wife, virgin, and mother.) The apparent contradiction in terms meant simply that a woman could become a nun or isolate herself at home, a credo that persisted until recent times. Or she could allow herself to be exploited as cheap labour.

Some call it the Quiet Revolution. Mme Michèle Jean, an eminent historian and the president of a Quebec commission on professionals, refers to it as the Turbulent Revolution, because, when it began in 1960, women were sure it would improve their lives dramatically. There was indeed reform of education and social structures, but, in Mme Jean's opinion, its effect on women was minimal. "We discovered the Quiet Revolution was not for everyone. It was mainly for men, particularly for technocrats and those highly trained for special work." To her, 1968 was far more significant than 1960. That was the peak of the student revolt and the blossoming of the feminist movement in the US; and that's when women in Quebec began to assert themselves.

Today how do women in Quebec stand in terms of liberation? Mme Jean feels they have now passed the US stage of development and that of other provinces. "We are more vigorous," she says, giving credit for much of this to the pioneers who brought with them a special strength, an abiding force for continuity and survival. Then she hesitates, lest she be accused of chauvinism, and says that if the Québécoise is not further ahead she is at least different. "We combine," she says, "the branches of three sources of culture – Latin, Judaeo-Christian, and American. The way we live and think as women is taken from all these sources."

The most advanced of the francophone feminists are almost invariably separatists. Yet, just as Mme Jean regrets that the Quiet Revolution did not fulfil female expectations, so do the most militant Montreal leaders feel betrayed by the Parti Québécois whose sweep to power in 1976 they helped to bring about. Louky Bersianik, a writer of rumpled appearance with a broad face much more youthful than her age (fifty-one) would suggest, is not very surprised by the Parti Québécois behaviour. Every revolution uses women and then discards them. She cites as an example the Algerian war of independence, in which women fired rifles and threw grenades alongside men. When it was over, they asked the victorious leader, Ahmed Ben Bella, what they could do next. "You will return to your cous-cous," he supposedly said. That is, back to the kitchen to prepare meals!

"The priority," says Louky, a person of enormous talent and imagination, "is not to fight for independence. I am an *indépendantiste*, but my energy is such that it is better for me to fight for my territory – which is women. Women worked hard for the Parti Québécois but the Parti Québécois has not done much for women. I cannot trust political revolutions. Men feel castrated by the feminist revolution because for the first time women do not want to be the mothers of men. Men are frightened." Oddly, though, she does identify more with members of the Parti Québécois than with non-members, simply because she feels a certain sensitivity is required to be any kind of revolutionary. "If men are not disturbed by the search for their own country they are not going to be interested in supporting the feminist movement."

Nicole Brossard, another author of great importance, visualizes a delicate nuance in the Quebec of the 1980's. "Now, with Quebec growing in identity," she says, "there will be a place for women. But we must be on guard. The men will want to retain the place they have gained – political and economic – as a new bourgeoisie. Men for the first time feel their new power in their new nationalism. They are no longer 'colonized' men. It's not necessarily more difficult for us, but we have to be careful that men, in enjoying their new power, will not try to send women back again to the kitchen."

Neither Rita Dionne-Marsolais nor Micheline Bouchard is likely ever to accept domestication. Each is brilliant, each is gorgeous, each is a product of Hydro-Québec, and each is representative of the young new breed of francophone women in important executive positions in Montreal. And each is married, combining the home and business responsibilities of ancestors.

Mme Dionne-Marsolais, whose husband is a lawyer (the Dionne is her surname, the rest his), was only thirty-two when she became, in 1979, vice-president, corporate development, for Le Groupe SGF, a conglomerate (shipbuilding, sawmill machinery, turbines, and generators), with sales in the $800 million bracket. She is an economist by profession, with her MA from Université de Montréal, but was surrounded by science in the first part of her career, working with "very innovative young people" at Hydro-Québec. "When I got here (SGF) my first thought was, 'Gee whiz, all we do is bend metal.' "

That, to her, was too conservative, and not in keeping with her belief that the future lay in high technology. One of her first achievements was to get her group to buy a company that specialized in the environmental sector and had a water treatment plant among its resources. Risky? Maybe, but Rita is, if nothing else, innovative herself – certainly unorthodox when it comes to economic theory. She expresses, in flawless and accentless English, "a very personal view" on how Montreal's fate accompanies the Canadian dollar. When the dollar is weak, Montreal thrives; when the dollar is strong, Montreal slumps. "Examine the 1960's," she says. "The dollar was low and Montreal had a building boom. In the 1970's, it was high and Montreal did not prosper. Now, in the 1980's, the dollar is low again – and look," and she points from her office windows on Sherbrooke Street at the construction cranes visible in several directions.

Never mind that the 1960's featured Expo 67; never mind that the Parti Québécois came into power in 1976 and this hurt business. Rita smiles a deliciously wicked smile and says, "I told you it was an unorthodox theory." But who knows? Other economists haven't postulated a unique connection between Montreal's fortune and the dollar's misfortune.

Rita's generation, educated in the 1960's and the 1970's, possesses a mentality much more alert and ambitious and self-confident than previous generations. "People before us," she says, "thought only of economic survival. But we, in the Quiet Revolution, were brought up in an environment that said, 'The world is yours – go out and get it.' And why shouldn't it be the world? If you confine your business to Quebec, that is your choice. But there's no law that says you have to restrict yourself to Quebec. We are only six million here. The big market is elsewhere. It's not even Canada with twenty-five million. You can't build an empire on those numbers." So she heartily approves of a Paul Desmarais and is trying to make her own people aware of the advantages of taking over businesses outside Quebec.

Plainly, Mme Dionne-Marsolais is ambitious. "I'm aggressive," she says freely. "I believe in success – whether it's measured in money or power." She also believes in feminism, in women banding together in self-interest. Thus she has helped to organize a network of thirty to forty women, mostly francophone and in their thirties, who have moved up from the ranks into top management. (Mitzi Dobrin, the mainstay of the Steinberg supermarket empire, might not qualify because she inherited her position.) Many are in law; quite a few are economists; others are accountants. They're in the $40,000 to $75,000 range – "and maybe more." Are those salaries on a par with male counterparts? Rita shrugs, and there's an enigmatic smile. But obviously one of the purposes of the network is to exchange information, to determine what positions are open, what salaries should be offered. Basically the motive is the same as any "old boys' network," kindred souls scratching one another's backs.

Rita Dionne-Marsolais is a stunning brunette. Micheline Bouchard is a stunning blonde. Tall and slender, she has light blue eyes and is two days younger than Rita. She also has Rita's old job at Hydro-Québec, as assistant to the president. It is a big and important job – working with vice-presidents in research and development, dealing with government officials, co-ordinating operations on the president's behalf – and her office shows it. An expanse of thirty feet by twenty is broken by settees and easy chairs upholstered in honey fabric only a shade deeper than Micheline's hair.

Micheline, like Rita, is poised, charming and, even in maternity clothes (this will be her second child), retains style. An electrical engineer, and former president of L'Ordre des ingénieurs du Québec – a professional association of some 22,000 engineers, the big majority male – Micheline is striking evidence that femininity and professional success are compatible. If Rita hyphenates her name in a compromise, Micheline clings exclusively to her maiden name. "I signed it to many technical reports before marriage," she explains. "It's very practical to be able to trace those papers. And identity is important. My husband wouldn't change his name."

Her husband, Jean-Paul Sardin, is from France. Thirty-six years old, he is general manager of the Montreal branch of a Paris electrical equipment company. In Micheline's own words, "he is exceptional for a Frenchman," supportive not only of her identity and career but turning down offers for promotion in the home office. Friends from Paris, visiting here, had warned how difficult it is for women in France to reach Micheline's position. If she worked there it would be in an inferior job.

Twenty years ago, she points out, the problem for women thinking of a professional career in Quebec was to gain entry to universities. Ten years ago, the problem was to find a job. Now the main problem is to get a promotion to the presidency of a company, or at least the board of directors. To keep pace with developments, and exchange intelligence information, Micheline has her own network – mainly of Hydro women and other engineers. She enjoys dealing with "the élite panzer corps," the thirty- to forty-year-old generation of francophone men. "They're not afraid to go in new directions. They work hard and believe in what they're doing." But there is a reservation. These men, while young and progressive, still play the role of father. Micheline is on the executive of the Chambre de Commerce, and she notes that if a conference is coming up – say, in Calgary – the other members, in discussing who should comprise a delegation, invariably consider men. "I will say, quietly, 'Don't you think a woman could be in the group?' They look uneasy and uncomfortable, but say, 'Of course.' It doesn't come naturally to them." A protective attitude towards women remains dominant.

Yet she finds Quebecers far more open minded than men in other provinces or in Europe ("they take a chance"), and it doesn't apply only to the thirty- to forty-year-olds. Older men, too, demonstrate faith – for example, her president. But Micheline does not want special concessions from a state organization such as Hydro-Québec, or even from legislation. "I want to be selected for a task, not because of official views imposed by a government, but because of my ability," she says. "An enthusiastic group of young women has emerged. This new involvement in society gives us a fresh mind. We're determined not to lose the opportunities our mothers missed."

Women have achieved high positions in other parts of Canada, but they're older than the francophones of Quebec. Having arrived at least a decade ahead, they're in their forties and fifties. This is part of the explanation for the youthful glamour of the Micheline Bouchards – but there is more. Quebec males, despite any paternalism, demand of their career women continued femininity and chic. The paradox was examined by Jennifer Stoddard, who moved to Montreal from Toronto in 1970, perfected her French, and specialized in the history of women, which she taught at the Université du Québec à Montréal while studying law at McGill University. In 1982, at the age of thirty-three, she entered the profession full time. Slender and pretty herself, she appreciates what is required of women here. "In any society you have to be an over-achiever in order to compete with males. But in addition, the Quebec woman is expected to conform more to traditional stereotypes than in Ontario. She has to be careful about wearing makeup and the proper clothing. She has to be both high powered and stunning. The same group of women in Toronto don't feel the compulsion to spend as much time on themselves. When I was teaching at the Université du Québec my counterparts in Toronto or Vancouver would wear jeans; no one said I couldn't, but the pressure here is to wear a dress."

How does Jennifer feel about it? "I resent," she admits, "the fact that I have to act this way when I'd like to be more myself. This is a time-consuming process – grooming and makeup and selecting the right clothes. It's a choice I wouldn't want for my daughters. Meanwhile, I will conform to Montreal standards. The culture here calls for more style-consciousness than anywhere else in Canada. In terms of long-range feminism that's bad, because you're expected to perform like a man but look like a woman. But in the short haul it's probably good; strategically it gives you an advantage. If you're packaged as a traditional woman you're not a threat. If you walked into an office wearing jeans and sneakers you would be. If you seem feminine and charming, you're ahead."

Even though it may be a dangerous game for the future, she concedes that women in Montreal are clever to use feminine wiles. There is also no doubt in her mind that they are at the forefront of the feminist movement in the world today. The explanation is simple: "It is easier to present radical solutions for conditions of women because they've thrown out so much of the past. My generation in Toronto doesn't show as much radicalism because we didn't start with so many restrictions. Pre-marital sex was not taboo, nor was contraception." But for Quebec women neither contraception nor divorce was simple until the late 1960's.

The result, statistically, is startling. The birth rate among Quebec women, who might have been brought up in a family of a dozen children, ranks with the lowest in the country. The divorce rate is the highest: one for every three marriages. It was 4.7 times higher in 1975 than in 1969; over the last three years the annual increase has been 40 per cent. There is acceptance of "union de fait" – living together. Changes in the civil code recognize its legality and reject any discrimination against what once was known as a "bastard." More unmarried couples are estimated to be living together in Quebec than elsewhere in Canada.

An examination of two magazines of the same parentage reveals a difference between the women of two cultures. *Châtelaine* of Montreal is avant-garde compared with its sister in Toronto. Both are published by Maclean-Hunter, but each has its own editor and writers. The English version published an article on questions of sexuality women are afraid to ask their doctors. It was rather clinical and vague. The French edition talked precisely of clitoral and vaginal orgasms and told readers that what they had heard all their lives was false – that it is, in fact, normal to have a clitoral orgasm. An issue was devoted almost entirely to death. *Châtelaine's* editor, Francine Montpetit, who is forty-seven, hesitated at first. "We knew people didn't want to read about death but we felt it was time that a magazine was able to face the subject." One article explained that modern society is frightened by death because it is not brought up to live with it. In earlier days the grandfather died in a room next to the kitchen. Today the gravely ill are shunted into hospitals, into remoteness.

Reader response was "positive and enormous," and Mme Montpetit takes special pride that even the editor of *Elle*, the Paris magazine, is envious of *Châtelaine's* ability to be daring, not so much in its subject matter but in its outspoken language. Yet if it deals frankly with lesbianism it also knows that its audience – the awakened Quebec woman of twenty-five to forty-five – retains an intrinsic interest in money value. The approach to fashions involves practical rather than expensive chic. It's okay, *Châtelaine* says, to spend $150 on a suit, "but use all the tricks you can to vary the combinations of skirt and blouses." In cooking, while "fun" dishes are condoned once in a while, the emphasis is on nutrition.

"Maybe it's our ability to face reality that gives us an advantage," says Francine Montpetit. "Historically, from Jeanne Mance on, we had to take more than other women, helping our husbands in work, raising large families. The reality has changed tremendously. Society has changed, youth has changed – and all within the last twenty years. We have problems dealing with change, but we can take it."

Mair Verthuy, the principal of Concordia University's Simone de Beauvoir Institute, brings an international perspective to women's studies. Born in Wales, she lived in France before working in Toronto for Oxford University Press, and then moving to Montreal. What Mrs. Verthuy finds remarkable about Quebec – and this makes it far different from any other part of North America – is the number of grass-roots groups taking stands on women's issues. Located in rural areas and small towns, they do not hesitate to act as lobbyists or to present argumentative briefs to governments. "Where else," she asks, "do you find farmers' wives established in strong organizations?"

Most impressive of all is La Fédération des femmes du Québec, which was founded in 1965 to commemorate the twenty-fifth anniversary of the right of women to vote in provincial elections. An umbrella agency, it includes forty-four affiliated groups with a combined membership of 130,000. Eighty per cent are francophone. The 20 per cent anglophone makeup is in proportion to population. But what was not typical was the election, in 1977, of Sheila Finestone to a three year term as president. Not only was she the first anglophone so selected, but she was Jewish. (A disdainer of labels, Mrs. Finestone has adopted the word "allophone," after the telephone, to include non-Wasp or non-French minorities such as Jews, Italians, and Greeks.)

Mrs. Finestone arrived at her feminism – she considers herself "militant" but compared with a Louky Bersianik she is really a moderate – accidentally. Active in Jewish community services for many years, she became vice-president, in 1972, of a drive for a home for the elderly. Of 1,800 applicants for residence, 1,200 were from women with an income under $3,000. Other than Ottawa's old-age pension there was no financial provision for them. "Because they'd stayed home to raise a family, instead of working, this was their crowning glory – poverty," says Mrs. Finestone. "I knew to change that condition I had to broaden myself, to move beyond my own Jewish community."

Still, there were elements of surprise and personal uncertainty when she was asked to run for the presidency of La Fédération des femmes du Québec. "I was extremely reluctant to represent Quebec women when I felt I was a member of a minority within a minority. I didn't know how I would be accepted." This was, after all, only a few months following the 1976 election of the Parti Québécois. She discussed it with her husband, Alan, who owns an advertising company, and her four grown sons, and concluded: "Either there is a place for me as a Quebec-born woman who shares concerns with my neighbours – regardless of race, language, and culture – or else I should leave Quebec." So she said she'd run.

The two other nominees, francophones with whom she had worked on committees and shared mutual respect, withdrew. Thus her election, at age fifty, was unanimous, a tribute not only to her but to the francophone women of Quebec. "It was a true example," says Mrs. Finestone, "that the concern of women transcends political philosophy, socio-economic levels, and cultural diversities." A Liberal, she works closely for the common cause with Parti Québécois members of the federation. As one result, Le Conseil de statut de la femme, a provincial para-government agency, was born. It is the best-funded and most militant council in the country, attracting the cultural élite: authors, singers, film-makers. Generally today the status of women in Quebec (as defined by issues like alimony rights and maternity leave), is at least as good as in other parts of Canada, and in some sectors much further advanced.

But it is only the start. Mrs. Finestone says: "We have arrived at the point of knowing where we need to go to achieve equality with our partners, the men. We must digest what we've attained. A change in law doesn't bring an immediate change in society. A bill of rights can decree non-discrimination, but to implement it would require thousands of inspectors. You succeed only with the will of society – getting your children to realize that women as well as men can be plumbers or electricians. We were excellent at that during the war."

Louky Bersianik, through her writings, has attracted attention not only in Quebec but in Europe as one of the fiercest of feminists. *Le Monde* allots much space to reviews of her books, as do other leading journals in Paris, Geneva, and elsewhere. Her first book, *l'Euguéli-onne*, dissected the language of repression of women. This was followed by *Pique-Nique sur l'Acropole*, a parody on the philosophy and nature of love. A kind of biting science fiction creeps in. In *l'Euguélionne* a woman from another planet is on earth only moments before she discovers that the situation is the same as where she came from – men dominate women. "Part of my struggle even with other feminists," Louky explains, "is to arouse an awareness that men still do not want to give up their mastery. Women have to understand; the revolution is not *against* men; it is *for* women." There is a phrase in Quebec that covers Louky's radicalism: "separatist-feminist." This does not mean separatism in the political sense, but rather the need for women to make their way apart from men.

Nicole Brossard, an author-feminist who is a great admirer of Louky's talent, displays a gentler approach. There is, she says, "a little Yvette" in every woman.

A Study in Contrasts

If November 15, 1976, the day the Parti Québécois swept into power, was a day of shock for anglophones (and some francophones), so January 6, 1978, must be recorded as another significant date in Quebec history. That was the day the Sun Life Assurance Company announced, to the consternation and dismay of anglophones and francophones alike, that it was moving its head office from Montreal to Toronto. Other firms had shifted earlier; some banks had transferred parts of their operations. But nothing – before or since – carried the impact of the Sun Life's decision, for this was the symbolic Montreal financial and business institution. The Sun Life's building on Dominion Square, massive and graceful with its fluted Corinthian columns, conveyed just the right impression of strength and dignity. During the Second World War, the Sun Life's vaults had sheltered the British treasury's reserves of gold. It was so secure that even members of Roger Lemelin's fictional Plouffe family took out their policies with Sun Life.

Yet hidden behind the grey, granite face of the building was a story that, in the piecing together now, tells much of what was wrong with the portion of the anglophone community that refused to yield to the times. Of twenty-one directors, two were French Canadians. Of 2,000 employees in Montreal, only 200 were French Canadians, an insulting and impractical ratio for anyone operating in the contemporary climate (and most of these 200 were engaged in "Quebec" rather than head office business). The first position of major responsibility, that of investment officer, had been given to a French Canadian only fourteen years earlier, four years after the start of the Quiet Revolution. But most significant of all in the Sun Life story was the fact that it was one man, a transplanted Scotsman named

Alistair Matheson Campbell, who decided on the move on emotional grounds. An effort at rational justification was made later. In essence it was reaffirmation for francophones, federalists as well as separatists, that old and theoretically dependable anglophone establishments could be relied on only when it suited them. January 6, 1978, was, in short, a black day for the community and for the nation.

All along, the Scottish influence in Sun Life was prominent, beginning with an immigrant from Aberdeen, Robertson Macaulay, who, in 1875 – four years after the company's founding – was taken on as secretary. Fourteen years later he became president. Robertson Macaulay was succeeded by his son, T.B. Macaulay. But another heritage was also established by Robertson. He believed the only good mathematicians or actuaries came from Scotland. Moreover, in true clan fashion, they had to come from his part of Scotland. As recently as the 1930's, 80 per cent of Sun Life's actuaries did in fact originate in Scotland. So it was not out of character when Alistair Campbell was recruited by Sun Life after he graduated, in mathematics, from the University of Aberdeen in 1928. He landed in Montreal at the age of twenty-three, and in a half century never learned to say more than "merci" and a few other trifling, patronizing words in French. He was obviously, in the description of a colleague who spent many of those years close to him, "a stubborn Scotsman." He was also hard working, rising to the presidency from 1962 to 1970, at which point he was named chairman of the board.

But Campbell – a tall, well built man of distinguished bearing whose full crop of greying hair disguised his age – was not comfortable. The Montreal he had known, from the Square Mile, the residential area of the old aristocracy, to the anachronistic Staff Common Room in his own building, no longer carried meaning. There was a distinct challenge to the established order. More French Canadians had to be hired for the sake of appearance. A former Sun Life man remembers how a public relations officer, Pierre Boileau, was showing around a group of distinguished European visitors. Later Campbell asked, "Who is that Frenchman?" Bothered by the rapidly changing environment, Campbell, while retaining an apartment in Montreal, moved his home to Ottawa. Of course he would hardly be receptive to Bill 101, which set out to establish the primacy of the French language in Quebec. Campbell fumed and made no secret of his frustration, claiming that conditions of language would render a head office operation such as the Sun Life's impossible.

At this point, the story takes on the semblance of high drama, with some characters remaining in a hazy background. But one possible script goes this way: a group of prominent Montrealers, sitting around their club and apprehensive over what was transpiring, listened while Campbell, the most vociferous, became so agitated that he said maybe it was time to teach the Parti Québécois a lesson. There was respectful silence while he built up to the point of threatening to pull Sun Life out of Montreal. Someone muttered, "Go to it, Alistair."

It was not a conspiracy in a legal sense, for no one else joined his crusade. But undoubtedly it was a moral conspiracy, for no one attempted to discourage him. In the words of one knowledgeable chief executive: "Campbell was being allowed to test the water." Camille A. Dagenais, chairman of the mammoth SNC engineering group, says he isn't sure the script worked out exactly that way. But he does say that "someone had to go on the block," so intense was the feeling over Bill 101, and the fiery Campbell was not an illogical choice.

Campbell guarded his plan closely, and of the 2,000 men and women who worked in the Sun Life building only three – Campbell himself, Thomas M. Galt, the president, and George F.S. Clarke, the executive vice-president – knew of it. None of the marketing people was asked about what effect a move might have on sales in Quebec; none of the public relations people was warned so they could prepare a coherent explanation. The board of directors, most of whom were Campbell appointees, approved. The announcement was made: the Sun Life Assurance Company, bedrock of the Montreal establishment for 107 years, was taking away its head office. The company, it said, could not live with regulations under the new language bill. The fact is that there were no regulations in effect at that stage. They were only under discussion, and other heads of corporations (A. Jean de Grandpré of Bell Canada, for example), were preparing to go to Quebec City to appear before Camille Laurin, the minister responsible, with demands and arguments for a reasonable approach. But the Sun Life made no such appearance. Instead, with a large number of routine proxies in hand, it called for a meeting of endorsation by policyholders (because it is a mutual company, policyholders are the equivalent of shareholders), on January 27 – in Toronto. There is little doubt that Toronto was selected so that officers would not have to confront Montrealers on their home ground. The reaction in

58

Quebec was swift and filled with condemnation, especially in the francophone media.

But anglophones were far from complacent. Richard Holden, a lawyer who was forty-six at the time, recalls the moment: "It was just by chance that I was a policyholder – and I hit the roof." Holden's seventeen-year-old son, Arthur, hearing his father expound on how terrible this was, what it would mean to morale in Montreal, how it would discredit anglophones generally and encourage separatism, said, "You're always writing letters to the press. Don't just let this thing drop."

Holden could be classed, if the drama is to unfold on storybook lines, as a typical Westmount "Wasp" – educated at Westmount High School and McGill University, and member of a prominent law firm. But he was prepared to take on a Wasp establishment. He remembered how, when he was a child, his father would drive him past the Sun Life and say it was the biggest building in the British Empire – and therefore solid and immutable. That was the image that stayed with him and made him so upset when he heard of the company's decision. Now he threatened Sun Life with an injunction, arguing it was illegal to use proxies given by policyholders over the previous three years, for general purposes, in an issue as crucial as this. Sun Life lawyers came to see Holden, but he was adamant. The Toronto meeting was postponed until April 25 to enable the company to collect fresh proxies specifically endorsing the move.

By now the argument had changed. There was no mention of language, merely, according to a brochure sent to policyholders, a general desire "to remove any uncertainty as to the company's future position." But plenty of allegations were circulated, among them that Sun Life agents had difficulty selling potential customers out west or in the US because salesmen of rival companies (particularly Great-West Life), were saying that policyholders would be paid in "Quebec" dollars. Sun Life officers also seized on a statement by Jacques Parizeau, Quebec finance minister, as implying a threat to make the company – two thirds of whose 932,000 policyholders lived in Britain, the US, Australia, and other places – invest heavily in Quebec. The fact is that every government since the earliest time of Premier Maurice Duplessis in the 1930's had urged Sun Life to invest a decent portion of the revenue it collected from *Quebec* customers in their own province. The company took the position that it should be free to allocate its resources any place in the world where it could gain the highest yield. In this context Quebec had benefited only when it served the company's purpose.

John Lynch-Staunton, who was a Montreal city councillor while working as an investment officer at Sun Life, remembers that during the period of the 1960's, when Montreal experienced a series of terrorist bombings, Lucien Saulnier, chairman of the city's executive committee, set out to raise a loan. The motive was to show the world that despite incidents of violence the city was stable. Actually the city's credit was good, but major corporations were now expected to underline this. The target was $40 million. Banks and credit unions responded swiftly and Saulnier anticipated $1 million from Sun Life. Lynch-Staunton was asked to act as intermediary. He came away with $500,000 and a lecture that this was gesture enough. It was his moment for disenchantment.

Under an old federal statute, The Canadian and British Insurance Companies Act, it was inconceivable that a provincial government could compel a company to invest any funds gathered elsewhere. No one was more aware of the legality than Sun Life itself. During the Liberal government which preceded the Parti Québécois, the minister of financial institutions, William Tetley, introduced legislation aimed at two automobile insurance companies which had transferred virtually all their Quebec policyholders' payments out of the province. The bill, similar to legislation in other parts of Canada, established as a condition for licence to operate in Quebec that a "reasonable proportion" of Quebec revenue must be invested in the province. The Sun Life, wanting a good law, lent one of its lawyers to Tetley's department. The bill was passed but never promulgated.

None of this was publicized at the time of Campbell's action. As far as the outside world was concerned there was now a secessionist government in office in Quebec. Who knew what would happen to insurance policies written by a company with its head office in Montreal? The proxies poured in. Richard Holden, meanwhile, was collecting his own, mostly from policyholders who had been reading about his campaign. The city council of Windsor, Ontario, sent its vote along with a letter of encouragement. Interestingly enough, Ontario business leaders and politicians appeared to perceive the danger to national unity more readily than did Campbell and his board of directors. Darcy McKeough, the Ontario treasurer, said in an interview that while he never liked to turn down business in Toronto this was one occasion he wished had never arisen.

The meeting of April 25 was held in the Royal York Hotel. Holden recalls riding down the elevator with one of the Sun Life directors, Ian D. Sinclair, at the time chairman and chief executive officer of Canadian Pacific. Sinclair was preoccupied. Parizeau's new budget had been tabled the week before, and in it was a provincial income tax rate that would make it harder to attract executives to Montreal. Any drawback, Sinclair told Holden, was not language but this kind of personal taxation. Yet the Campbell decision – which Sinclair had supported – was based ostensibly on Bill 101.

The vote went as anticipated. No one would reasonably expect that policyholders who lived outside Canada would be concerned about the country's internal problems. Eighty-four per cent approved of the move. Among those who voted against it were Mitchell, Douglas, and David Bourke, the sons of George W. Bourke, Campbell's predecessor as president of Sun Life. What were the repercussions of the battle? To Arthur Holden, who is now heading for a law degree at McGill, his father was a hero. To some of his friends, Richard Holden was a Don Quixote, tilting fruitlessly. But to himself, to this day, there remains a sense of satisfaction. "At least I slowed them down a bit," he says.

What would T.B. Macaulay have done? "He would have told the government to go to hell, and he would have stayed," says J.W. "Jack" Popkin, a Manitoban who, in 1930, fresh with a Bachelor of Commerce degree from Queen's University, was one of the few non-Scotsmen to be hired by Macaulay as a mathematician. Now retired, Popkin, who spent the last twelve of his forty-two years at Sun Life as chief economist, looks on the dislocation not in any political or social context but rather in economic terms: the expenditure involved in moving 300 men and women. No precise figure is available, but a rule of thumb is that it can cost $50,000 to transfer a family, depending on the differential in home prices. Thus Sun Life might have spent $15 million, a figure that has not shown up as such in any annual report, but, probably spread over a couple of years, is included in general operating expenses. Popkin, ever practical, merely would have waited for results of the expected referendum; a step towards separation or sovereignty-association would have been all the reason required. "But obviously, after the referendum, as it turned out, there wouldn't have been any reason to move," he says.

The curious fact – and it is underscored by many chief executives – is that Montreal directors of Sun Life, such as Ian Sinclair and

Jock Finlayson, vice-chairman of the Royal Bank of Canada, saw their own companies remaining in Montreal. The reality is that language regulations did not turn out to be insurmountable; indeed, for internationally-oriented companies they were relatively light. But more pertinently, federally-chartered financial institutions, including the francophone Banque Nationale, have refused as a matter of principle to apply for so-called francization certificates – and they have done so without repercussions. The Sun Life would have fallen into the same category.

The company now designates Montreal as "the national office," within which operates the Quebec division headed by Pierre Boileau, the "Frenchman" whom Campbell once wanted identified. Boileau refers an author's delicate questions to Peter R. MacGibbon. In 1978, as vice-president and secretary, it was MacGibbon who signed the notice that went out to policyholders. Now vice-president for corporate affairs, and based in Toronto, part of his responsibility is public relations – that is, restoring the image of Sun Life.

MacGibbon is a pleasant, soft-spoken, mild-mannered man with a white fringe of hair. A Winnipegger, he joined Sun Life in 1947 and personally approved of the move in 1978, because, "Let us say Quebec had separated. Policyholders would have had to collect in Quebec." But in all the statements and press releases at the time, did the company's officers not make it clear they were not afraid Quebec would separate? Yes. Then why didn't Sun Life attempt to offset the sales pitch of competitors by rebutting the canard that policyholders would be paid in "Quebec" dollars? "We couldn't, in all fairness, tell people there wouldn't be complications. Look at what happened in Cuba." What did happen in Cuba? Well, Sun Life had been burned there – back in 1953 when the government of Fulgencio Batista (the dictator who was overthrown in 1959 by Fidel Castro), enacted a law that said all insurance contracts had to be in Cuban pesos. The Sun Life had been writing these in US dollars for its many Cuban policyholders who wanted guarantees of redemption in dollars, not pesos. On the quiet, Sun Life made private deals, guaranteeing at least a portion in dollars. Batista never knew of this. "It was a complex situation," says MacGibbon with a sigh.

Is he equating Quebec with Cuba? No, of course not; but there was a fear of the Quebec government taking some kind of drastic measure. Why didn't the company say so at the time? "Why?" he repeats. "Because we didn't want to add fuel. We were in the position banks have been in the past. Would you go out and broadcast there's a run on the bank?" But doesn't the Federal Insurance Act offer protection? It does and it doesn't. "It's fuzzy." Then, suddenly, MacGibbon asks a question: Isn't it possible that the Sun Life action led to the subsequent decline in Parti Québécois fortunes? "We were like the little boy who pointed and said, 'Look, the emperor has no clothes.'" MacGibbon is referring, of course, to the defeat of the Parti Québécois on the issue of sovereignty-association. Apart from the fact that no one would seriously accept that Parti Québécois fortunes have indeed declined, in the light of the 1981 election results, there are obvious and interesting dimensions to the MacGibbon thesis. This rationale was never thought of at the time of the move, or at least talked about publicly. If anything, it reinforces the conspiracy theory – that Campbell's intention was to show up the emperor.

The paranoia and insensitivity that prevailed in 1978 are not yet over. MacGibbon admits he never felt comfortable in Montreal. "I made French Canadians nervous when I tried out my French," he says. But what bothered him most, when the move was announced, was the reaction of anglophone members of the Board of Trade: "They were hostile." Why does he think they were hostile? "Because if they were in advertising or similar fields they were afraid they were losing a good client." Isn't it possible they were hostile because they felt Sun Life was betraying the anglophone community? MacGibbon nods. "Yes, especially if they came from Westmount."

The Sun Life lost 30 per cent of its agents and its business in Quebec. McGill professors called off their policies. On a bigger scale, the Sun Life had written 40 per cent of Hydro-Québec's group life and health insurance policies. Hydro-Québec cancelled. More important, Sun Life lost substantial fees as principal administrator of Hydro-Québec's life and health plan. A francophone insurance company, La Sauvegarde, was the immediate beneficiary, its holdings rising in one leap from $2 billion to $3 billion. "It was the contract of the century for us," says La Sauvegarde's president, Clément Gauthier. "It made headlines, and this you cannot measure in dollars." But other reaction, persisting to this day, was less publicized. The Molson Brewery labour agreement is such that no pension policy or any other involving personnel may be taken out with Sun Life. The prestigious C.D. Howe Research Institute, disdaining any connection, even indirect, eliminated the address which it had once displayed on its letterhead: the Sun Life Building. It now lists itself simply as 1155 Metcalfe Street. Other tenants, as leases expired, moved out. The cost in that sense was incalculable.

Yet the Sun Life, at its annual meeting in Toronto on February 10, 1981 – at which Campbell, having reached age seventy-five, retired as a director and chairman of the executive committee – proudly announced that it had attained more than $1 billion in premiums in 1980 for the first time in its history, an increase of 9.9 per cent over 1979. There was no claim that the increase might have been due to the departure from Montreal, but the suggestion was not discouraged. Ignored was the fact that in the past Quebec had accounted for one third of the company's Canadian business, and the annual report might have looked even more impressive without the setback sustained there. Most telling, however, was the 1980 performance of Great-West Life. Its business was $1.3 billion, a 17 per cent increase. James W. Burns, who is president of Paul Desmarais' Power Corporation but retains the title of chairman of the Winnipeg-based insurance company, calls the Sun Life performance "almost flat" – meaning that in view of inflation, 9.9 per cent was no real gain.

What about the accusation that agents of Great-West had told potential Sun Life customers they would be paid in "Quebec" dollars? Burns shakes his head vigorously and says, "There may have been individuals saying it – there are in any business, the GM salesman saying his cars are safer than a Ford – but it certainly was not company policy." Anyway, he is aware from his own experience that in the US, where Great-West does more than half its business, "Ninety-eight per cent of the people hardly know Canada. They buy a policy from an agent, not a company." Since the Sun Life – with regional headquarters in London, England, and Wellesley, Massachusetts – derives most of its business from outside Canada, one assumes the same principle applies. Burns adds a stark point: "The Sun Life could have said a takeover was impossible. Federal laws protect insurance companies. If it had been us, we would have given our agents copies of the act and said, 'Forget that nonsense.' " In August 1981, three years after the switch, and despite the claim that Montreal remained "the national office," the Sun Life surreptitiously moved its archives to Toronto. Included were portraits of the Macaulays and other great figures of the past, enough memorabilia and linkage with Montreal to fill a forty-five foot van. The packers and truck drivers were told to keep silent.

One of Richard Holden's law partners is a French Canadian

named Jean-Paul Cardinal, who grew up in the working-class district of St. Henri. When informed recently that as far back as 1964 a French Canadian had been appointed to a senior post in Sun Life, Cardinal said, "Sure, they changed his broom for a vacuum cleaner." In such bittersweet humour is a reflection of the ability today of French Canadians, in their new self-confidence, to look back on an unpleasant and unnecessary act, not as ancient history, but as a constant reminder of the unreliability of some old masters. The miracle of the Sun Life affair is that it did not contribute to separatism. Time had a cooling effect. If the referendum had been held immediately after the company's pronouncement – instead of two years later – one wonders what would have been the outcome.

There were earlier Scotsmen – the McGills, the McTavishes, the Macdonalds – among the staunchest of Montreal's builders; and there were those who came after Alistair Campbell who were determined to make a positive mark on the city. J. Stuart Spalding, a native of Edinburgh, says of Campbell, "He was of another generation."

Spalding is vice-president and treasurer of Bell Canada. He is a forthright, practical financial man with a soul. Tall and slender and deceptively youthful in appearance at forty-seven, he refuses to be pressured by what he regards as emotional arguments about why money should be packed up in bundles and sent off to Toronto (if not literally, at least in computers), to be handled by experts who are in a position to exchange exclusive investment information. He calls this "a bit of nonsense." In an age of instant communications, the same knowledge and speed of action are available to everyone. "We're in the telecommunications business," he says. "If we don't know what's happening, everywhere, who does?"

All of Bell Canada's corporate and pension money is handled by Spalding's staff of twenty-five specialists, including some former members of Sun Life who refused to move to Toronto. He regards his people as equal to the best anywhere, and maybe even a little better. The pension fund, covering employees in Ontario as well as Quebec, consists of assets of $1.5 billion in bonds and mortgages. In addition, the corporation itself raises large sums to finance its operations. Before and after each transaction there is loose money on hand – at any given moment something like $500 million. This enters the money market, flowing in and out of the kind of short-term investment Spalding and his team consider proper. No executive of Bell, he avers, has ever put pressure on him to emulate Canadian Pacific and switch his department to Toronto or anywhere else.

All shareholders' activities are also run from Montreal. Records are kept by Bell itself, in contrast to other big corporations which assign this function to trust companies. It is a huge operation, involving 265,000 shareholders, 80 per cent of whom live outside Quebec. In the last couple of years not a single anxious query has arisen, though in 1978, during the period when Sun Life was in the news, a few men and women phoned to ask about the safety of their holdings. Answered by employees who plainly were not anglophones but spoke English with a French accent, some of the callers obviously felt uneasy, for they followed up with letters. They appeared satisfied by the reassuring responses which Spalding or staff members sent back. Spalding declines to condescend to any explanation that Bell Canada operates under a federal charter that is inviolable. He prefers, rather, to argue: "We provide an essential service. This is what justifies us being in business and is your best protection."

Spalding earned his degree as a chartered accountant in Edinburgh in 1957 and immigrated that year to Canada. He worked two years in Toronto before engaging in money management in Montreal. He joined Bell Canada in 1972. He is an intelligent and sensitive human being, a credit to his company and the community which he adopted twenty-two years ago and in which he learned to speak French. He does not dismiss out of hand those who question whether alternatives for running his financial department might be preferable. Maybe, he says, their arguments have a point. But the test is how much of that point is logical. "I like to think I deal reasonably well with all propositions, so long as they're not made purely on the basis of emotion. So far, no one has been able to demonstrate there would be any financial saving or advantage for Bell Canada not to be operating out of Montreal, or that we could be any more effective than we are now in dealings with New York or London or Zurich."

His concept runs deep. It is the concept of a modern corporation man who believes that service and value establish the strongest sales position. Bell Canada, he says, has been responsive to the needs of customers: "Francophones in Quebec think as well of Bell Canada as anglophones do in Ontario. Without this goodwill, you run into trouble."

66

Not long after Alistair Campbell decided to move, David M. Culver, president and chief executive officer of Alcan, Canada's biggest multinational, was faced with a similar decision: where to shift the head office. Montreal had been the base for the Aluminum Company of Canada for forty years. There had been a transfer once before in 1939 – ironically *to* Montreal from Toronto, where the company was established in 1928 after the monolithic Aluminum Company of America divested itself of foreign operations. More whimsically still, Toronto was not even in the running now. Nor was Calgary or any other city. It was simply a question of how to cope with the administrative size of Alcan, which, like its parent before it, had grown too big. So the decision was made. Aluminum Company of *Canada* would remain in the existing offices in Place Ville Marie. But Alcan Aluminium Limited, which embraced the entire global network with operations in thirty-five countries and revenues of $5 billion a year, would separate itself – to quarters a half dozen blocks away, on Sherbrooke Street.

Culver was content once the dilemma was resolved. A native Montrealer, he had spent long and pleasant hours strolling along Sherbrooke Street. A certain elegance in himself responded appreciatively to the stately mansions sheltered by tall old elm trees. Afflicted by disease, not many trees were left; nor were there many of the old mansions. But one that had always attracted him, at the corner of Stanley Street, was still there. Indeed, it was in the process of complete overhaul, at the instructions of the Shah of Iran, to serve as a trade mission. (Some whispered that the cost of renovation alone was $500,000.) But revolution had swept Iran and the place might be available.

So it was, and so it came about that Alcan bought that building and others adjacent to it, including the old Berkeley Hotel and two three storey town houses. Another structure, a few storeys taller, was planned for construction in the rear, to link up with the acquisitions and form a world complex for Alcan at a cost of $40 million. But Culver's own office, when everything is in readiness in 1983, will be located in that outstanding mansion he had so admired: the former residence of Lord Atholstan, founder of *The Montreal Star*. Three floors in height, the antithesis of the high-rises that dominate modern cities, it is to Culver's taste, not only for aesthetic reasons but because, as he perceived it, "Alcan was purchasing a home."

That is important to bear in mind: the kind of symbolism that the Sun Life once represented in a massive twentieth century structure was now to be assumed by Alcan in a building dating back to 1895. Alcan was here to stay, regardless of any political upheavals. Solidity and continuity, to say nothing of inherent wealth, were manifest in an effort to retain the commercial importance of a city without destroying its character or gentle landmarks. If there was ever a city-state mentality in Montreal it was reflected here, at the corner of Sherbrooke and Stanley Streets, in a place at one time dominated by a Wasp press baron, and now taken over by an industrial giant with its own empire. But there was a profound difference. Neither individuals nor corporations dictated the affairs of city or province.

What did dominate today? One might say governments, but that would be only part of the truth. In Alcan's instance the force that kept it here was raw power in the form of rivers and hydroelectricity. Alcan was impotent without the bauxite which it brought in from other countries, and the energy with which it could convert it to aluminum. Since Quebec possesses the energy, and allows Alcan to tap it cheaply, the cynics say the company enjoys a convenient marriage; divorce would be unthinkable. Alcan pulling out? Setting up head offices elsewhere while taking advantage of Quebec resources? What would the provincial government – not only the Parti Québécois but any party – do? Probably nationalize Alcan's existing generators and smelters in the Saguenay area. They are worth billions.

That might be the obvious course but it would not take into account the fact that Alcan has an exceptionally fine record as a corporate citizen. Many years before Bill 101, labour contracts were written in French. (A unilingual anglophone executive, if he needed to understand a passage, had to call on a translator.) Long before the Parti Québécois came to office, its members in the Saguenay-Lac St. Jean region, the traditional heartland of separatism, acknowledged that Alcan was a good, sensitive employer. More currently and more specifically, five months after René Lévesque and the Parti Québécois won the 1976 election, Alcan was confronted with a major quandary: whether to build a new and expensive smelter at Grande Baie to replace aging facilities at Arvida. Since many anglophones saw only gloom ahead, with the possibility of Quebec's secession, it took a courageous president and board of directors to think it out.

Culver recalls clearly the morning in April 1977 when they met in the huge circular boardroom which dominates the thirty-first floor of Place Ville Marie. A sixteenth century Japanese silk screen painting on one wall might have lent a perspective of serenity and composure. But the atmosphere was far from tranquil. A great amount of money was involved – half a billion dollars. The first point raised by Culver, and accepted immediately by his colleagues, was that the Parti Québécois was only one of five or six governments that would come and go during the lifetime of a smelter. With that as a premise, the next questions were analyzed academically and practically. What about the risk of civil war? One chance in a hundred. How about "ethical standards" slipping – that is, intensified hostility of francophones towards the anglophone community culminating in a takeover? That scored ten in a hundred chances. And so Culver and the directors went down the list all morning, ending with agreement that on balance there could be only one course: to proceed with the erection of the first new Alcan smelter in Canada in a quarter of a century.

Culver is frank enough to admit that there was no alternative site in British Columbia (Kitimat is another important Alcan location), or anywhere else that would have made sense. The choice was simply to proceed then or to wait into the indefinite future when the Parti Québécois might be replaced by a government more to the liking of anglophones – and in the meanwhile, foreign rivals could pull ahead. "We're paid to take risks," says Culver. "In any case, our real support in Quebec is not the government but the people of Saguenay."

They are indeed a special breed. Not perhaps the Unipeds which Indians told Jacques Cartier inhabited the area – men with one enormous leg capable of outracing any animal. Nor was "le royaume du Saguenay" abounding in oranges and almonds and mines filled with gold and silver. But there was strength in the settlers, who long ago began a movement to break away from the province because they felt ignored economically by Quebec City. And there was wealth in the powerful rivers. With innovators bringing the two together, and creating, in 1925, the new city of Arvida as a centre for aluminum production, the Kingdom of the Saguenay became a reality. Alcan is the principal employer, with 10,000 on the payroll. The $500 million spent on the new smelter was only the start; a program to replace Arvida facilities piece by piece will add up to $2 billion by 1999. Meanwhile, Grande Baie has already paid off. Even with the smelter not fully operational by the end of 1981, Alcan, for the first time in its history, was neck and neck with its main competitor and onetime parent, Alcoa, in the contest to rank as the biggest aluminum producer in the world.

David Culver, fifty-eight, is slender and dapper with a mind that ranges far beyond the ability to manage a giant multinational corporation. Characteristic understatement is illustrated by the physical makeup of his office in Place Ville Marie. Unlike that of other chief executive officers, whose space can rival a squash court, Culver's measures eighteen by twenty feet. The designer asked him: "What do you want, a Rolls Royce or a Cadillac?" Culver immediately opted for a Rolls Royce, and that is what one senses in the unostentatious quality, from the pegged flooring to the exquisite eighteenth century French table that serves as a desk. The decision to move in 1983 to a low-rise building was "a matter of personal preference and style." Culver concedes that decisions of big companies, where one expects highly computerized or dispassionate analyses to govern, "are often made on a personal basis." He quotes a celebrated maxim: "A business organization is a group of people helping one man do a job." But it is one man, who, in most instances, dominates. There are, fortunately for Montreal, at least as many Culvers as there are Campbells.

Of Sports and Sex

There were strong men before him – for instance, the legendary Grenon, whom Wolfe's soldiers called "the Hercules of the North." And there was Joseph Montferrand, trapper and lumberjack, who whipped the best boxers in the British garrison in Montreal. But no one rose to the height of attainment or idolatry of Louis Cyr, whose name remains immortalized in French-Canadian folk stories and whose statue, as massive in bronze as he was in real life a century ago, occupies a corner of St. Elizabeth Square in the working-class district of St. Henri, where he grew up. In his day, Cyr was billed as "the strongest man in the world," but the statue is not content with such a limiting superlative. There stands Louis, his powerful arms folded, enormous chest thrust forward, bar-bells lying conquered at his feet, with the dates 1869-1912 and the inscription: "L'homme le plus fort de tous les temps."

If he was not the strongest man of all time, who's to dispute it? Certainly not his descendants, who paid for the casting, or the City of Montreal, which spent $25,000 for the base and concrete emplacement. What makes it so intriguing is that the resurrection came about in 1973, when French Canadians had more recent heroes they could call upon, such as Maurice "Rocket" Richard. Even more pertinently, the need for glory had declined in the rapid rise of French-Canadian political assertiveness. But the fact is that sports figures have performed a particularly significant part in the history and evolution of Quebec, more perhaps than in any other area of North America, because of the distinctive composition of the two cultures and the perennial rejection by many francophones of the British "conquest." Throughout the published works of French writers, most notably the book of E.Z. Massicotte, *Athletes Cana-*

dien-Français, published in 1909, two themes dominate: exploits of endurance and a fervent nationalism. The usual protagonist is dignified and slow to anger, but once incited he knows how to deal with his goaders, *les Anglais*. Thus he emerges as the symbol of the hardiness and determination of his own people.

Louis Cyr stood for these virtues when he took the battle to London, right to the heartland of the English, and, in 1889, before a crowd of 5,000 and in the presence of the Prince of Wales, lifted a 551-pound weight with one finger. The British were charmed by Cyr's friendly and unassuming manner, but at home he was regarded by anglophones with some misgiving, the ultimate in French-Canadian individuality, the loner as contrasted with the team player. There had been an earlier period when the English and French of Montreal participated in team activities, even joining together on the same sides. In one of the first ice hockey games on record, held on a rink at the corner of Dorchester and Bleury Streets in 1837, names like Charlebois, Peloquin, and Guilbeault were mixed with Mc-Clune, Stapleton, and Knox. But by the 1870's a different pattern had emerged: English Montrealers retained much of the ceremony and tradition of their ancestry, continuing their interest in cricket, rugger, and other team events; French Canadians engaged more in personal outings such as snowshoeing, tobogganing, paddling, and horse-racing. Thus there were two separate worlds in athletics as in other activities.

It may be that the Catholic Church dissuaded French Canadians from social contact with Protestants. Certainly there was little encouragement in parish organizations for them to engage in team activities – indeed, in sports of any kind. But Graeme Decarie, the Concordia University historian, believes that French Canadians were limited in team events not because of any influence of priests, but because of simple economics. In the 1880's and 1890's lacrosse was played by some French groups against the English, but that was about the limit. Other sports cost too much in equipment. Moreover, the French-Canadian community was hardly in a position to afford the club house and other facilities of the Montreal Amateur Athletic Association, the preserve of the English community.

However, secular influences did reach French youngsters, and by the 1920's the church itself, emulating the successful Catholic attitude towards recreation and sports in the US, followed with similar programs of its own. The ultimate in team participation was hockey, especially professional hockey, which carried with it a rivalry that suited Montreal's temperament. When the Montreal Maroons played the Montreal Canadiens there was no question that much more than hockey was involved; it was war between the English and French, the continuation of the conflict of nearly two centuries earlier. Tim Burke, a sports writer for most of his forty-eight years, remembers how, as a four-year-old, the first thing he asked his father in the morning was: "Did the Maroons win last night?" A defeat was a blow at *les Anglais.*

Ironically, a division of loyalty existed among the English, especially those who were devoted followers of Howie Morenz of the Canadiens. Even though the Maroons played their last game in 1938 (having started in 1924), Burke figures there are still a number of what he calls "unreconstructed" fans floating around. These are of his father's generation, or the sons and grandsons who were either original supporters or brainwashed in later years. Burke points out that the Forum is the only rink in the National Hockey League circuit where "a solid core of local people roots for the out-of-town team." Among these "unreconstructed" Maroons there's a special affection for the Boston Bruins, probably because of the link with New England held by Maritimers living in Montreal. But Burke's childhood memories, or his *Gazette* columns which reflect a redneck hue from time to time, do not prevent him from acknowledging that today the Canadiens possess a special and positive meaning. "If any outfit ever demonstrated how the anglophones and francophones can get along it's the Canadiens. Half the players are English, half are French. No sports dynasty has ever lasted as long as the Canadiens or done as well – not even the New York Yankees." Nor is there any doubt in Burke's mind that "Rocket" Richard was the greatest hockey player of all time. "To me he represented the flair, the will, the desire to do better than anyone else. The bigger the game, the bigger the goal."

Few dispute the eulogy. Andy O'Brien, who retired several years ago after forty years as one of the country's most widely read sports editors, says: "Howie Morenz was exciting and unafraid. But he didn't have the lightning-stroke charisma of the Rocket. Richard was the complete professional. He gave everything he had, and the fans recognized they were getting their money's worth. I cannot remember a Canadiens' loss when the Rocket didn't blame himself." That is why the now famous, historic incident of the 1954-55 season has been so widely written about, so extensively interpreted and misinterpreted. One of the most celebrated of folk heroes, Maurice "Rocket" Richard was suspended for rough tactics. (Opposing players, anxious to keep him from the puck, were always going after Richard, and he struck back with ferocity, so much so that in his eighteen National Hockey League seasons he piled up penalties equivalent to twenty-five games.) But the timing in 1955 was unfortunate, for it barred Richard from the Stanley Cup championship playoffs. Even more disquieting was the fact that the man who decided on the suspension, as president of the National Hockey League, was Clarence Campbell. Many of the Richard devotees were convinced that Campbell felt only disdain for French Canadians and would never have imposed such a severe sentence on an anglophone player.

On Thursday, March 17, the Canadiens appeared at the Forum, their star banished. But the enemy was on hand. Richard fans went wild, pelting Campbell with tomatoes and eggs. The younger ones stampeded through downtown Montreal, smashing shop windows and overturning cars. Though it was hardly recognized at the time, it was a classic example of built-in frustration – racial, political, economic, and every other variety – aroused at the suggestion that *les Anglais* were again committing a terrible act against the people of Quebec. Essentially, in the fans' minds, when Campbell suspended Richard he suspended the entire French-Canadian nation, and they were going to do something about it. But the rioting, which took police four hours to bring under control, was, in retrospect, not the *first* modern manifestation of French-Canadian fury as so many analysts thought, or traced back, when separatism became an obvious and live issue five or six years later. It was the *last* of the warnings. French Canadians then turned from idolatry of sports figures to other outlets for discharging feelings of anger and frustration; for instance, towards trade unions and the strike weapon. Lester Pearson was one of the few politicians to interpret the Forum upheaval for what it was, and later, as prime minister, brought such Quebecers as Jean Marchand, Gérard Pelletier, and Pierre Elliott Trudeau to Ottawa.

What, in retrospect, has Richard to say about it, what is his assessment? This very kind and gentle man, aged sixty (only his handshake, with a massive grip seemingly capable of holding ten sticks at once reminds you of his onetime power on skates), says he does not feel qualified to make pronouncements about the past. To him, the Campbell affair had nothing to do with politics and to this day he cannot or will not delve into whether it marked the beginning of the French-Canadian revolution. "I've never made a statement about it, and I still won't," he says. "I've got my own ideas but I don't know if they are right or wrong. So why say anything? I know one thing. I'm not for separatism. That's the only thing I'm against." As for the old concept of war between the French and English represented on ice, he says: "It never came to my mind to think about it, whether someone was English or French. When I was on the ice I was out to win – for the team and for myself." Then, after some prodding, he admits that occasionally after a game he would say, if he had played particularly well, how good it was for the French-Canadian image. But his definitive word on the subject, and he appears sincerely to mean it, is this: "The only thing I went for was the goal – trying to get goals, not the other guy."

Richard, who dresses smartly, with a tendency towards grey suits, gives every impression of being a successful businessman (wholesale fishing equipment, heating oil, public relations), and tends to dismiss the notion that French Canadians needed sports figures as heroes. His own idol as a youngster was an Ontarian, Hector "Toe" Blake, with whom he later wound up as a team-mate. But the reverence paid Richard is still obvious, even among Quebecers who were not born for his final game twenty-one years ago. When he walked out on the Forum ice for a presentation in 1981, he received a bigger ovation than Guy Lafleur, the current Canadiens' star who occupies Richard's former right-wing position. And when the Montreal Expos reached the playoffs for the National League pennant in 1981, it was Richard who was invited to toss out the ball in the last game at Olympic Stadium. Thus the mythology lingers, and despite the outlet in politics today hardly a French Canadian of at least middle age does not venerate Richard. Representative is Pierre Marion, who, forty-two years old and a public relations officer with Bell Canada, remembers how, as a child, his teachers always pointed to "Rocket" Richard as a symbol of "determination." He was told that if he wanted to get ahead in life he should pattern himself on Richard. It was only later that Marion, as an adult, identified the Rocket and other luminaries as symbols of the conflict with *les Anglais*. But the influence, he says, must have been there all along.

A more recent Canadiens' star, Ken Dryden, agrees with Richard that hockey is not a kind of crusade. "There's no doubt that what Richard said about thinking only of scoring is true for other players. You play for the team, and that's where the emotion stops. Others can make of it what they will." In other words, fans may – or at least did at one time – perceive the Canadiens in a special aura. Dryden, the six foot three inch Torontonian who joined the Canadiens in 1971 as goalkeeper, vividly relates his own perception as he sits over a meal and recalls his most dramatic experience – the night of November 15, 1976, when the results of the election that put the Parti Québécois into power became known:

Usually in a dressing room, preparing for a game, players are not too thoughtful. They're wound up, so there are just quick expressions of little things. Someone refers to something that happened on the last road trip, and someone else mentions the girl he'd met on that trip – kind of off-the-wall conversation. The night of November fifteenth it was much the same, with a couple of insignificant bits about the election. It started as a boring game; we were playing St. Louis, not an exciting team. Only as time went on did you begin to feel it wasn't just another game against St. Louis. The atmosphere in the Forum was restrained. There'd been a good play around the nets, the kind that usually caused the crowd to leap up, but in this case there was no response. Maybe there was a slight rise in the buzzing, nothing more. The first election results were flashed on the scoreboard – something like four seats to three for the Liberals, or eight to six for the Parti Québécois. I don't remember, but it was so close there was very little reaction. Then a sudden "Ah" from the spectators, as though they were watching the flashing of a score at a critical game out of town. It would appear one letter at a time – P.Q. – so there was some suspense, and the "Ah's" became louder and louder as the figures became bigger and bigger. Looking back, I realize the number of *péquistes* was larger than was first apparent, and the early restraint was maybe due to caution and discounting. Then, in an instant, the controls were off, and even we, the players, became caught up in the excitement. You'd hear a roar and know a goal wasn't scored. You'd be flipping your head up to catch the results; you'd become as much a spectator as the other spectators. You'd be fighting yourself to concentrate, telling yourself, "C'mon you've a game to play." After that bit of pep-talk you'd flip your head again and give yourself another pep-talk. In the dressing room, between the second and third periods, it became something really to comment about, and it was mostly gallows humour. Someone would say, "I think our next game is in Toronto. We'd better get our passports ready." Then, in the third period, when the results were clearer and clearer, the roars came as though they were for full-blown goals, as if Guy Lafleur had done something special. The last flash on the board, letter by letter, said "nouveau gouvernement" and there was an explosion of roaring and singing.

Dryden remembers that the Canadiens won that game, but he cannot recall the score. What stood out for him was the history of the moment, and though perhaps he did not see it this way one can link that night in the Forum with the night, two decades earlier, when Richard was barred from playing. Hockey again reflected the mood of the people watching it. The political movement that developed with the rioting over Richard's suspension culminated on November 15 with the triumph of a nationalist French-Canadian party. Dryden recognized its significance when, a few days later, he sat down with Maurice Podbrey, the artistic director of the Centaur Theatre. Dryden had been retained as adviser on a play called *Les Canadiens*. The play was still being written, on fairly standard lines, about the exploits of a hockey team. But the two men concurred in how it should be reshaped. As Podbrey, a sports fan, puts it, "It was never the same team again, filling the old role of French Montrealers, taking care of their frustrations. Politics had assumed that function. The Canadiens remained a marvellous, skilled professional group. But it was no longer the team that embodied the hot and cold of this province. No longer was the mystical quality of old times required."

Going into the theme more broadly, if one listens to some professional experts and onlookers such as Mordecai Richler, one concludes that hockey as such has declined in stature. Richler, when he is not immersed in writing his novels, follows sports zealously, emerging with some distinctive thoughts. For instance, in his mind the Toronto Maple Leafs replaced the Maroons as the anglo rivals of the Canadiens, but even this no longer applies, mainly because the National Hockey League has become so enlarged that old passions have waned. Besides, the centre of attention has shifted to baseball and the Expos. "The Forum doesn't attract the same crowd it once did," Richler believes. "Bosses give their tickets to their secretaries." He concedes that French-Canadian "honour" was once tied in with the Canadiens, but says this is no longer so – and that's only to the good. Richler, whose subject matter usually refers to the Montreal Jewish community, recalls how Jewish youngsters used to identify with the Golden Gloves, the top amateur boxing competition in North America which sometimes led to professionalism. In the US the Golden Gloves produced such champions as Benny Leonard and Barney Ross; and in Montreal it produced Maxie Berger, the last of the outstanding Jewish fighters of the 1940's. "Then the Jews became more sophisticated and didn't need the Golden Gloves," Richler says. "It's the same for the French Canadians and their need for idols."

Yvon Giguère, the head of sports programming for Radio-Canada, the CBC's French-language network, insists that hockey is still a religion with French Canadians, though the emphasis on individuals has faded. The Canadiens as a team still are in demand. If they are not televised on Saturday night, and Radio-Canada shows two other good teams, the audience drops by one third. Equally, however, there is no doubt about the new dedication to the Expos. "Richard," says Giguère, "was a special type who happened to be French Canadian. But you get the same devotion to the Expos – and there's not a single French Canadian on the team." This offers further evidence of a maturing of the Quebecer, a sense of confidence that no longer demands the deification of an individual.

At the same time, what is hardly understood outside Quebec is Montreal's traditional fondness for baseball. Giguère, who is forty-six, grew up in Rosemount, a bilingual neighbourhood. In high school, he remembers, anglophone kids played football while the francophones played softball. It was a question of money rather than taste. Football required a lot of expensive gear, while the other called for nothing more costly than a ball and bat. Giguère points out that such was the popularity of baseball that even after the Montreal Royals, of the minors, played their last game at Delorimier Stadium, in 1960, Radio-Canada continued to air NBC telecasts of major league games every Saturday. This love for the professionals was kept alive until the Expos arrived nine years later. The first Radio-Canada television crews to go out of town to cover the Expos invariably ran into problems with US broadcasters, who, believing that Canadians knew nothing about baseball, felt they could dictate where all cameras should be placed. But the fact was, as sports writers in the US quickly discovered, that the Canadians were as up to date on statistics or strategy as any American buff.

Giguère recalls a reverse touch of irony. In the early days, as a producer covering a game in Philadelphia, he hired local cameramen and technicians instead of importing his own crew from Montreal. Working from inside a mobile unit, he wanted Camera Three, which was concentrating on first base, to swing to the bullpen where an Expo pitcher was warming up. So, in common parlance (Giguère is fluently bilingual), he said into his closed-circuit microphone, "Camera Three to bullpen." Camera Three didn't budge. He repeated, "Camera Three to bullpen." No move. Finally, frustrated and unsure of himself and the terminology, he turned to the Philadelphia technical director who was in the mobile unit and said, "Do you use the same word here – bullpen?" "Sure," said the American. "But the cameraman doesn't understand English. He's Puerto Rican."

In the era of the Royals, the tendency of French-Canadian broadcasters and writers was to translate literally from English to French. A "shortstop" became "un arrêt court." Now, there's a simpler, invented word, "enper," which means "in between." "Bullpen" has become "enclos." This change in linguistic style came about, not because of pressures from nationalist groups or Bill 101, but simply to standardize sports parlance. So many commentators were calling plays in their own words that audiences were confused. Today's accepted guide is a handbook distributed by the O'Keefe Brewery. The game is still referred to in French as "le baseball," but some phrases continue to cause problems. A "squeeze play," according to O'Keefe, is "risque-tout" (to risk all), but it lacks the proper ring, so some narrators cling to the English.

The Expos had a lot going for them right from the beginning. The name itself followed on the success and pride of Montreal's great Expo 67. But what counted most was that this was big-time stuff – indeed, the first major league operation outside the US. In the first season, which the team ended forty-eight games behind the leader, someone came up with a slogan, "Nos Expos, nos amours." It provided just the right note, so that hardly a man who has ever joined the Expos can forget the infectious spirit of the fans, the dancers bouncing up and down the aisles, and other flashes of showmanship. But mainly it is the open enthusiasm for the team as a whole that makes playing for Montreal a special experience. If a

French Canadian, especially of the calibre of "Rocket" Richard, ever attains membership, fanaticism unquestionably will follow, even if idolatry no longer is required.

Yet, oddly – and again, this is a little known fact – Quebec has produced its share of first-rate baseball players. Dink Carroll, who, having celebrated his eightieth birthday, was still writing a regular column for *The Gazette* in 1981, once conducted a study of French-Canadian baseball players, including such personalities as Adelphi "Del" Bissonette, member of the Brooklyn Dodgers in 1928. Though Bissonette was born in Maine, he was regarded by French Canadians as one of their own. Another celebrated product of the great Quebec migration to the US of the 1890's was Leon Cadore, who became a Brooklyn pitcher in 1915. But the province itself should not be ignored. Carroll calculates that by 1968, a year before Montreal received its National League franchise, fifteen Quebec-born players had reached the majors.

Charles Bronfman, the deputy chairman of Seagram Company Limited, may have been unaware of this history when he became the principal owner of the Expos. But he did know what a lot of other anglophones did not know – something about the popularity of baseball among French Canadians. Before investing in the Expos he conducted a quiet survey and discovered that more ball is played by young people in Quebec than in any other part of Canada. His explanation reaffirms that of Yvon Giguère: "It's an inexpensive, non-violent sport." Beyond this, Bronfman has always been a baseball zealot. A touch of romance creeps in when this mild-mannered man, who is now in his early fifties, recalls childhood days of waiting for the Royals, not only for the play but for the sensation of a new season's arrival. "Baseball means a lot in our climate," he says. "By March, when you're aware of the spring training, you feel you've survived the winter and you have hopes for the summer. The season opens with the Expos at Olympic Stadium early in April, and ergo, spring is here."

Bronfman says he could talk three hours straight on the subject of baseball, and it soon becomes clear he does not mean this in a meandering sense; he can cite who hit the most home runs in the National League in 1972. It is plain that he loves the game. But equally he has an abiding faith in its importance as a cultural link between anglophones and francophones. When the Expos were launched he insisted that season tickets be sold in such a way that

80

French and English would not be placed in separate enclaves. He told his sales people to judge from the names of purchasers and, wherever possible, to seat those who sounded French alongside those who sounded English. That practice is still carried on. "It's a sociable game," says Bronfman. "You talk to your neighbour, and it's not so important whether your team wins or loses."

Thus Charles Bronfman possesses, like the Molson family in their interest in the Canadiens, a sense of community responsibility that goes beyond the commercial. "That's why I went in," Bronfman claims, and one takes him seriously. "I thought it important for Montreal, for Quebec, for Canada to have a major league team." He hardly regards his backing of the Expos as a profitable financial investment, since he was stuck with 45 per cent of the shares when other expected partners pulled out. He says the team has never really lost money; nor has it made money. In any case, in his income bracket it is difficult to figure out the balance sheet precisely; there are tax write-offs. But if, in fact, he did lose a lot of money, what would he do? "No one wants to sustain a continual loss in any field," he says. But this is hardly a satisfactory answer. Thus he adds that if he did sell it would only be "because of the state of the industry." But what if this meant the National League franchise going to another city, the Expos moving? Bronfman pulls for a few moments at his pipe and finally concedes: "I'd have grave difficulty deciding." And he repeats: "There is something important psychologically about a major league team."

Here, of course, is concurrence with Mayor Jean Drapeau, who pushed and encouraged men like Bronfman to buy a National League franchise. Drapeau's concept is one of quality, and his demand is for the best, because he believes that Montrealers are entitled to, and expect, only the finest in their athletes. Red Fisher, the sports editor of *The Montreal Star* for many years and now of *The Gazette*, agrees: "French Canadians cannot stand anything less than top quality. They're quick to criticize anything inferior." It may be one reason why the Alouettes, as contestants in the Canadian Football League, have never truly caught on. But Montrealers watch American football widely on television, and Drapeau, a shrewd judge of his own people, is determined to gain a National Football League franchise for the city by 1983.

The late Yvon Robert reigned as the "World's Wrestling Champ" in Montreal from 1955 to 1962, when in fact no such title was recognized internationally. But to Montrealers he was Number One and that was all that counted. Louis Cyr was glorified in slightly exaggerated terms as the strongest man of all time. At least his statue speaks for him. But poor Joseph Montferrand, the boxer who defeated "le champion de la marine anglaise," hasn't fared so well. A wood carving of Montferrand – twenty-four inches tall on a base of ten inches – was kept prominently on display at the Château de Ramezay, the museum in Old Montreal, for many years. But in a renovation in 1976 it was relegated to storage space in the basement. It emerged in 1981 to accompany other Quebec figures on a travelling exhibition in Ontario. But now it is back in the basement. The symbolism is not difficult to interpret. Quebec's sports heroes had their time and place, but today's public nonchalance, to say nothing of self-confidence, predominates. Perhaps most revealing of all is the reaction to Wayne Gretzky, the youthful Edmonton Oiler who demolished old National Hockey League scoring records. In Montreal in 1982, T-shirts bearing Gretzky's Number 99 outsold those with Canadiens logos.

If the Montreal fan is a special breed, so is a newspaper publisher, Pierre Péladeau, who has cleverly capitalized on sports to turn out the biggest French-language paper in North America. Péladeau's *Le Journal de Montréal*, with a circulation of 330,000, is well ahead of the much more sober *La Presse*, and the cornerstone of a publishing empire that once included the US. Péladeau did it all on a loan of $1,500 and a formula that is as simple as it is successful: sports (commentaries, reports, pictures in great abundance), and, to a lesser degree, scandal and sex. Péladeau, who is sufficiently unorthodox not to worry much, shows only the mildest irritation when an interviewer quotes reprovers who sneer at what they call his "Three S's" – sports, scandal, sex. He says, for one thing, that *Le Journal de Montréal* and his other papers are relatively light on sex; they display none of the nudity that stamps the pages of a big Australian counterpart, Rupert Murdoch.

Anyway, Péladeau deserves to be identified at least as much by the "Two B's" as by the "Three S's." These stand for Balzac and Beethoven. When one asks Péladeau where he obtained his concept for turning out newspapers of great mass appeal – there was no training or family proclivity towards journalism, his father having been a lumber merchant – he says, "It was the reading I have done, especially of Balzac." The French author's message, throughout his works, was: "Know your neighbour." For Péladeau the theme was easily translated when he instructed his editors to go after neighbourly material – gossip about sports figures, about television stars, and, equally important, about events commonplace in everyone's life. Beethoven? His music reflects the struggle of a handicapped man, the conquest of inner turmoil after deafness. This comes close to Péladeau's own strength in defeating alcoholism.

Péladeau, fifty-six, is a true Montrealer. He took a degree at Université de Montréal, majoring in philosophy and writing his thesis on Nietzsche; then he went on to McGill University for a law degree. But it was a chance to buy a suburban weekly, for which he borrowed the money, that turned him towards the career that led to the construction of his company, Québécor Incorporated, which controls tabloid dailies in Montreal and Quebec City. It also controls twenty-one Quebec regional weeklies; a half dozen "pop weeklies" which are more lurid than the dailies; and various other communications organizations, including his latest venture, a book-publishing house that specializes in self-help and success stories always based on the same precept he learned from Balzac.

Péladeau has many detractors, but he is a personable man – short in physique with sandy hair swept long at the back and huge, rimmed spectacles – who is absolutely frank in conversation. He appears to hold back nothing, except the size of his fortune (Québécor does a volume of $200 million a year). When one mentions that he is two men, both the intellectual and the publisher who does not aspire to lofty heights of quality, he says that, judging only from his own education, there is no discrepancy. "In philosophy you deal with thoughts, in law, with facts." As a publisher he is purely a businessman, out to make money because money means power. And making money is related to giving the public what it wants. All Péladeau really does is to emulate television. He doesn't try to compete with it, as serious papers still seek to do in analyzing in detail what audiences might have caught in a glimpse of the screen. Péladeau's papers, in addition to their television-like visual emphasis, offer only capsules of the events readers have already seen the night before. But if they are inquisitive, and want to know what others think, they are handed a variety of commentators. His papers carry no editorials and take no sides politically. Not uncharacteristic of his formula approach, he prefers to allow columnists of different shades to express their own opinions. René Lévesque, before his Parti Québécois won office, and even before he could boast his own seat in the National Assembly, was glad, Péladeau claims, to become a commentator for *Le Journal de Montréal*; it helped the future premier to learn, through a feedback of letters from readers, something of the varying and unpredictable moods of Montrealers. (Lévesque says he still cannot come up with a simple definition of the Montreal voter. But the fact that the Montrealer chooses a federalist like Trudeau as prime minister and someone like himself as premier is not strictly a Montreal phenomenon. "It's a French-Quebec phenomenon" – the need to maintain an insurance policy. He likens it to a man who wears suspenders and, for extra security, also a belt.)

Péladeau, when the Parti Québécois rose to prominence, asked himself, "Is there anything harmful in what they advocate?" At first, by his own admission, he could see little that was potentially disruptive because he thought Quebec might be able to make it on its own. Later he became less certain, and in the 1981 election personally favoured Claude Ryan, the Liberal leader. But he does give Lévesque credit for one essential contribution: "He reduced considerably the danger of social upheaval that was prevalent in Quebec in 1976. That is, people, in their insecurity, were turning more and more to the militants in unions. But Lévesque gave the individual self-confidence as a Quebecer." Péladeau has had his own share of fights with trade unions entering his papers. He tried to prevent certification, but once this became a reality he accepted his defeat with grace. Today, reporters on *Le Journal de Montréal* are the highest paid in the city.

Péladeau is frank about his bout with alcoholism. He was only, by his own definition, a weekend drinker. But he feared that drinks on Sunday would lead to several on Monday and throughout the week. So he joined Alcoholics Anonymous, which he calls "the greatest fraternity in the world." He illustrates: on a flight from Montreal to Frankfurt, his plane was held up by a strike in Paris and he was stranded there overnight. His favourite hotel, The Plaza Athénée, could not accommodate him; a survey of other hotels led nowhere. Finally, Péladeau reached into his briefcase for a list of AA members in Paris, and found that one man was identified as "realtor." He called him, asking if he would be able to rent an apartment for the night. The Frenchman – "remember, he was a total stranger" – told Péladeau to wait for him at the airport, was there within twenty minutes, drove him to his own apartment, presented him with a key and said, "You are my guest."

Péladeau responds in even more lavish fashion. As a helper of other AA members, he usually invites a half dozen or more guests for weekends at his year-round Laurentians home in Ste. Adèle (he drives the sixty kilometres to his office each work day). Among them were members of the staff of his *Philadelphia Journal*. He entered that market in 1978, despite the presence of three competitors. The *Journal* was slow to take off, but Péladeau applied a technique (besides his formula of sex-scandal-sports), that he had learned in Montreal: to sell papers through corner groceries and other stores. Péladeau was not interested in establishing a home-delivery service because of the built-in expenses and problems. Street vending machines cost $150 each and were broken into often by thieves or vandals. Péladeau, after exploring Philadelphia himself, told his circulation people: "Go after the corner stores." They argued that it had never been done that way, but it turned out to be a profitable outlet. It was in keeping with his faith in Balzac. The corner grocer or tobacconist had intimate contact with regular customers who came by for a carton of milk or a pack of cigarettes.

Nonetheless, the Philadelphia venture lost money and Péladeau conceded defeat in 1981. Most of the time now he is in Montreal, looking after his Canadian interests which include a printing plant in Toronto and the English-language *Sunday Express* in Montreal. Usually he takes lunch at the Club St. Denis, where it is obvious, judging from the number of other members – businessmen, lawyers, bankers – who drop by his table to shake his hand or trade a few comments, that he is held in esteem despite the questionable character of his products. If he is an enigma, he gives no signs of caring. He admits that he would like to own *La Presse*, and from time to time makes overtures to Paul Desmarais, whose Power Corporation is in control. There is no apparent jealousy of Desmarais even when he concedes that Desmarais can read a ledger and he, Péladeau, cannot (that is why he hires the best accountants and pays them the highest salaries). Then why does he want *La Presse*? Prestige? Péladeau shrugs non-committally. Does he want to be part of the high order that extends beyond the Club St. Denis? Now he shakes his head. He saw Desmarais and other tycoons on the CBC television series, *The Canadian Establishment*, making a round of cocktail parties, and says, "The small talk would drive me crazy." His idea of relaxation is to stay home with his wife and listen to Beethoven. "The establishment," he says, "may have the money, but I have power because I know tricks they don't know. I know what my people want."

Decline of the Wasps

When John Molson, a determined and self-confident young Englishman arrived in Montreal in 1786 with forty-six bushels of English
barley, a small bundle of hops, a little equipment, and not much
capital, he established more than a brewery. He set up a dynasty that
lasts to this day, seven generations following each other with an eye
to success and a place in the community. No family in North
America, not even the du Ponts, can claim greater continuity in the
original business. Nor, in Montreal, does any anglophone name
come close to reflecting the Molsons' credo for service and responsibility beyond the pursuit of money. On the contrary, their story
underscores the decline not only of the old English aristocracy but of
the failure of the newer rich to respond to community obligations
and needs. An example is the McConnells, who lasted hardly two
generations in sustaining *The Montreal Star*, at one time one of
Canada's most successful and profitable newspapers; its death in
1979 was a sharp blow to the morale of English Montrealers.

The president of Molson Breweries of Canada Limited today is
Eric H. Molson, a shy, slender, pleasant man of forty-five who, on
first contact, modestly says he knows little about the family history.
But later it develops that he is indeed interested in his ancestry, and
that a few years ago he made a surprising discovery. On tracing the
lineage he learned that, through marriages, two French-Canadian
families, the Héberts and the Taschereaus, have contributed their
genes. So the Molsons are not pure "Anglo-Saxons." Eric recounts
this revelation with satisfaction, for he dislikes the use of hyphens in
a racial or national context. He feels, anyway, that Molsons are not
regarded by francophones as "English Canadians." They've been
around so long they're "Montrealers." Moreover, he wants to be

known simply as a brewer. "We've been lucky," he says, "that we've had someone in each generation who was interested in the business. I'm not a crackerjack financier. But I know brewing. I love beer. I love to smell it, think it, make it. My father had the same feeling."

One does not, of course, equate the current master with the simple, strong-willed Lincolnshire immigrant who opened shop two centuries ago, even though a small oil portrait of John Molson is tucked in a corner of Eric's wood-panelled office. More pertinently, near it is a diploma from Princeton University testifying that Eric Molson graduated *cum laude*, honours chemistry. He had already spent summers in the brewhouse, acquiring practical knowledge. But he fondly recalls his adviser at Princeton, a Russian-American, who, with heavy accent, asked him, "What are you going to do when you graduate?" "I'm going to make beer," said Eric. "Then," said his adviser, "we must study yeast." So for two years Eric Molson learned everything there was to know about yeast and wrote his thesis on it. This dedication to detail is quite in character with the rule of conduct laid down by a forebear, of the third Molson Canadian generation, who, on the eve of his death, dictated a final message: "The Molson family has maintained and preserved its position and influence by steady, patient industry, and every member should be a real worker and not rely on what it has been. All that is good and great of the family should not be underground."

Physically, as well as spiritually, the Molsons operate from the same site where John established himself, on the bank of the St. Lawrence River, alongside what is now Notre Dame Street East and in the shadow of Jacques Cartier Bridge. The same water from the same river – filtered and purified, of course – goes into the same product. The cellar of the original brewhouse still exists, storage space in a huge complex that turns out beer, not only for Quebec (there are Molson branches in nine other locations across Canada), but for the US market. That part of the modern story is remarkable enough. Molson, which began to invade the US seriously only in 1970, is now the Number Two imported beer sold there. "We've room to move," says Eric quietly; explaining that while Heineken, the Number One import, is available in all fifty states, Molson has barely touched half of them. Equally noteworthy is the fact that after years of sliding, in the face of competition from Labatt, Molson in 1981 again became the biggest brewer in Canada.

The sales burst, especially in the US, resulted from a shrewd advertising and marketing campaign combined with the Molson faith in Montreal as a continued base of operation. While hardly any construction was going on elsewhere in the city during the gloom of the 1970's, cranes and derricks were heartening, visible signs of expansion at Molson. The Molson companies now also embrace a variety of interests, including Beaver Lumber (with 250 do-it-yourself retail stores); the Diversey Corporation, which produces chemical products in thirty-two countries; and Willson Office Specialty Limited. The Diversey operation is handled from Chicago, while Beaver and Willson executive offices are located in Toronto. But the head office for the conglomerate remains in Montreal, partly because brewing accounts for about half of the annual total sales of $1.5 billion, and largely because the Molson family, who still own major blocks of stock, want it that way.

Eric's uncle, Senator Hartland deMontarville Molson, honorary chairman of the board at the age of seventy-four, is almost apologetic about the diversification. But he points out that even in the earliest days the family was involved in steamboats, railways, and banking, in addition to brewing. In any case, the emphasis, the mainstay is simple: the family clings faithfully to Montreal. It was Senator Molson who sounded a widely cited cry of defiance when the Parti Québécois came to power. "We've been here 200 years," he said. "I'm damned if I'm going to leave now." Other business people may have headed for Toronto or Calgary, but more than a few were persuaded to hang on because of the senator's attitude. Yet he is magnanimous towards those who have departed. "There has been so much uncertainty," he says, "that I thoroughly understand people leaving in order to simplify their lives, especially as they grow older. Some say, 'My roots aren't all that deep. Why should I put up with uncertainty and high taxes?'" Then why haven't the Molsons left? Apart from the obvious fact that roots are deep, he says: "We don't know anywhere we'd rather be. That doesn't mean we like excesses such as Bill 101."

Eric Molson, who functions bilingually, thanks in part to his experiences in the brewhouse ("I know beer inside out in French"), offers a candid footnote to his uncle's comment. He recalls attending a private meeting that Robert Bourassa, at the time Liberal premier of Quebec, held with anglophone leaders of Montreal. Bourassa warned that unless he could go ahead with Bill 22, which would give French language pre-eminence over English, he would be destroyed politically. There was intense hostility to the legislation and Molson felt he was the only one in the room who understood what Bourassa was saying. That took sensitivity and prescience, for Bourassa was indeed turned upon by the anglophone community, contributing to his downfall and the emergence of the Parti Québécois in 1976, and subsequently to the enactment of Bill 101 which was much more restrictive than Bill 22.

Eric Molson is a little less forgiving than his uncle on the question of the anglophone migration from Montreal. "I understand both positions – of those who go, and those who stay," he says. "But naturally, I have a lot in common with those who stay. If there are more jobs in Alberta I appreciate why someone goes there. But if I were a young man, even without roots here, I'd still end up in Montreal. We – and I include my children – like it, and everything about it, a lot. There are no negatives as far as we're concerned. We feel this is a better place to live than anywhere else in North America – more challenging, more exciting, with better business possibilities. When there's emigration, and we've had some, it obviously means a vacuum has been created. If a dentist quits, he leaves behind his clientele, and that makes room for another dentist to move in."

But factors other than any exodus because of a dislike for the political situation affect even the Molsons. A century ago the descendants of John Molson numbered more than 100; no fewer than forty-two, in the family by lineage or marriage, served in the First World War. A close count is unavailable today, but not many Molsons are left. In the 1920's and 1930's some wandered off to British Columbia and elsewhere. There are none in Toronto; but a Molson lives in New York and another, a banker, in London. Most of the rest remain in Montreal, and Eric calculates there are, all told, a dozen Molsons – distant cousins – between the ages of ten and thirty. His own three sons constitute direct descent, seventh generation, and he considers it likely that at least one (Andrew, fourteen, or Justin, thirteen, or Geoffrey, eleven), will carry on with the family business.

Senator Hartland Molson was brought up in the family home on what was once known as Ontario Avenue, today called Avenue du Musée. It was a lovely red brick house, standing on the corner of what is now Avenue Docteur Penfield, formerly McGregor Avenue. The name changes do not distress the senator as much as the fact that the old home is now the Soviet consulate. "If my mother knew that, she'd turn over in her grave," he says. Why his mother rather than his father? His father died in 1938, before the Soviet Union became a superpower; his mother only a decade ago.

But other profound alterations have swept away the character of what used to be referred to as the Square Mile. That uptown territory – bounded by Pine Avenue and Dorchester Boulevard in the north and south, and by University Street and Côte des Neiges in the east and west – was, for more than three quarters of a century, the enclave of the men who built not only Montreal's prosperity but that of much of Canada. Here dwelt the railway barons, the shipping giants, the sugar merchants, the bankers and directors of the largest insurance companies, and a host of other prominent figures, from leading physicians to McGill University principals. What they had in common was not only wealth and power but an ancestry that was almost entirely English or Scottish; few of French descent made it to the Square Mile.

Equally, they later shared in the abandonment of the district – through death; through movement to Westmount (a suburb that earlier had been regarded distastefully as "new rich" or "middle class"); or through departure of offspring for other places in Canada or abroad; so that by the outbreak of the Second World War in 1939 the Square Mile had shrunk to mere pockets of old families who clung to habit or tradition. By the late 1940's the process was more or less complete. The slow and steady erosion of the White Anglo-Saxon Protestant establishment preceded by many years the entry of the Parti Québécois. It was a natural process that few take into account when they talk today of the change in Montreal's makeup. In simple words, attrition was at work long before politics.

The Allans may be an extreme example of the erosion; nonetheless, in their own drama they depict much of what befell the old English élite of Montreal. For nearly a century, from small beginnings in 1819, the family operated a fleet of sail and steam ships that dominated routes between Canada and Europe. Then, in relatively recent years, one tragedy after another took its price, eventually ending the dynasty. In 1915, two daughters of Sir Montagu and Lady Allan, Gwendolyn and Anna, perished when the *Lusitania* was sunk by a German torpedo. In 1917, their only son, Hugh, was killed in action. The surviving child, Martha, dramatist and actress and a leader of the city's cultural life (she founded the Montreal Repertory Theatre), died in 1942. A year later the elderly Sir Montagu parted with the last visible link between the present and the past – Ravenscrag, the mansion on a slope of Mount Royal at Pine Avenue, that dominated the Square Mile.

Today, as the Allan Memorial Institute, it serves as the psychiatric wing of the Royal Victoria Hospital. In more opulent times, gabled, columned, and porticoed Ravenscrag, with its grey limestone walls of enormous thickness, was the scene of Montreal's most lavish balls and banquets – 400 guests partaking of nine or ten courses. Even though of lesser stature, other great mansions came into prominence, such as the Van Horne home on Sherbrooke Street; the red sandstone baronial house of Sir George Drummond, also on Sherbrooke Street; and the elegant residence of Sir Mortimer Davis, at Pine and Peel, said to have been designed by Stanford White. Murray Ballantyne, a historian who grew up in the Square Mile, has recollections of the staffs of servants required to maintain these homes. In his own family's town house there were usually nine, including coachman, groom, chauffeur, butler, cook, kitchen maid, and table maid. Ballantyne, now in his early seventies, has kept an academic's interest in the area, and notes that not a single mansion of the old times is privately occupied today. Some have been demolished, others converted to institutional use.

On the fringes, and immune from simple classification, are a few buildings on Redpath Crescent, a satellite of Pine Avenue, many of them owned by foreign governments for use as residences by their consuls-general. In a touch of modern drama, the chief British diplomatic representative was preparing to go to his office one October morning in 1970 when members of the Front de Libération du Québec, burst in on him. The kidnapping of James Cross, culminating a period of terrorism, denoted a new phase in Canadian history. No longer was this a land immune from violence or the upheavals familiar to Europeans and Latin Americans. And no longer was Montreal the most solid of cities for investment and growth. Ironically, James Cross was not the desired prime target of the FLQ. They had set out initially to abduct the US consul general, who lived across the road. But they were discouraged by the complications inherent in two entrances to his residence. Equally ironic was a postscript which the writer learned from Cross in London in 1978. His street had been a busy one, with students from the nearby medical school of McGill University using it for parking. But a neighbour complained to the police about the excessive traffic. From then on parking was restricted. Cross believes – and he says this with a trace of bitterness – that he might not have had to endure his ordeal if the kidnappers had been frightened by the kind of street activity that had gone on earlier.

Among the last of the Square Milers who live in the district, though not in his original home, is Eric Reford, who was born in 1900 on a site at the corner of Drummond and McGregor streets now occupied by an apartment block. Several years ago, Reford, whose forefathers had built up a prosperous shipping agency, bought a relatively modern mansion dating back to around 1912, three blocks from his birthplace. In 1981, still active in the shipping business, he enjoyed entertaining occasionally at lunch at home, with a staff that, though small, was enough to remind him of the old days. To reinforce memories he also continued to pour for himself a vodka laced with ground pepper, a drink (so he was told by a onetime neighbour, a Russian nobleman), that had been popular among Czarist cavalry officers. Reford remembers the first move ever made by a Square Miler to Westmount, that of a stockbroker named W.R. Millar. Square Milers thought it justly fitting that after Millar built his new home its view was obstructed by construction of St. Joseph's Oratory.

So much has changed. If Westmount is now considered the sanctuary of the wealthy anglophones who remain in Montreal, the Square Mile today represents transition of another sort. Depending on one's interpretation of events, it may be regarded as one of the most interesting, cosmopolitan areas of Montreal. In the centre of the city, it is a desired location for people who are tired of suburban life and commuting. One can walk to work from there, and find shops and discothèques and myriad restaurants. Apartments and new condominiums abound, and in them live francophones as well as anglophones. Premier René Lévesque in 1982 owned a condominium unit in Le Noble, which faced Pine Avenue but backed onto Rue de la Montagne, from where he could obtain a magnificent view of the city below, with beacons rotating atop Place Ville Marie and the sheen from Sherbrooke Street on a wet day throwing out the reflection of passing vehicles. There may no longer be the sight and sound of horses and carriages, but then this no longer is the era of exclusiveness or Ravenscrag.

One wonders if René Lévesque contemplates any of this as he

looks at the city below. When the question is put to him, he says, "To tell you the truth, it never crossed my mind that this was the old establishment corner, or that there was anything abnormal about living anywhere." Indeed, Lévesque lived for several years in this area – what he calls "the west end" – before moving to Old Montreal and then ascending the hill again. Even though he considered returning to Old Montreal, the Square Mile suited his purpose. "You have a better chance, especially in the kind of job I'm in, to isolate yourself." Pine Avenue and its surroundings ("very quiet and a bit remote"), offer privacy. Yet, oddly, he is concerned about isolation in terms of really knowing what English Montrealers think and feel. Lévesque wants anglophones to join the Parti Québécois to provide a better knowledge of what is on their minds. While he doesn't expect to sweep the ranks of old Square Mile types "like a tornado" (he says this with his characteristic nervous laugh), he does hope to appeal eventually to younger anglophones.

The decline of the Wasp community was gradual and inevitable in the context of an outflow of younger generations; an inflow of masses of immigrants, particularly after the Second World War; and, coincidentally, the assertion of French-Canadian identity. But if a single event is needed to underscore that decline, the "incident of St. Léonard," as it became known, provides it. St. Léonard in 1968 was a northeastern municipality of Greater Montreal made up of about 53 per cent francophones, 32 per cent Italian immigrants, and 10 per cent Polish and Ukrainian immigrants with others of Eastern European extraction. Fewer than 5 per cent were "Anglo-Saxons." Schools were of two types: French or bilingual. There were no English schools. "We didn't want them," says a man named Robert Beale, who, with a French-Canadian mother and an Irish father, wanted his children to be fluent in the two tongues. It was an attitude shared by many of the inhabitants, for the bilingual schools featured an interesting approach: all subjects were taught one week in French, the next in English. But Beale, who was thirty-seven and just an average working man – a process operator at an oil refinery with habits no more violent than watching baseball on television or drinking the occasional beer with friends – suddenly found himself thrust into the most awesome experience of his life.

The local school board had decided to abolish the bilingual

system and make all schools French only. Beale attended a meeting of parents who were opposed to the change. It was designed to be a quiet gathering, with no outside publicity. But Beale spoke up and urged that they immediately form a board of directors and go public – that is, deliberately invite in the media. He was voted down on it, a not uncharacteristic reaction of new citizens with a European reluctance to buck authorities. Beale persisted, and two meetings later was elected president of the Association of Parents of St. Léonard. That was when the battle was formed and the disenchantment began to creep in. For one thing, Beale was convinced that this was much more than a local issue. The Union Nationale party was in office, and Daniel Johnson, the premier, was pushing for "special status" for Quebec. Beale, along with others, felt that Johnson was purposely making an effort to challenge the constitution, using education as the key; by agreement with allies on the school board, St. Léonard was to be the test.

For a supposedly mild-mannered type – even today, with his short stature and curly hair, he looks quite benign – Beale turned out to be a gifted fighter. He organized a march on Ottawa. It was one of the largest ever held, with 14,000 Montrealers, mostly from St. Léonard but including other sympathizers, descending on Parliament Hill for the opening of the House of Commons. Italians made it in cars and buses laden with cheese and wine and salami. Wholesale television and press coverage achieved what Beale had in mind: "I wanted everyone to know this was discrimination that could spread." But Premier Johnson, who was not to live much longer, refused to budge. The only course left was legal action, and so another non-member of the establishment, Claude-Armand Sheppard, paunchy lawyer extraordinary, was called in. Sheppard, born in Belgium in 1935, was brought up in Flemish Ghent by French-speaking parents, and for six years had experienced German occupation. By the time he arrived in Canada at the age of fifteen he had a special affinity for the underdog. He did brilliantly at McGill, and as a young lawyer became involved in celebrated causes, among them the defence of the first FLQ group accused of bombings. After two years of court hearings, Sheppard won back for parents of St. Léonard the right to send their children to bilingual schools.

Sheppard charged nothing for his services. What distressed him about the St. Léonard episode was the discovery that the anglophone community wanted no part of it. He was shaken by how old Wasps turned their backs on the Italians, as though it was beneath their dignity to become connected with a squabble involving an immigrant group. Any immigrant group. Twelve years later he was able to link St. Léonard with the introduction of Bill 101 – to him an inevitable result of English-Montreal passivity. Why were young anglophones leaving? He did not ask the question rhetorically, for as an "outsider" (a phrase that enables him to view Montreal, which he loves, with some objectivity), he felt he knew the answer: "Their parents in effect told them they could no longer enjoy the élitism their class always enjoyed in the past."

Sheppard, who is fluently bilingual, tends to relate more to francophones than to anglophones. Yet principles take priority. He deplored publicly, in an address to the annual meeting of the Canadian Bar Association, the meekness with which anglophones accepted the Parti Québécois demand that they would need to subjugate themselves as a minority and swallow language and other restrictions. He called this "cultural suicide." Later, in private conversation, he said that if this were required of blacks or Jews in the US there would be a revolution or at least an enormous outpouring of resentment. "I sometimes wish there was an anglophone equivalent of the Jewish Defence League," he comments, not facetiously. Instead, "the English have gone from a position of arrogance to humble apology." The judgement may be excessively harsh (as noted in a chapter dealing with how some anglophones, including the younger generation, have in fact responded in a variety of constructive fashions to what they regard as abuses under the Parti Québécois government). But it is difficult to rebut his reminder that in the St. Léonard episode the anglophones did not even contribute money to help residents there combat the school board.

This is borne out by Robert Beale, who says bluntly, "If you want to put blame on anybody, look to the anglophone businessmen, the hierarchy of the community. They were apathetic and indifferent – and ignorant. Five years later I had prominent people coming up to me and asking, 'Bob, is that St. Léonard affair settled yet?' But at the time, when we needed them and I knocked on the doors of big business – department stores, corporations – to say we had to raise $50,000, they said, 'Hey, take it easy. We have to do business with the French.' They missed the whole point. We were fighting for French rights, too; francophones who wanted their children to be bilingual appreciated it. But to businessmen the buck came before the principle."

One can still ask today: where was the anglophone leadership in 1968? Why was it left to relatively obscure men like Beale to co-ordinate an effort of concern to all Montrealers? The answer, sadly, is that there was no anglophone leadership. The unnecessary bitterness that resulted from the St. Léonard episode later encouraged Beale to make other efforts. He formed the Quebec Student Intra-Exchange Program, to bring together Quebec youngsters from ages ten to thirteen, and later two other groups, the Canada Student Exchange Program and the Hockey-Cultural Exchange Program. Interestingly, distinguished citizens, both francophone and anglophone, now act as sponsors.

But the pain in St. Léonard has not entirely gone. Joseph Reda still recalls with mild horror how he watched from the balcony of his house as a crowd of demonstrators marched through the streets with placards that said, in French: "Wops Go Home." For Reda, who felt betrayed by Montrealers, English and French alike, it was a shattering chapter in what, up to that time, had been a happy romance. Born in the small village of Cozenza, just south of Naples, he had decided in 1955, when he was twenty, to emigrate to Canada with $50 in his pocket and "a dream." It all came true. A year later, on a waiter's income, he was able to bring over his two brothers and two sisters, and a year after that, his parents. By 1968, the beginning of "the incident," he had a wife and family, owned a duplex, and was a successful insurance agent.

Today, as president of the Canadian-Italian Professional Businessmen's Association, Reda is a leader of Montreal's Italian community of 250,000, of whom between 35,000 and 40,000 still live in St. Léonard. He loves the district, which is colourful and boasts its share of affluent homes, shops, and restaurants, and if anything is trilingual: French, English, Italian. There is no quandary over Bill 101. Reda accepts it, though he was unhappy when local Parti Québécois supporters held a reception for René Lévesque and tables were decorated with Italian and Quebec flags, to the exclusion of the Canadian emblem. But he makes no argument over Bill 101's ruling that new immigrants, those who came after him, must send their children to French schools. He simply says, "We live in Quebec, and French should be the first language." But, he adds, "I don't want to have to look over my shoulder if I want to use English." Basically, he feels that Italians make up a sound community, at ease with both anglophones and francophones. This gives them, in his mind, a dimension that is ahead of Toronto's Italian community, which is about double Montreal's size. While the image of "Wops Go Home," still haunts him ("I felt we didn't deserve that kind of treatment"), in many ways he now thinks that what happened was actually beneficial. "We had to remain what we are," he says. "We knew no one else would fight for us."

Stephen Leacock once wrote that "the name of Molson echoes down the history of the city in the throb of the steamship, the tinkle of the bank teller's coins, the whisper of the college library, and the roar of the college stadium." Few will challenge the impact the family has had on the life of Montreal, its benefactions etched in buildings dedicated to education or healing or culture. The sense of duty to the community carries on in a multiplicity of enterprises that includes a hockey team, the Canadiens. One can be a trifle cynical and argue that there is a direct relationship between the rise and fall of the Canadiens' fortune and Molson beer sales. When the team traded Pierre Bouchard, a defence player, to Washington a couple of years ago, someone fired a gun at a Molson truck in reprisal. Certainly it is clear that beer consumption goes up appreciably during playoffs and Stanley Cup finals. And if the biggest competitor, Labatt's Breweries, makes a move to acquire the Canadiens, it should be enough to arouse all of Molson's business instincts. Yet, equally in fairness, one must give credit for some altruism in the Molson dedication to the hometown team.

For three generations the Molsons had held shares in the Canadiens, but not until Hartland bought control in 1957 could it be considered as part of the family "trust" – the word Eric uses to describe it. David Molson, a second cousin who had worked at the brewery as a vice-president, left in 1964 to run the Canadiens and the Forum, which was part of the package Hartland had acquired. Four years later, with his brothers Peter and William, he took over Hartland's controlling interest for an estimated $5 million. In December 1971 they sold out to Peter and Edward Bronfman, cousins of Charles Bronfman of the liquor dominion, their own wealth augmented by the variety of their Edper Investments. The figure mentioned unofficially for the Canadiens purchase was $15 million.

To this day, Senator Hartland Molson declines to comment on the transaction. But he was obviously disturbed. He had been on a holiday down south and David and his brothers had not notified him in advance of the sale; he felt it was virtually a family betrayal. All Eric will say is that his uncle had "les Canadiens in his blood." Personally, Eric felt that with the Bronfmans the team was in "good Montreal hands," but there was a fear that the Canadiens would be sold again, this time to the deep rival, Labatt's. Not only could such a deal affect the sales of Molson's own products but it would mean that a revered Montreal institution would be run from Ontario. As a precaution, the brewery bought back the Molson interest in the team in 1977 for a reported $22 million, a fourfold jump since the original transfer. (The Bronfmans retained the Forum, which the Canadiens now rent at $1 million a year.)

David Molson, fifty-four, a low-keyed individual who has exercised a lifelong affection for Canadian art by operating the Continental Galleries, among his other activities, says: "The most remarkable thing about the Molsons is that usually in an old family there is one generation that puts an end to everything. In our family, whether a member was involved in the most minimal task, like teaching school, he has done it with the same sense of responsibility. The family has not existed on grandeur." Here he quotes the celebrated deathbed injunction of "steady, patient industry." He also likes to mention that "it has been remarkably free of family feuding," and dismisses the notion that Hartland carries a grudge over the Canadiens affair; they meet from time to time "in amiable relations." But a main feature of what David Molson has to say relates to the sense of continuity and dedication. A Molson, he points out, cannot automatically expect to enter the family business. He must be "invited," regarded as worthy. This applied equally to David, who recalls his father, named John after the founder, saying that he expected his son to join the brewery "but first you'll have to learn French." How does David feel about Montreal? "My roots are here," he answers. "I have never for one moment considered living anywhere else."

Eric Molson was "aghast" over the Sun Life's decision to move, and attributes it to a lack of knowledge by officers of the company on the reaction it would involve. But regardless of any detail, it is clear that the decision offended his sense of accountability to the community one is supposed to serve. He will not comment directly about a family's obligation to keep alive a newspaper like *The Montreal Star*, especially since Derek Price, a fellow Princetonian and an old friend, was in a position of decision-making. But he does cite the analogy of the Molsons and their determination to preserve the Canadiens for Montreal, even at a high cost.

J.W. McConnell could not, like any Molson, trace his success in Canada back to the eighteenth century. What he achieved he did on his own, starting early in this century as an office boy and bond salesman, and then acquiring great wealth and power through acquisition of sugar and flour mills. When he became proprietor of *The Montreal Star* – a flourishing newspaper that was started in 1869 by young Hugh Graham, later Lord Atholstan – he resigned from fifteen directorates. That was in 1938, though in fact he had for several years quietly controlled the paper financially even while Lord Atholstan was alive. That was the way J.W. McConnell liked to operate – backstage and discreetly. His contributions to universities, hospitals, and other institutions were enormous and almost always made without publicity, though after a while he became dubbed, sarcastically but accurately, as "Canada's best known anonymous benefactor." He was a hard bargainer, not untypical of the mercantile barons who ruled Montreal, and from it much of the rest of Canada, in the 1920's and 1930's. He was also a tough father whose sternness with his three sons, Wilson, John, and David, was to undermine rather than bolster their self-confidence. His daughter, Kit, he left unscarred in the belief that a woman had no place in a competitive business world.

Wilson later operated the sugar side of the family interests (St. Lawrence), David the flour (Ogilvie), and John took over the newspaper. John's apprenticeship had been a challenge. At the start, J.W. deliberately gave him *The Standard*, a Saturday paper with a circulation of only 78,000 and a likelihood of imminent collapse. Instead, John McConnell built its circulation to 350,000 and converted it into *Weekend Magazine*, a supplement appearing in forty-one newspapers with readership in the millions, in its era the most successful publication in Canada. By the time he took over *The Montreal Star*, in the early 1950's, his life was dedicated to journalism. Shy and modest, he was also a naturally gifted publisher, with an unerring eye for quality of content and appearance. His main concern was the editorial product, and he was prepared to spend as much money as necessary to attain excellence. His concept of serving the community was to provide readers with what he believed to be the best possible coverage of local, domestic, and international news. He won enormous respect, warmth, and loyalty from his staff. His private life was less successful, accented by a faltering marriage and chronic uncertainty of personal worth. His health suffered, he was frequently unavailable for important decisions, and the time eventually arrived for a change in leadership.

There was never any danger of the paper failing financially. Its profits contributed indirectly to the McConnell Foundation; with an estimated value of $600 million it was the biggest in Canada in 1981. But direction was needed. Both of John's brothers were dead, David a suicide. None of the dozen of J.W. McConnell's descendants were capable of, or interested in, operating a newspaper. (John's own adopted son, Royden, became a playboy who liked to race around town with the ambulance service which he operated.) The only candidate was a member of the family by marriage – Derek Price, whose wife, Jill, was Wilson's daughter. Price had worked briefly for a bank and for Wilson in the sugar refinery, and then moved over to *The Montreal Star*, serving in various departments, including editorial, to develop a feel for publishing and what was required of it. A decent, likable, handsome man, he had the proper motivations, including a sense of duty. (His father, Brigadier John H. Price, who led Canadian soldiers trapped by the Japanese in Hong Kong during the Second World War, maintained into his eighties an office to care for any of his veterans who needed help.)

But Derek Price, in his early forties, never felt at home after he became publisher of *The Montreal Star* in 1969. In particular, the editorial process, which had been John McConnell's great forte, baffled and bothered him. He found it difficult to accept criticism of editorials from friends; or to deal with family members who would call over trifling matters of headlines – standard hazards for any publisher. Price was honest enough in his own analysis to realize he lacked the kind of stamina or fire to carry on, and within eight years decided to resign as publisher. The problem that had driven him into the post in the first place remained: who, in the family, could take over? There was no one. Thus a great community property, with profits ranging from $6 million to $8 million a year, became part of an impersonal organization, FP Publications, based in Toronto.

The deal was straightforward. In relinquishing ownership of *The Montreal Star*, members of the McConnell family acquired 25 per cent of the shares of FP Publications, which included Toronto's *Globe and Mail*, the *Winnipeg Free Press*, *The Vancouver Sun*, and five other papers. The man appointed to serve as publisher, William Goodson, had started with *The Montreal Star* as an office boy at the age of sixteen, and proved over the years to be a shrewd businessman, converting the plant of *Weekend Magazine* into such a commercially viable property that it even printed the opposition magazine, *The Canadian*, and several other journals. FP Publications also hired a new president, George Currie, who, fresh from a management consultant firm, possessed no newspaper background. Less than three months after Currie's appointment, *The Montreal Star* was shut down by a strike. Price, who served as the McConnell representative on the FP board, told Currie to keep out of it. Goodson, he said, would know how to cope.

The strike, which began on June 15, 1978, was seemingly over a simple issue: manning in the press room. That is, how many persons would have to be engaged to keep the several presses rolling. The union had already established the ratio in bitterly contested battles with *Le Soleil* in Quebec City and *La Presse* in Montreal – battles which involved strikes of seven and eight months. It could not sign a contract that was different from that of the other newspapers and print shops generally. Goodson saw it another way. Any yielding on this issue, which management regarded as "featherbedding," would have repercussions throughout Canada, especially affecting other papers in the FP group. Goodson had, he says, both Currie's and Price's concurrence, because even broader issues were involved. Coming up were negotiations with other major unions at *The Montreal Star*, and any substantial yielding on the press room front would work against management in overall settlements.

Goodson brushed aside the fundamental weakness and insensitivity in this argument when it was pointed out to him by others on the staff. One could no longer fight in a global sense against a union, made up of both francophones and anglophones, which had won a long battle in Quebec against French-language newspapers; one simply had to accept the fact that *The Montreal Star* was located in

Quebec and not in English Canada, where rates continued to be lower. But Goodson had been a pilot in the Second World War, and, before long, union members felt he was trying to fight the Battle of Britain all over again. It did not help when someone in Goodson's own office, or in the office of an aide, anonymously sent all the crafts a photocopy of a confidential document setting out company strategy that contained elements of union-busting.

In any event, the strike, which management had estimated would last no longer than three months – the relatively quiet business period of summer when advertising losses would not be serious – dragged on. It became a traditional pas de deux. When the company began to yield, the unions dug in, and vice versa. But on this occasion the pas de deux proved fatal. By the time the paper resumed publication eight months later, meeting virtually all the original union demands that could have been negotiated earlier, it was too late. The opposition *Gazette*, which had steadily lost $2 million annually for several years, had shrewdly capitalized on *The Montreal Star*'s absence when it became apparent, after three months, that the strike was not going to end. *The Gazette*'s owners, the Southams, increased the paper's budget substantially, while its editors surveyed *The Montreal Star*'s readers to find out what they most missed about the absent paper, and then provided them with these features. *The Montreal Star* never regained its lost audience (it had, before the strike, 57,000 more subscribers than *The Gazette*'s 115,000), or its advertisers.

Thus, on September 25, 1979, a newspaper with a record of involvement in community affairs, of intelligent and delicate awareness of the changes in French Canada, ceased to exist. There were many touches of tragic irony, including the fact that acceptance of the press room manning clause would have involved the salary of half a man a year – $15,000. The paper had been closed in panic, at the very start of a new and encouraging promotion campaign. George Currie had argued that the heavy and continuing losses of the FP's onetime most solid property endangered the future of the whole chain. Yet a few months later, FP Publications was sold to Thomson Newspapers for a very substantial price that enabled the McConnell family to benefit. Its share came to $41 million.

The post-mortems go on to this day, and one suspects that even Derek Price concedes that the strike should never have been allowed to happen. If management had accepted the union's case early on, it would not only have saved the paper itself, but in all likelihood it would have driven the shaky *Gazette*, unable at that stage to match new labour contracts, out of business or forced it into a merger. Yet an even deeper question, and one which is possibly not so speculative as it might seem, must be asked. What would John McConnell have done? McConnell, whose fully-clothed body was found floating in the lake of his Laurentian estate not many years after his forced retirement, would in all probability have spent his own wealth to keep the paper alive. Certainly he would not have tolerated a labour situation to reach a strike position. None took place on *The Montreal Star* during his tenure. But the story is a sad and complex one, a confluence of events and factors: absentee landlords, an individual publisher's ego, a union striving to assert its Quebec identity, and a family's indifferent attitude. Even John McConnell's sister, Kit (Mrs. Peter Laing), the closest to him in spirit and devotion, was disappointing in her reaction. Asked how she felt about the closing of *The Montreal Star*, she said, "To be truthful, I've been more concerned that *The Times* may be finished." This was said by her when it appeared that *The Times* of London, then in the midst of a long labour dispute, might not re-open.

If one assumes that a newspaper is like any other business and must rise or fall on its profits and losses, then only a pro forma case can be made to sustain a weakened publication. However, if one regards a newspaper in the same category as a university – that is, ennobled by public trust and responsibility to the community – then the conclusion must be different. The collapse of *The Montreal Star*, especially in a period of disquiet for the anglophone community of Montreal, a community that had enabled it to build handsome profits and a family fortune, denotes abrogation of that responsibility, to say nothing of how mismanagement of an institution can undermine society at large.

Modern Explorers ...

If only one could call him a country bumpkin. In a way it wouldn't be inaccurate. He was born in Thetford Mines, Quebec, which is not exactly a big town, and brought up in Sherbrooke, hardly a metropolis, and his first job paid only $5 a week. Then why not call him a country bumpkin? Especially since it would lend a nice touch to a success story – one of the most remarkable of all Canadian success stories. After all, he did invade Montreal, home of a lot of sharp businessmen; and then he absorbed an Ontario company twice his own size; and in the span of the next decade he became the biggest food merchandiser in Canada, with sales of more than $3 billion in 1981. Well, even there one must be careful. Depending on how you want to define it, Loblaws might be bigger. But then again it might not.

Anyway, a couple of things about Antoine Turmel can be said with certainty. First, he was born on April 25, 1918. Second, he is a francophone; and not only proud of it but blunt in admitting it gave him determination to leap ahead in an anglophone world. Third, he is no country bumpkin. He doesn't even look the part. He looks more like a surgeon – which is what he wanted to become – and a prosperous one at that. Of medium build, with black hair carefully brushed back and parted at the side, he wears rimless glasses and expensively tailored conservative suits. He is what he is: a brilliant innovator, a careful master of acquisition (despite the speed of his growth in recent years), and a man who hires as executives MBA's half his own age. He talks about "the human resources" needed to keep afloat and enlarge an operation such as Provigo, his flagship, and figures it is more sensible to let business administration school graduates learn about groceries than it is to expect clerks to understand modern methods of distribution. While Turmel is chairman and chief executive officer, his president is Pierre Lessard, an MBA from Harvard, who, barely forty, has been with him since 1967. Turmel's thirty-three-year-old daughter, Hélène – one of four children – took her MA in criminology and worked for the provincial probation office; then she decided to head for an MBA, and the likelihood is she will join the several other young women at Provigo.

Oh yes, there is something else about Antoine Turmel. In his empire, which stretches across Canada, down into California, and over to the eastern US, he sells not only food but pharmaceuticals and sporting goods. He is also examining the prospects of restaurant chains. He works on five year plans, just like the Russians, and though he is hardly a Communist his method of franchising carries with it a kind of egalitarian élan. His current five year target is to reach sales of $5 billion by 1985 – there's hardly a doubt about it – and to capture 2 per cent of the food market in the US, double his present slice (no one has more than 5 per cent).

But let him do some of the talking: "I think the English Canadian is beginning to treat the French Canadian with a bit more respect." There is an edge to that remark – not exactly biting but possessing sufficient querulousness to remind one that Provigo was not always given the financial support from the Wasp establishment that should have been forthcoming. Even to this day the Royal Trust Company, with its office just a few doors from the building on Dorchester Boulevard where Turmel makes his headquarters, acts in a kind of bewildered astonishment that a francophone could have made it so big in food, one of the most highly competitive and hazardous fields of all. Turmel's largest single source of backing, and therefore confidence, is the Caisse de dépôt et placement du Québec, the government institution responsible for Quebec's pension funds. One quarter of Provigo's stock is held by the Caisse, not a bad investment when one considers that a share bought at $8 in 1977 was worth $70 three years later.

Antoine Turmel sits in his fifth floor office – it is comfortably furnished and fairly big but it does not even occupy a corner with a view – and reflects on a life with a well-to-do father who lost everything in the Depression; his own initial failure at a business enterprise; and his discovery that what merchants needed was produce at the lowest possible price, for which they were prepared to pay cash. Much later he found that what impressed the consumer was shopping of convenience and quality. His father was the first francophone to move into what had been an entirely English-speaking district of Sherbrooke, the North Ward. Antoine was then nine years old and, as he recalls it, the move was beneficial for him. Within three months he had made friends and was on his way to learning English which today is impeccable, honed by studies in later years and a determination to be as good as any English Canadian. But life was not great for his father, a Coca-Cola bottler. Antoine, just a teenager, observed that Turmel senior's own delivery people were cheating him, and he warned him to introduce some sort of system to check loads. But his father couldn't bring himself to do anything that might suggest to his old employees that he thought they were dishonest. So he went broke, and Antoine learned a lesson he later applied in the food field: with margins too low to permit such losses, a system is necessary.

But in the interval, he suffered his own economic disaster. As a sixteen-year-old he went to work for a local food wholesaler, staying on the job for eleven years and taking correspondence courses in business administration with the Alexander Hamilton Institute of New York. By the time he was twenty-six he was ready to move upward – but not in the food business. Acquaintances who manufactured children's rocking chairs asked him to come in as general manager, provided he put up $4,000. It didn't strike him as being exactly right, particularly since they refused to show him the last year's audit. But with his entire savings of $3,000 plus $1,000 borrowed from a bank, he plunged ahead. The first thing he discovered was that workers, paid by the hour, would saw by hand little more than 150 rocker parts each day; if rewarded by the unit, they could turn out 1,000. The second thing he learned was that, with plastics encroaching, this was a dying field. So, after six months, he accepted $1,000 for his supposed partnership and paid off the bank loan. The lessons he bought for his $3,000 savings were twofold and everlasting: the importance of incentive to people who undertake franchises to operate a business on their own; and the absolute necessity of carefully examining figures before contemplating any takeover.

In any event, Antoine, in 1945, returned to the field he knew best: groceries. Big supermarket chains were rapidly knocking out the corner stores. But Turmel saw an area that was waiting to be handled with daring and imagination: the wholesaling of food to which he had been introduced as a youth. His approach was unique. Unlike the traditional wholesaler who provided clients with long term credit in exchange for markups of 12 to 15 per cent, Turmel was content with 2.5 per cent – and cash payment. With two partners, he took over a small tobacco and confectionery wholesaler in Sherbrooke, Denault Ltée, expanded it into groceries and applied his concept. He could work it by moving his stock before his own suppliers demanded payment. The lower costs kept some of the independent grocers alive and allowed Turmel to see his sales reach $1.5 million within five years.

In 1968, a car accident invalided Turmel for six months – enough time to think out current strategy and look ahead to the future. On the immediate front, he saw that with $50 million in business he had saturated the Sherbrooke market. In longer range he anticipated that his role as a wholesaler had its limitations. Now he says simply, "I came to the conclusion that Montreal, with half the province's population, was right for me." The move upward has been calculated and steady ever since. First came a complex merger with two other wholesalers, one in Chicoutimi, the other in Montreal, so distribution could be both province-wide and attractive enough to persuade Montreal grocers that Provigo-brand products – eventually exceeding 500 – would allow them to compete with the low-priced labels of the chains. Turmel, who bought out the interests of his two original associates, became chairman and chief executive. The formula is uncomplicated: for the affiliate, Provigo provides financial management and co-ordinated advertising, in addition to quality control. In turn, the franchiser buys his meats, groceries, vegetables, fruits, and other items from Provigo.

More than 2,000 grocers in Quebec thus are linked; and 900 of them bear Provigo's name in one form or another. These range from big supermarkets (240 called Provigo), to tiny Jovi corner stores (with the latest count at 277). In between are 281 medium-sized Provibec stores, and 160 Provi-Soir convenience stores. Provigo, in addition to its mainstay of wholesaling, is also now in the retail end, directly operating forty-seven of the supermarkets. In a ten year period, sales rose from $200 million annually to more than $1 billion. Then they shot up another billion, through Turmel's acquisition, in 1977, of M. Loeb Limited, an Ottawa wholesaler. Provigo had been quietly buying Loeb stock for three years, but the final takeover was done so discreetly, at a bargain price, that it even shook Bertram Loeb, the company's chairman and son of the founder, Moses Loeb.

What caused financial men to pay attention was that here was a Quebec company buying an Ontario company twice its own size. Apart from inheriting Loeb's 200 Independent Grocers Alliance (IGA), outlets, Turmel also got Loeb's Horne & Pitfield Limited, an Edmonton wholesaler with 340 affiliates in the west. Since Horne & Pitfield had its own little empire, Turmel fell heir to a grocery wholesaler in Santa Rosa, California, and to National Drug Limited, Canada's largest distributor of pharmaceuticals and other items to retail druggists. In one venture Turmel thereby transformed a regional business into an international one, with 60 per cent of sales outside Quebec. But that was hardly enough. Late in 1980 he closed a $100 million deal to take over the Quebec division of the Toronto based Dominion Stores Limited – eighty-seven supermarkets. Turmel is almost apologetic that three years elapsed between the Loeb and the Dominion Stores manoeuvres; but that was in keeping with his five year plans. "We had to restructure Loeb," he explains, "and then we were ready to move on."

Purchase of Dominion Stores was impelled by the awareness that Provigo was strong, in retail as well as wholesale trade, everywhere in Quebec except Montreal. Of the seventy-one Dominion Stores in Montreal, many of them in superb locations, Provigo runs some on its own and franchises the others to independents. What does this now do to Turmel's standing in the industry? Market analysts quibble whether Loblaws, part of the George Weston Limited group, or Provigo is now master. Turmel is satisfied to quote from the *Financial Times*, which says that Provigo's $3 billion business makes him Canada's largest food merchandiser. He reads it aloud with obvious gratification and confesses, "I can't help but feel proud. If Bombardier is able to do it, and Paul Desmarais is able to do it, and now I am able to do it, it should give French Canadians greater self-confidence." That is always close to his thinking – the self-image and the national image of fellow Quebecers.

Does acquisition of Dominion Stores mean that he is going to make war on Steinberg, the other giant supermarket chain in Quebec? "No," Turmel says clearly. "It's always been my philosophy to watch my own business. I haven't got time to worry about competition. If they come out with something sensational we'll read about it." Then a pause – a significant pause – and an almost reverential tone for a fellow marketing genius. "I had tremendous respect for Sam Steinberg. We had something in common. We both started from nothing." In return, the late Sam Steinberg demonstrated his esteem for the self-made Antoine Turmel. He owned shares in Provigo, which is something he never deigned to do with the institutionalized Dominion Stores, his direct and principal competitor.

Provigo has meanwhile acquired a sporting goods chain, Sports Experts Incorporated, with 100 outlets in Quebec, one in Ontario, one in Manitoba, and three in the Maritimes. What is a grocer doing in sports goods? "Our expertise has always been in food distribution," Turmel answers. "But distributing sports goods is to us the same thing – a matter of organization." It is Provigo's first deliberate invasion of an area outside food (National Drug was part of the Loeb package), and to Turmel it offers special opportunities. He sees more and more leisure time ahead for the public. In addition, it relates to the service field which he regards as important to the future of Montreal. Does this imply that French Canadians, like their ancestors who explored and traded into the midwest of the continent, will be sending pioneers to the hinterland? "Right on," he replies, not quite English in accent but certainly in choice of expression.

Turmel is not only a frontiersman but a practical one. "We were the first to come out with discount food stores," he points out. "That was in 1969, but we started to get out in 1980 when others went in. We feel the majority of shoppers don't want discount settings. They want better display and better service. The price difference is not so great. It's not 30 per cent, as some operators say. It might be 30 per cent on one product but on the average the saving is more like 5 to 7 per cent. People still want national brands and are willing to pay for them, especially if the children are grown up and you don't need a giant box of corn flakes."

This ability to adapt has inspired the boy from Sherbrooke to restore the old fashioned butcher to the modern city scene. La Boucherie was opened in 1980 in Candiac, a dormitory town south of Montreal. The counters are wooden, just like the ones he remembers from the Sherbrooke of a half century ago, and, even though Provigo employees now total 13,000, there are individual butchers to cut the meat just the way the customer wants it. La Boucherie proved so successful that three more were opened in the Montreal area in 1981, with several additions scheduled for 1982. The objective is to cover the desires of middle and upper income shoppers who are prepared to pay a little more for personalized service.

If the experiment continues to work well, Turmel will be ready to go farther afield with La Boucherie, across Canada and into the US – just as he has done with Provi-Soir convenience stores that are linked to gasoline service stations. That took a little selling to the oil companies, until Shell agreed to try and others soon clamoured to join in. The concept is elementary. You need a loaf of bread and a litre of milk – and you also need gasoline. So, instead of having to make two stops, why not do it all at one location? The same franchiser sells you both. Turmel's inspiration for the Provi-Soir link with gas stations was based on an awareness of how the women's liberation movement has changed buying habits. Career women simply haven't the same time or patience to spend on shopping for food as their mothers did. Any merchandiser who ignores this, says Turmel, "risks entrapment in the old social notions of his youth."

Turmel is also looking into the fast food business, another form of service or convenience to the public which he builds on. But he is in no hurry to enter it until he knows more about trends. If gas goes beyond $2 a gallon people won't want to drive to the outskirts of a city as they once did to a Howard Johnson's. "We're examining whether locations should be in the core of a city," he says, admitting that conditions, at least in 1981, did not yet encourage a major decision. "When gas prices stabilize we'll know more about where to go." Meanwhile, little is left to luck or chance. That old cautious streak of wanting to examine the books keeps reasserting itself. Provigo owns ten shares of every public company selling food in North America – restaurants and groceries – just so Turmel's team can get their annual reports and see how they operate and perform.

Once he decides on fast food expansion, one can presume that since Turmel believes in expertise ("human resources"), he'll acquire a flourishing concern and retain executives who know the business. The odds are that this will be in the US. Why not, say, Europe? Not interested, says Turmel, because he doesn't know the market there. "We go by the possibilities of markets, and there are many possibilities in the US." California alone, he notes, boasts a $20 billion food market – about $4 billion more than all of Canada. Since he already runs eight food distribution warehouses there (in addition to others in Maryland and Washington, DC), California is an obvious attraction, along with the Sun Belt in general.

Antoine Turmel always possessed vision but he is not exactly the same poor boy who started to work at $5 a week. He holds 10 per cent of Provigo's shares, worth $20 million in 1981 prices on the Montreal and Toronto stock exchanges. His salary is presumably in the range of $300,000 a year. How does he regard the future for francophones, for the coming Turmels? "When you see Paul Desmarais looking at opportunities all over the world," he says, "my impression is that there are no more barriers for us. The opportunities are there. But as we go along you'll see more and more large operations and fewer small ones. Inflation separates the good businessmen from the marginal. So the old image of a small Quebec entrepreneur will vanish." What has already gone, of course, is the traditional Quebec limitation of a career as a notary, a doctor, or a priest. Indeed, Turmel at one time aspired to a career in medicine, especially surgery. If the Depression had not forced him into a job instead, a continent might have been deprived of a marketing brain, and the French-Canadian people missed an inspiration.

Turmel is no separatist. Nor is he in any sense a bigot. But he does bear scars that many French Canadians of his generation, and other generations, recognize very easily. He speaks of an incident of two decades ago when he attended a meeting of prominent businessmen in the Sherbrooke-Magog area. The Quebec minister of finance began to address them in French, and the man sitting next to Turmel, an English Canadian who was president of a large textile mill in Magog, switched his earpiece to the English interpretation. Later, Turmel turned to him and asked, "Don't you understand any French?" The response was: "None. Can't understand a word." It was said almost in braggadocio, and this from a resident of Magog, which was half francophone at the time. "I can accept it when an English Canadian is awkward in speaking French," says Turmel. "But not to understand a word?" Since the episode occurred so long ago, why did he recall it now? There is a lengthy pause, and then Turmel replies, "I felt hurt."

He was, and still is, hurt too by the attitude of the Royal Trust Company, which for years he tried to get to invest in Provigo. There was deep symbolism behind his request, for the Royal Trust maintained its head office in Montreal – even though, since 1978, it has answered to the parent company, Royal Trustco Limited of Toronto – and he sought acceptance from local anglophone institutions. "We have the best return on equity of all food companies in Canada, and probably in North America," he argues. "It's not a fly-by-night record; the summary of our financial report goes back a decade. I've always felt an obligation to protect shareholders. I won't dilute their holdings by acquiring other corporations through equity. I've preferred to borrow from the bank. The Royal Trust knew our record and yet they've never bought a single share in our company."

Turmel made a comment to this effect in *Executive* magazine in September 1980. It pushed a reply by the Royal Trust that it had bought some shares under a nominee's name in addition to others for its own portfolio. Today Turmel shrugs this aside with the observation, "Whether they later bought ten shares or 10,000 was insignificant. The question is: Where was this trust company, the biggest in Canada, when it would have had meaning to us?"

Why does he think the Royal Trust acted so coldly? It comes down, in Turmel's mind, to a single word: prejudice – the kind that tells an English Montrealer that a French Montrealer must be limited in his outlook. "If we had been a company in Ontario I think they would have behaved differently," Turmel says. Nonetheless, he is optimistic about the future, about collaboration between anglophone and francophone. "With the right kind of give and take, both groups will be able to live comfortably together."

The office of Power Corporation is in the old Canada Steamship Lines building on Victoria Square. It would be rash to guess from the outward appearance of this modest granite structure – a throwback to 1912 – that it shelters such a huge organization. On the board listing occupants are a couple of lawyers and architects, and the lobby is spotted with glass showcases of models of the sailing vessels and steamboats that once sailed the St. Lawrence River. But nowhere is there a reference, even a clue, that Power Corporation is here. Nor is there any automation. You must ask the elevator operator for the office of Mr. Paul Desmarais and slowly you ascend to the seventh floor, to a hall blocked off by full-length glass doors behind which sits a receptionist who, after a casual glance, buzzes an electronic lock.

It is part of the circumspect security system, of course, but the next thing you know is that there he is in the outer office – a tall man (six feet four inches), lean, with grey hair in just the slightest disarray, sleeves rolled up and vest showing a little too much shirt in the back. Paul Desmarais, with the assistance of two girls and a young man, is prying open a crate and lifting a painting out of it. He takes another painting off its hook on the wall – an A.Y. Jackson, a Goodridge Roberts? One does not dally glancing at it, for the other sight is too intriguing: this giant of a man, financially as well as physically, doing what is obviously a labour of love.

The painting from the crate goes on the wall. It is old and it shows a boy holding a bundle of newspapers, but there is still no inclination to examine it closely, for the fascination is with Desmarais and the impatient grimace when he discovers it hangs so low that it rests on the back of a leather chair. "Do something," he instructs the aides as he leads his visitor to his office. During the walk he explains that he had seen the painting once at *La Presse*; it vanished mysteriously and, just as inexplicably, reappeared. He liked it and took possession of it – and suddenly he swings around and guides the visitor back to the reception area to see why. By now an assistant has moved it to another wall where it hangs freely; the boy is holding copies of *La Presse*. The artist is unknown, but, judging from the boy's costume, it must go back many, many decades. Later, when he talks and expounds on *La Presse* it becomes clear why the painting has so much meaning for Desmarais. Of all his acquisitions, it is the newspaper – and the intellectual stimulation it provides – that he loves the most.

This is an unpretentious man, as friendly and informal as though he is still operating a shoestring bus company in Sudbury, Ontario. His jacket is draped sloppily on the back of a chair as he sits with his guest in a corner of the handsome, but quietly toned, office, its dominant object an old sea chest with brass corners. He holds or chews on a long yellow pencil while the visitor says he has a question, suggested by a mutual acquaintance, Minda Bronfman, the Baroness de Gunsberg; but it can wait until more pertinent material is dispensed with. "No, what's the question?" he says, an impatient little boy, inquisitive about what would intrigue the Baroness de Gunsberg. "Well, she said, 'Be sure to get him to tell you the story of how he bought his first bus company in order to get a date with Jacqueline.'"

Desmarais is puzzled and agrees that maybe the Baroness had romanticized things, for he was already owner of the bus line – for which he paid $10. But he does volunteer the following glimpse of a courtship: "Jackie was a nurse, and there was a bus stop a block from the hospital. I used to wait there, in my car, and say, 'C'mon, I'll give you a lift.' She'd say, 'No, I'm waiting for the bus.' This went on for a couple of weeks and everyone else at the stop knew it was a kind of game, and they'd say, 'Go on Jackie, take the lift.'" So he kept the buses running and he married Jackie and they have lived happily ever after.

The story of Paul Desmarais has been well chronicled in word and picture. It was by far the most attractive subject of a widely viewed 1980 CBC documentary series, *The Canadian Establishment*, an adaptation of Peter C. Newman's book. But it remains endlessly fascinating, for no story can quite match it. In little more than a quarter century Desmarais emerged from obscurity in Sudbury to become the most important francophone in Canadian industry and possibly the outstanding performer in the whole of the Canadian business world. He is as much a "bumpkin" as Antoine Turmel, though he does like to refer to himself as "the little guy from Sudbury" who grew up in the company of French gangs who were always getting into fights with the English guys. Desmarais reached law school in Toronto but dropped out in order to take over the family's ailing bus company. What he received in return for his token $10 payment was a fleet of sixteen dilapidated vehicles and $385,000 in debts. The initial struggle was such that he would count the coins left every night in the fare boxes in the buses – until he began to haul miners to International Nickel Company sites at nearby Copper Cliff.

That was the only encouragement he needed; from that point onward his ambition took the form of acquisitiveness. Once he had accumulated $100,000, he set out to buy the Gatineau Bus Line of Hull, Quebec. But that required a loan of $175,000. The manager of the Banque Canadienne Nationale argued that, as a Franco-Ontarian, Desmarais did not understand Quebec. He could cope with Sudbury, but not with a Quebec which was under English control despite a French-Canadian government. Turned down, he went to the Royal Bank and obtained a loan. From Hull it was but a simple step, in his mind, to Quebec City and acquisition of Québec Autobus. That was when he met Premier Maurice Duplessis, who, at the height of his power, repeated what the bank manager in Sudbury had said: a "little guy" didn't have a chance if he thought he could enter the terrain of the English or even the French establishment. Québec Autobus was swung around from a loss of $60,000 to a profit of $350,000, and this propelled Desmarais to the Provincial Transport Company and the goal he had aimed at – Montreal, the big league, in 1960. "It was," as he remembers it, "a marvellous time to arrive in Montreal." The spirit of the Quiet Revolution was positive and infectious after the Duplessis era.

It had taken Desmarais nine years. But while he was not an innovator in the sense of originating new enterprises, what he brought with him was the capacity to see what others missed: how to dismantle disorganized companies and put them together again. He also learned what he calls a trick: the reverse takeover, a perfectly legal manoeuvre. For example, J. Louis Lévesque, the francophone financier from New Brunswick, wanted to sell his diversified holdings, but Desmarais lacked the money. Lévesque suggested an exchange of shares, and Desmarais wound up still in control of Provincial Transport and its Voyageur buses, along with new outfits. In 1980, when Desmarais was fifty-three, he controlled – as chairman and chief executive officer of Power Corporation – 190 companies with profits of $120 million, and assets worth more than $8 billion.

If you read a newspaper the chances are it was printed on paper supplied by Desmarais' Consolidated-Bathurst Limited (with 18,000 employees): most certainly this is the case if it is *La Presse*, or publications in three other Quebec cities. If you buy insurance, the odds are good it was from Great-West Life Assurance Company, the biggest today in Canada. The list goes on and on – everything from trust companies to cement plants. Desmarais holds 70 per cent of the voting shares in the myriad corporations and it is all done from the old-fashioned little building on Victoria Square where only about three dozen men and women work directly for Power Corporation. There isn't a public relations man in sight; none exists in Power Corporation as such. In his infrequent interviews Paul Desmarais makes his own decisions: who he will see, what he will say.

For instance, a writer is equipped well in advance with a beautiful quote from Roger Lemelin, one-time publisher of *La Presse*, who speaks of his boss with awe and admiration. "He came not from Quebec but from a small town in Ontario. He had no complex at all about Quebec. His complex was in his own community. But when he came here and saw people had no reason for a complex but were complaining, he got so mad that he said, 'To hell with them. I'll transform everything.' He wanted to transform Quebec and Canada and then the whole world." What does Desmarais have to say in comment? One word: "Bull." There is concurrence about Lemelin's dramatic proclivities.

116

But what about the warning Desmarais received from his old bank manager in Sudbury and from Duplessis about how the Quebec establishment would gobble him up? A flat rebuttal: "I was well received by everyone – the French, the English, the bankers, the others. What's so marvellous about Montreal is that an outsider coming in is better treated than someone already living here." There is a theory that anglophones sheltered Desmarais because, as a French Canadian of importance, he could provide some protection against the rising phenomenon known as "separatism." But that is a highly fanciful notion. The fact is that the business community, anglophone or francophone, had no choice but to accept the upstart from Sudbury. He was original, he was daring, and anyway, as he puts it, "I wasn't all that successful when I arrived. Claim to fame came later, with Provincial Transport. If anything, there was a feeling, 'Here is a young Ontario boy, let's give him a break.'"

With it all, Desmarais was, and remains, shy and – odd to say – conservative. Two people close to him choose, by chance, to seize on the same descriptive word, "haphazard," in order to refute it. Jacqueline, his wife, notes that Paul may seem "haphazard" in his ways; in fact that is what he says of himself. He maintains that "luck" often plays a part in his achievements. But in actuality, she emphasizes, he misses nothing; when they are out socially, he listens – just as he does in business lunches – and he never forgets an observation or remark he regards as important. James W. Burns, the astute head of Great-West Life, whom Desmarais brought to Montreal to serve as president of Power Corporation, says simply: "Paul has French-Canadian characteristics in him – his exuberance, his waving of hands to emphasize a point. But it's a disarming advantage. Behind it is a mind of steel. He's not haphazard." Desmarais himself concedes the truth of these observations. It was while he was in Toronto that he heard casually over a dinner that Great-West Life was for sale. The next morning he flew to Winnipeg, the home of the insurance company, and by telephone and personal contact raised the $76 million necessary to beat competitors in the race. "Quite often, when I've gone somewhere, something unexpected has turned up," he says in retrospect. "Who'd ever have thought I'd wind up with Great-West Life? Certainly I hadn't thought of it."

Then how about his diversification, his apparent interest in branching out, not only into multiple fields, but into the world – the kind of conquest Roger Lemelin talks about? Here James Burns steps in with a word of caution. Desmarais and Power Corporation already enjoy entry into the US through sales by Great-West Life, and into Germany and the UK through Consolidated-Bathurst. Burns' own view is that the US is the place to aim for; it's nearby and it's familiar. "The thing to remember," he says, "is that you don't do business in the US. You do it in a *region* of the US. California's population is one and a half times bigger than Canada's; it's richer than France. I argue: why run around the world when we know the US?" Then he returns to the cardinal point. "Paul is very conservative and careful. He's not out to conquer the world."

Yet there is a kind of boyish wonderment about Desmarais when he recounts the trips he has taken to China and Saudi Arabia. He recognizes that there are not one billion potential customers in China. There is just one customer: the state. "But once you're in, dealing with one agent is easier than with one billion." As for Saudi Arabia, he thinks of the potential in a field with which he became acquainted early on: trucking and transportation. "And most important," he throws in, almost as an afterthought, "is looking after their investments." Thus one cannot be sure just where Paul Desmarais' fertile mind is taking him. "When I started out, in the bus business, we had a strike and I decided to go into life insurance," he relates. "The two couldn't have been more different. Then you diversify on a provincial basis, province by province, across Canada; and then you go into other countries."

The point, therefore, is to strengthen yourself through multiformity? He nods. But doesn't that suggest another element: global power? Now he shakes his head and says, "I haven't saturated any area, so why should I go after the world? I can be busy all my life here." And then he lapses into a moment of reflection, stressing that it is important to get out, to meet as many people in as many places as possible, because that's how ideas and opportunities unexpectedly present themselves; the Great-West Life example is cited again. So what will Paul Desmarais of the 1980's be like? A man on the world route of acquisition? Back to China, back to Saudi Arabia, out to Timbuktu? James Burns' knowledgeable assessment of his boss is not to be tampered with injudiciously, but an outsider can only wonder if one day newspapers will carry headlines about Paul Desmarais engaging in a reverse takeover in an exotic far off place. In 1981 they told only of his decision to sell his bus, trucking, and other transportation holdings, and to become the biggest single share-holder in Canadian Pacific.

Meanwhile, there is a more parochial question. With his empire scattered so widely in North America, why does he live in Montreal? His instant answer is: "Because I bought Provincial Transport." But then he hesitates, as though he has never considered the question before, and indeed admits he hasn't. Initially, Montreal was the ultimate, the big time, especially for a French Canadian; but then, as though spiritually scratching his head, he says, "Yes, I suppose I should be in a lot of places: in Winnipeg, because I bought Great-West Life; in Toronto, because I bought Imperial Life." He skims through the list a bit, and stops abruptly, as though finally he knows what he was groping for. "Power Corporation's head office is here." And then, the ultimate confession. "We saw a home and bought it, and love it here. We raised a family in Montreal and they love it. There's good shopping, good restaurants." So he's not maudlin; he's very practical. "I've never thought of it," he says again. He agrees with a view that becomes more and more evident as one presses into the question of why head offices move or stay: the basis is usually personal and emotional, the rationale follows.

When one remarks that he is looked upon today as a great example of how a francophone can succeed, Paul Desmarais says that makes him feel all right, but deep down he isn't satisfied with himself. "I wonder if I could have accomplished more," he says. A pause. The visitor says: "But you are barely in your mid-fifties." A rejoinder: "One is always critical of oneself. Aren't you? I could have done more up to now." Is that a reference to his failure to take over Argus Corporation, the bastion of the Toronto establishment? Not at all. He's not bothered by missing out on Argus. He tried and lost; that was fair enough. "It's the things that I didn't try and should have – and missed. That's what bothers me." Again, when the visitor points out that his is an outstanding story of achievements (just look at all those adjectives and glowing descriptions, "a myth writ large," used on the CBC program), he says, "That's the perception others have of me. I have my own perception of myself. I wake up in the morning making notes of what I should be looking into." He halts and repeats, "But I didn't do enough in the past."

So here is this enormously likable, restless man, confessing, with a barely traceable speech impediment that only adds to his warmth and human quality, that he finds his perception of himself lacking. He is far more introspective, far more philosophic, than he often lets on. And maybe the clue is contained in that painting that hangs in the outer office, the newsboy holding copies of *La Presse*. Dozens of canvases are scattered through Power Corporation's two floors that resemble a big, rambling, elegantly furnished home – paintings by Tom Thomson and Emily Carr and Clarence Gagnon and Jean-Paul Lemieux, to say nothing of the three Krieghoffs in Desmarais' own office. But the little unknown newsboy seems to stand out. Of all his holdings, Desmarais admits, *La Presse* is his first love. "Journalism is a fascinating world," he says. "The people in it. The events. There's always something new. And it's a community responsibility. During a big issue, such as federalism, it's important that we write about it and explain why it makes sense." He doesn't lose sight of the fact (indeed, he reminds the visitor), that "a newspaper is a business, and *La Presse* is well run." It makes money; and "it has always made money, and despite strikes it still comes out ahead. Mind you, it's no picnic." He bought it as a business venture but found an intellectual challenge and a world beyond the other world with which he was familiar.

Desmarais retains responsibility for the editorial policy of *La Presse*, though it is evident that he and his publisher, Roger Lemelin, who resigned late in 1981, not over policy but to pursue new projects, shared identical views. He met with Lemelin, whom he refers to affectionately as "that romantic," two or three times a week, usually at lunch. In the twelve years since his proprietorship, Desmarais has allowed an article to appear only twice under his own name. The first was in February 1976 when his administrative assistant, Jean Parisien, suddenly fell ill. Desmarais rushed into Parisien's office just in time to catch him as he slumped from his chair, dead from a heart attack. Desmarais wrote a tribute about the associate who had been at his side since the earliest days in Sudbury. The second occasion was in November 1980; Desmarais wanted to pay his respects when Jules Léger, the former governor general, died.

Clearly his attraction to *La Presse* relates to many factors: not only the power implied in ownership of an important newspaper but, in this instance, language and heritage. Desmarais is a francophone, and by adoption a Montrealer. He is interested in the flourishing of a culture and a city. How does he regard Montreal's future? "We've been through a difficult period," he says. "We've gone about as low as we can go, but that is history now. All the future can do is improve. Look at the construction going on, look at those bright, young, aggressive people you see all around you. We're over the hump." In his travels abroad, Desmarais is struck by the questions foreigners ask. He gives a direct answer. "We've had our problems, but if you want to invest you've got to think long term. It's better and cheaper to come in when all is not so rosy. It's more expensive when everything is rosy." He also notes that Europeans remark on how "civilized" the behaviour of Quebec was during the referendum, "so different from the experiences they have had in trying to settle similar problems."

And the future of anglophones? "Just let them," he says, "continue as they are. They've got as great a future as the francophones. It's better to speak French but it's not essential. Look at the tourists from the States or the visitors from other parts of Canada who spend a couple of weeks here. They've no problem. If you live in a French milieu you'll survive even if you don't adapt to the language. You punish yourself, you miss something if you don't go to French theatre. But a lot of people come here and don't go to theatre." Is he this generous – much more so than others who say anglophones must learn French or they'll fail in business – because he is a French Canadian from a town in Ontario? Does this give him a special perspective? He can't answer that. Maybe it is because he is himself such a practical person that he calculates the factors that add up the most: business ability, the willingness to plunge.

Desmarais also makes a point, whenever Toronto enters a conversation, of commenting, "Some people say you've got to be on Bay Street to feel the market. I've never been on Bay Street." He is a master of drollery. At a reception he gave in the Ritz-Carlton gardens, in honour of his brother, some of the guests became overly enthusiastic. After appropriate toasts, they hurled their glasses onto the flagstone pavement. "What the hell," said Paul Desmarais with a fatalistic shrug. "We own Dominion Glass."

Of this triumvirate in tales of success, Bombardier, Incorporated, stands on its own, for it is in the manufacturing sector. "We've taken on the world in a different way from Paul Desmarais; not so much by acquisition but by building by ourselves," says Laurent Beaudoin, the company's chairman and chief executive officer. But the degree of attainment, apart from an intense desire to prove French-Canadian ability, remains similar to that of Desmarais and Turmel. No corporation in Canada can compare with Bombardier in the production of mass transit equipment. Budd, the only organization in the US that is bigger, leans on a much longer history; and Bombardier is growing at a faster clip. The range is astonishing: from motorcycles for the Belgian army to locomotives for Via Rail. The locomotives are built in Montreal, the subway cars in the Quebec town of La Pocatière, with components in four other Quebec factories. In addition, Bombardier now operates an assembly plant in Barre, Vermont (for commuter rail cars), and two plants in Austria (for tramways and light engines). Production lines in Ireland turn out buses.

This multinational operation arose from a cumbersome machine known as a snowmobile – invented a generation ago by a man named J. Armand Bombardier – which later became streamlined and lissome as the Ski-Doo. The Ski-Doo, after defending a market contested by more than 100 imitators, still accounts for 40 per cent of Bombardier's business; and the Ski-Doo is still Number One in the world, most of the other snowmobiles having melted away. But it is in the dynamic and challenging business of mass transportation, particularly the development of the Light-Rapid-Comfortable (LRC), train – used for commuter and inter-city transportation – that Beaudoin looks to the future. He estimates that by the mid-1980's the Canadian and American markets alone could reach $1 billion a year. Bombardier expects to win a major share of these markets, ensuring a significant growth rate for a company whose sales totalled $500 million in 1981. The start will come at Barre, with $100 million worth of commuter cars for the state of New Jersey – the first big thrust into the US market.

Beaudoin enhanced his career by marrying the boss's daughter (they met when they were students at the Université de Sherbrooke), and reciprocated by advancing the company to its present dimensions and concept for the future. His father-in-law had the mind of an inventor, not the preoccupation of a businessman. When Beaudoin joined in 1963, Bombardier's volume was a modest $9 million a year, based on sales of 7,000 Ski-Doos, the new recreational vehicle, mainly in Ontario and Quebec. Beaudoin saw the potential in enlarging the territory. But that meant talking J. Armand, who had started his business in 1942 with $1,500 and a cautious attitude, into accepting an advertising budget of $40,000. Beaudoin remembers the precise reaction as though it were yesterday. "For that price," said his father-in-law, "you can build a nice house and see something tangible." But to Beaudoin, a commerce graduate and a chartered accountant, the choice was clear. Because of growing competition from Americans and Japanese, Bombardier had to go in for Ski-Doos in a big way or give up making them. The big way meant capturing the market fast, and this in turn meant developing a vast distribution organization.

Reluctantly, J. Armand accepted the $40,000 advertising budget, which led to marketing, familiarization of the name Ski-Doo, and a network of 2,000 dealers in Canada and the US alone. But J. Armand Bombardier did not live to witness the lightning ascent. He died of cancer the next year, 1964, at the age of fifty-six. A decade later, the company that once was known only for its snow gadabouts, veered into the mass transit field. Beaudoin set high sights: to build the cars for Montreal's subway extension. The main competitor was Canadian Vickers. But Vickers failed to follow specifications, particularly on the car couplings. The effect of this was to make Bombardier, at $117 million, the lowest bidder. Vickers, chagrined, turned nasty, issuing pronouncements that a snowmobile manufacturer lacked the experience to handle the sophisticated demands of an intricate subway system. The impression of some anglophones was that a francophone outfit simply could not deliver. The cars turned out to be of the highest quality.

Knowing he was dying, J. Armand had told his son-in-law, "It's too bad I'm going. We would have made a good team." Beaudoin interprets this to mean the inventor plus the organizer. Bombardier was happiest in his workshop, tinkering, developing new equipment; and Beaudoin thinks the company might have taken a different orientation under the founder. "I don't imagine he would have been very happy acquiring Montreal Locomotive Works. He would have preferred to develop his own, maybe a new-type locomotive, as he had the snowmobile." Actually, buying Montreal Locomotive Works was the only substantial acquisition the company did make, in contrast to building or expanding its own facilities. And there is irony to that. The locomotive firm was three quarters of a century old, and, though renamed MLW-Worthington Limited, still carried a romantic image. Beaudoin wanted to continue to diversify. Moreover, he anticipated the rising demand for rapid public transportation and thought the answer lay in MLW because of its long experience. The purchase was made in 1976, for $16 million. "As a French-Canadian group with very little tradition we thought we could learn something from MLW – like management style," says Beaudoin. "To our disappointment the company had let itself age." The challenge then was to revamp management and install quality control. It was francophone expertise that did it.

The reputation of Bombardier's new product is high, and Beaudoin proudly points out that "we are the only company in Canada which makes a complete locomotive, including the diesel engine." (General Motors maintains an assembly plant only.) The hope is that the LRC will lead to a major overhauling of the railway system in North America. Amtrak would be the potential major customer. Meanwhile, Bombardier has orders from Via Rail, the Canadian system, with $70 million worth of locomotives and coaches being built. Such is the impact of the operation that early in 1981 Bombardier received a $14 million contract from Guatemala for ten diesel freight locomotives; a later order, valued at $150 million, to build trucks for the Canadian Armed Forces (under licence from American Motors Corporation); and, most pleasing of all for Beaudoin, a $100 million deal with Mexico City for subway cars similar to the rubber-tired vehicles running in Montreal's métro.

Beaudoin, a rather shy person, works from an unpretentious office (in the same Dorchester Boulevard building as Provigo), that is in keeping with his personal style. He is, at forty-three, the antithesis of others of the new generation of francophone executives; that is, he does not exude the kind of super-confidence of some of them. Instead, he is rather quiet and reserved, knowing, for instance, that 1980 was a bad year for snowmobiles (a mild winter knocked industry sales down to 190,000 units from 260,000 the year before). But he is confident of the future, thanks to the infusion generated by the LRC. Most of all, he is proud of the attainments of a francophone company. "People used to say that French Canadians weren't much good at taking raw materials and turning them into finished products; or that they couldn't cope with large volume, with organizing big-scale production. These are myths that have been exploded." Also on the upbeat, he makes an interesting point: "We have been one of the biggest schools in Quebec for French-speaking business management types. I see our graduates today all over the place." There are, he estimates, at least 100 Bombardier veterans in senior executive positions in engineering and manufacturing companies.

Beaudoin does not blame the anglophones for the mythology; it is, rather, the fault of the old francophone upbringing and the old set of values. Beaudoin was born in a village called Laurier Station, twenty-five miles west of Quebec City, and, as he recalls it: "My father was a moderately successful businessman – a grocery whole-saler – but the curé didn't look up to him. Business was not a good tradition, especially in a rural area. Maybe it was all right to be a road contractor, but nothing else. I was lucky, because my father encouraged me to think of a business career." Starting with Beaudoin's generation, "our frontiers and approach opened up."

One of the first discoveries he made at Bombardier was that the US was potentially a bigger market for Ski-Doos than Canada. Beaudoin also found, at conferences of distributors and customers, that Americans are much more responsive than English Canadians. "They like the flavour of an accent, whether it is German or French. I never felt that because we were French Canadians we were limited. In the States it was a plus to be a French Canadian – we were thought to have flair, a different approach." In English Canada? He is not so sure, but answers this way: "I recall in Wisconsin an international snowmobile competition and race – an annual event where we always put on a big show because we were the biggest in the industry. We brought along some participants from the Quebec Carnival; men and women in raccoon coats and typical costumes. The people in Wisconsin were charmed, and we all sang French-Canadian songs. We tried the same in Peterborough, Ontario, but the reaction was not so warm. There wasn't the same feeling."

He says this in a manner of realism, not bitterness; yet, as is apparent from the next sentence, there is a depth of challenge for the French Canadian to demonstrate his ability to the English Canadian. "When we set forward to build up the company with a basic product of Ski-Doos, one of the goals was to show that a French Canadian could in the long term succeed. If, in the short term, we had been interested in selling out, we could have done so many times." Was there a "mission," then, behind Bombardier? He dismisses that word as "too grand," but he admits that part of the task was to avoid what so many French-Canadian businessmen did in the past when they only built up to a certain stage, saying to themselves, "If I can sell out I'll be able to leave my children with some money and they won't have to face the problems I did." This mentality is changing, and Beaudoin says simply, "I want to build an organization that will not die with me." Yet it is still very much a family affair, with 67.6 per cent of the 3.9 million shares held by Bombardier's own kinfolk.

Now that the initial challenge has been met, the one ahead lies in continued expansion. Bombardier is spending $60 million over a three year period enlarging three of its factories producing snowmobiles, rapid transit cars, and locomotives. Beaudoin is convinced that the trend towards the LRC is inevitable because of the high fuel costs for individual motorists. He is clearly at a loss to speculate about what would have happened if the man he so obviously admired and respected, J. Armand Bombardier, had continued to live. But he does say, "When he died he was just finishing development of the snowmobile. Afterwards, he would have started something else." What? A shrug of the shoulders and one word: "Unknown." Maybe something symbolic of the restless, expanding world of French Canadians? Like engines powered by liquid hydrogen? In any case, in May 1982 the company, against stiff international competition, won the largest export order in Canadian history: manufacturing one billion dollars worth of subway cars for New York City.

... and Young Innovators

Laurent Beaudoin, if only because of his relatively young age, forms a link between such giants as Paul Desmarais and Antoine Turmel, who are in their fifties and sixties, and a youthful new breed of francophone executives who go by an irreverent yet telling label: "the élite panzer corps." The fact that the man who thought it up, Pierre Robitaille, a leading chartered accountant, wasn't even born when the wartime phrase "panzer" was synonymous with lightning German armoured attack, makes it even more tantalizing. The use of "élite" is really redundant, but, as a French word, at least appropriate. What it amounts to is that there are scores, maybe hundreds, of French-Montrealers, mostly in their thirties, who have emerged in recent years, either to replace anglophones in senior positions or to work alongside them. And what they have in common is a high level of education, expertise, and the kind of ambition and drive that makes them a challenge to competitors everywhere.

Often they also share a rare combination – experience in government that proves invaluable in business. Pierre Lortie is an example. In 1981, at the age of thirty-four, he became the youngest president in the history of the Montreal Stock Exchange. Handsome, with greying hair, he not only looks the part of an energetic administrator but shows it in his enthusiasm for all things Montreal and in a fresh perception that enables him to break down the modern period into three parts. The 1950's was the age of the entrepreneur – the small businessman. The 1960's and 1970's saw the rise of the intellectuals, when academics entered government. The 1980's again turned into the age of the entrepreneurs, but with a vast difference: it embraced the skilled hands and minds of government veterans who possessed confidence and knowledge absent in earlier generations. Most important, they could think globally rather than within the parochial limitations of the earlier group.

Lortie himself, after earning degrees in engineering at Université Laval, business administration at the University of Chicago, and a diploma in economics at the University of Louvain, joined the Quebec civil service in the late 1960's. By 1970 he was executive assistant to Raymond Garneau, minister of finance in the Bourassa government. "But there are only so many jobs government can provide," Lortie points out. "In the early 1970's a general freeze was placed on government hiring. There was no longer any choice – the doors of the business world had to be opened. Francophones began to penetrate in such large contingents that they shattered the doors." Lortie became a senior partner in Secor Incorporated, a Montreal firm of marketing consultants specializing in strategic studies. "I do not pretend to be well versed in the sociological aspects of the emergence of a new élite," he says. "My observations are impressionistic." But the fact is that his work with Secor placed him in a position to test and confirm some favourite theories.

For instance, even though a predominantly francophone society in Montreal displays basic cultural differences from those of English Canadians, he feels the aspirations of both are much the same. "French Canada is still often pictured as a North American haven of *joie de vivre* and of proverbial Latin attitudes not often associated with hard work and the dour accumulation of riches. It's a stereotype that does not conform to reality. The 'Protestant work ethic' is still alive and well in Quebec nowadays. In fact, it's paradoxical to encounter an underground Calvinistic revival in the same period as the break by French Canadians with the traditional Catholic values that used to make them such interesting sociological artifacts. This paradox makes it necessary to treat the arrival of a French-Canadian business élite in the broader framework of the evolution of Quebec society."

Lortie commands a swift style in coming up with catchy and appropriate illustrations. For one thing, he disdains the use of "entrepreneurial" in a current context, preferring to call it a "managerial" class. And, bringing this down to even simpler language, he says the dominant character of a francophone manager is that he is "a gamesman." That conclusion originates from a study conducted in 1980 by Secor, in which nearly 150 middle managers in ten large

128

Quebec based organizations were interviewed. The Secor summation knocks out any image of the Quebec manager as sluggish or unimaginative. Instead, "he is calculating, driven by ambition, motivated by personal recognition and financial reward. If he leaves his organization, it is to pursue a better opportunity elsewhere. And if he seems attached to Quebec, it is because he recognizes that this is presently the land of opportunities."

Lortie, when he talks this way, may sound like a Chambre de Commerce type. Indeed, he was elected its Montreal president for 1980-81, and remained chairman in 1982. But he is genuinely fervent – and able to reinforce it with statistics and facts – in his belief that not only has the major phenomenon in Quebec in the past two decades been the rapid multiplication of the francophone managerial type, but that despite "the tired gloom" which characterized the Montreal business community a few years ago, the level of productivity in Quebec today is higher than in Ontario. Lortie predicts that Montreal will expand, and that in twenty-five years Toronto will be like Detroit, a decaying city. One reason he cites is the American swing away from branch plant operations, which they find costly and out of tune with modern international trade.

Montreal, by contrast, is made up of what he calls "immigrants" – that is, people who may have lived here 200 years but only recently migrated to an industrial society, bringing with them new spirit and ideas. Bombardier is an obvious case. Lortie now finds that the Toronto business approach is "conservative," an inevitable attitude after a period of aggressive and rapid expansion. He sees the future of Montreal industry related more to US rather than Canadian (specifically Ontario) markets. "The Ontario market is tougher to crack than the American, so we'll be heading towards the US in the 1980's, with a very distinct impact by the end of the decade." Provigo provides the example even today. And this, he argues, will happen whether or not the Parti Québécois remains in office. The key point here – and Lortie does little more than reiterate what many of his background and generation feel – is that francophones are not nearly as uptight as anglophones about the Parti Québécois or about dealing with its cabinet ministers and senior civil servants. Since so many of the young entrepreneurs or managers are themselves graduates of government, they treat government to their advantage because they understand it. In his old firm of Secor, for instance, one colleague prepared a report for Claude Ryan, the Liberal leader in the 1981 election, while another partner worked on a project for the Parti Québécois.

Lortie contends that he would leave Quebec if it ever separated. "But it won't separate. The Parti Québécois is basically a conservative party. We can see this more clearly every day." Lortie, who was appointed to the Economic Council of Canada in 1981, also believes that Quebec is the most North American of all provinces. To him, the Carter administration in the US and the Parti Québécois were somewhat similar in style. He cites cases of Secor working on nuclear projects with Carter officials and finding that they were precisely the same as Parti Québécois types – the same kind of educational framework, the same general concept. The American swing later to Ronald Reagan was matched by a turn towards conservatism here. "Not a swing, really," Lortie adds in qualification, "because Quebecers have always been more in favour of private enterprise than socialization. Much more so, say, than Ontarians."

Lortie plainly is a man who likes to debunk myths, and he carries this practice into the field of language. While he recognizes that many anglophones, especially the younger, accept that the battle is over, that French is indeed the principal language, some of the older anglophones are still apprehensive – not because they fear a loss of culture but because they perceive, even if unconsciously, that Bill 101 is "expropriation without compensation." The fact is that if anglophones cannot adjust, they give up by default their business opportunities to the bright young francophones who form the new élite of the 1980's.

Lortie has ambitious plans for the Montreal Stock Exchange – that venerable institution which once dominated the country but now ranks as Number Three after Toronto and Vancouver. "It's a challenge," he says simply, focussing on a prime weakness. Montreal is a national exchange; it possesses no Quebec roots. This is unlike the Toronto market which was built largely on the Ontario economy, with about 60 per cent of its listings from Ontario based companies. "You can count on the fingers of two hands Quebec listings like Provigo," Lortie says. As many as 100 Quebec companies now privately owned could, or should, go public: such large firms as Forex-Leroy, a family held lumber goliath of Abitibi; or Canam-Manac, one of Canada's largest makers of steel joists and pre-fabricated industrial buildings. Located in St. Georges de Beauce under the proprietorship of Marcel Dutil, Canam-Manac does a volume of $210 million a year. Dutil, thirty-nine, is something of a folk hero to Quebec businessmen, though he is hardly known by the public at large.

Lortie is not sure why so few of the Quebec companies that should be public, aren't public. He does not attribute it to the old entrepreneurial attitude of a man making just enough money to be able to leave a legacy for his family. It is, rather, in the case of Dutil, the style of an individual who likes to buy small and build big – starting a company and seeing it grow. Paul Desmarais, in contrast, is a genius at making acquisitions, of putting together the ingredients of a complex deal. (Lortie, like other young francophones, has great respect for the way Desmarais sprang from obscurity. Desmarais bears, in the phrase of Lortie, "the scars" of the first part of the industrial revolution of francophones.) But Lortie is counting on Dutil accepting the advantage of a stock exchange listing. He has taken it upon himself over the next two or three years to do a promotional job of persuading the men who are builders of large industries to turn to the Montreal Stock Exchange, though he doesn't delude himself about one point. If they do go public, the chances are they will want to be listed in Toronto as well.

Meanwhile, Lortie puts his faith in the future of the Quebec economy and the conviction that conservatism will continue to mark Parti Québécois policy. For one thing, the government has overreached itself, hence the moves by Jacques Parizeau, the finance minister, towards curtailing social services. Lortie says: "It certainly means they have less leeway when they have less money." Lortie is not in the slightest bit concerned by the occasional Lévesque comment that the Parti Québécois has not abandoned the notion of sovereignty. "You would have to be pretty naive not to expect him to say such things," he comments; pointing out that Premier William Davis of Ontario sometimes appeals to rednecks in his constituency, while President Reagan constantly reminds conservatives of his commitment to them. Some 20 to 25 per cent of the electorate in Quebec is attracted to the concept of sovereignty-association, "so once in a while Lévesque has to rekindle the flame." But Lortie, who understands the anglophone community as deeply as he does the francophone, feels that some English Montrealers remain so paranoid about the Parti Québécois that his words of reassurance won't have much impact.

The paranoia of the anglophones has been a bonanza for the franco-phones, especially a hyperactive, breathless type like Jean de Brabant. With lean elegance, de Brabant, in his early forties, is a kind of high-strung thoroughbred. On his father's side he traces ancestry back to Belgian aristocracy of the sixteenth century. His mother, a French Canadian, was a member of the Marcil family prominent in business, government, and banking. Though he is sometimes taken for an Englishman (because of an accent acquired partly at McGill University, with the proper tailoring adding to the image), he is deeply and proudly francophone. And he is very, very breathless; especially after fifteen years in law practice which he finally decided was not to his taste. Now he has found himself. The flight of anglophones and the slump in real estate values has turned him into a superb - and impatient - innovator and entrepreneur. You visit his office on Rue St. Jacques. "Come," he says, before you even sit. "Something to show you. It'll blow your mind - blow your mind!" Into the street to get a cab; no overcoat - never mind the winter or the snow. A quick ride to inspect Les Atriums...incredible, truly mind-blowing. Then another taxi dash to look at La Caserne ... less unique but still daring in vision. Then a rapid walk through Place d'Armes (past the statue of Maisonneuve, the founder of the city-state to which de Brabant belongs), back to his office (in a building which he owns). All this tour, breathlessly, inside one hour.

What was it all about? Les Atriums, La Caserne, and others of a similar nature? It is a field - real estate, property, development - that de Brabant entered only in 1977, with virtually no money of his own. What he did have was tremendous imagination, a belief that the market in Montreal had hit bottom (this was eleven months after the Parti Québécois had taken over), and financial backing from a Swiss. He was right about the condition of the real estate market; and he made all his acquisitions from that date until October 1979 when prices, along with confidence in the future of Montreal, began to rise substantially. De Brabant bought out most of his Swiss backer's interest and estimates that his own worth now is at least $10 million. He rates every penny of it, and as testimony one needs only to examine Les Atriums, formed in what was Depuis Frères, a depart-ment store that went bankrupt a few years ago. What once consisted of floor after floor of display counters is now wide open space - two gigantic atriums rising eight storeys. One has the sensation of being, not in a building, but in the wild, tropical outdoors.

Atriums are not new to Montreal, but the size and added dimension of waterfalls lend to the de Brabant creation a special aura. And it is *his* creation. With an architect, he visited thirty atrium buildings in Dallas and Houston and was surprised to discover how many trees there were. "Imagine," he declared, "trees indoors in Texas. Who needs trees indoors more than Canadians?" He next brought in a landscape specialist who agreed that trees were no problem but also demanded to know whether de Brabant had gone mad in wanting water cascading from a height of eight floors. Technically, said the landscape man, it couldn't be done. But a way was invented to engage a score of waterfalls, tumbling from the eighth to the sixth floor, or from the fifth to the third, at irregular intervals throughout the atriums. What de Brabant finds so droll, in recounting this bit of experience, is that developers are usually regarded as staid and cautious – and designers complain they are unable to let themselves go. Here it was he who had to sell the artistic type. In any event, the result is stunning. Workers or shoppers disembark at the Berri-de-Montigny station, a crossroads of the métro, where a direct entrance takes them into Les Atriums and its two levels of boutiques and restaurants and the offices higher up. It can be in the midst of a blizzard, but one would never know it. Palm trees fifteen to twenty feet tall, orange bushes, and flowering plants rise not only from the lowest point but from each floor.

Thus office workers enjoy a choice. They can look in one direction, wide open in front of them, and see oleander, poinsettia, bougainvilia, hibiscus, and scores of other tropical flowers – or they can look in the other direction, through the windows back of them, and catch a glimpse of Jacques Cartier Bridge or rooftops covered with snow. De Brabant calls it the largest interior tropical garden in the world, but whether this can be proved is incidental. The point is that it is tasteful, exciting, and in keeping with the eye of a lawyer who found hidden flair as a developer. His other most satisfying project, La Caserne, is a ninety-six unit condominium on St. Paul Street in Old Montreal. Once it was Cassidy's Warehouse, a squat building constructed a century ago with 300 small windows. But de Brabant had a simple answer to that one, apart from ripping out the interior and creating attractive apartments, each with a fireplace. There are 300 window boxes, maintained by a full time gardener. "I like flowers," de Brabant explains; and if this isn't satisfactory to a potential buyer, there's no deal. De Brabant is, at the moment, busily engaged in other "mind-blowing" projects, one of them so daring in concept – and really quite tantalizing – that the visitor for whom he unrolls blueprints and goes into details must first swear an oath of secrecy. Breathlessly.

The contrast between Jean de Brabant and Pierre Robitaille is not only one of manner but of content. Apart from conjuring up a colourful expression such as "élite panzer corps" (and that was done largely facetiously), Robitaille is fairly formal in business methods, not inappropriately in view of his background. This includes education at L'Ecole des Hautes Etudes Commerciales, where he obtained a degree in commerce; and later, an MBA from McGill University. Now, aged thirty-eight, he is partner in charge of the Montreal office of Ernst & Whinney, the international firm of management consultants and chartered accountants. Since he comes from a bilingual educational background, and his work continues to keep him involved with anglophones as well as francophones, he considers the mix stimulating. But the key is when he admits, "I am an achiever. I want to do great things." And he goes on: "An achiever creates his own opportunities, but if the environment is good, he's going to create more. I was born on a farm fifty miles northeast of Quebec City, and something beautiful happened to me. When I was seven my father moved to St. Catharines, Ontario, to work on a hydro project. We lived in a 'ghetto' area – Poles, Ukrainians, French Canadians – and we had two things in common. We were all Catholics and spoke no English. I was lucky. I was never motivated by a Quebec nationalist theme. When I arrived in Montreal it was in an environment that was favourable to me, and to my thinking, and I've never looked back." That environment included a demand by industry, not only in Montreal but in Ontario, for francophone administrators. All the francophones in his class (at the time McGill was the only college in Montreal offering an MBA degree), were swept up in job offers, and he took one with Labatt's Breweries in London, Ontario. He felt the opportunity was there because people at Labatt's wanted to know what was going on in Quebec.

That, he admits, was reverse discrimination, but it still required the recipient to prove himself. "It's like getting a university degree. It opens doors, but after that you have to show you have the right stuff." The right stuff, he is convinced, exists among today's generation of francophones. When he joined Ernst & Whinney in 1969, the Montreal office consisted of fifteen professionals. Today there are sixty-five, of whom 85 per cent are francophones. In 1969 most of the firm's clients were subsidiaries of US corporations, and many of these later moved to Toronto. "So," he points out, "while we lost a big chunk of our base, we managed to build a replacement business, much of it among francophones." Today the Ernst & Whinney operation in Montreal is autonomous.

Robitaille believes Montreal is now at a significant juncture, and the élite group will have a great deal to do with what turning it takes. "We know that because of the exodus we need to find new ventures to sustain Montreal's viability internationally. The exodus created a vacuum, and unless it is filled we are in danger of becoming another Boston. People like myself – in the Chambre de Commerce, in the Board of Trade – are in a position to influence the Quebec government, primarily in fiscal policies that would attract new banking, new industry, and high technology and communication." One of Robitaille's thoughts is to persuade the Quebec government to establish Montreal as an international "booking centre" – that is, foreign exchange market – in the fashion of Singapore. This would enable banks with head offices in Montreal to escape taxation on loans made to non-residents in foreign currency. Robitaille acknowledges that if Quebec could achieve this, within federal banking regulations, Ontario would quickly emulate it – "but we'd have a head start." Singapore a decade ago was not a "booking centre." Now it challenges Hong Kong. "In effect you'd create another stock exchange with all the spinoff benefits," Robitaille says.

Whether or not such a concept ever reaches maturity (and Robitaille heads a joint committee of the Chambre de Commerce and the Board of Trade to push for it), he at least demonstrates the kind of originality that is characteristic of his contemporaries. He blames much of what happened negatively in Montreal on Parti Québécois policy which, in setting out initially to create an independent Quebec, was blinded by the philosophy that "small is beautiful." All its early actions derived from the fixation that Montreal would be the metropolis of a separate Quebec, in contrast to its old position as metropolis of Canada. "I say that the attitude should be, 'big is wonderful.' And it is a consideration that goes beyond Canada. All of us in my age group are motivated by the same thing. We believe in ourselves, and, because we have been underdogs...we've developed fighter instincts. Our appetite is far greater than that of our franco-phone predecessors and our anglophone peers." But this does not mark him as a chauvinist. On the contrary, he says, "I would like to think that the anglophone who is bilingual has a brighter future than a francophone who is unilingual."

While the visitor sits in the comfortable waiting room to see Claude Perron, president and general manager of Canadian National (CN) Express, he picks up a copy of *Horizons*, the fortnightly magazine for employees of the one-time CN satellite, Air Canada. Of twenty-four retirements listed – men who joined the airline twenty-five to thirty-five years ago – three were French Canadians, all mechanics. The others, anglophones, included pilot-captains and maintenance or sales managers. Inside the office of Perron, a comfortable and expansive area thirty by forty feet on the twenty-sixth floor of a modern building, the visitor mentions the message contained in *Horizons*, and the president of CN Express agrees: "Quite a change."

Quite a change indeed. Canadian National, whose late president, Donald Gordon, once caused a near-riot because he said he knew of no qualified French Canadians who could fill responsible senior positions, is now headed by a francophone, J. Maurice LeClair. Five vice-presidents are also francophones; and one of CN's principal subsidiary companies is headed by a French Canadian: Perron. There is some irony to the appointment of Perron, who has the thankless task of curtailing the express function. But he is doing it, according to all accounts, with skill and compassion that may well be traced to his own heritage. Perron's background is multifold. Born in Chicoutimi in 1942, he studied engineering, then moved to Montreal to take business administration at L'Ecole des Hautes Etudes Commerciales, but won his MBA at McGill, having mean-while taught himself English. He worked for a textile company as director of financial planning, and for the Université du Québec à Montréal as director of the department of business administration. He was general manager of a centre engaged in research and man-agement studies for francophone firms; and finally, in 1978, joined CN as vice-president, marketing.

A year later, at the age of thirty-seven, Perron was appointed president of CN Express – a company with 5,600 employees, of whom only one fifth were francophones. But that was not the significant statistic. The important number was 2,800, the size to which it had to be reduced by the end of 1981. And it had to be reduced further, to 2,500, by the close of 1982. The world of CN Express has altered dramatically from the days before air and truck freight, when railways held a monopoly on the movement of people and goods. Railways still do well on carloads, but, in small packages, business in 1980 was down to one quarter of the 1960 volume, with CN Express sustaining a loss of $53 million. Yet under the Railway Act it is compelled to provide a service to Canadians which commercial organizations, if they find it unprofitable, can shun. Perron says, "I doubt if we will ever make a profit, but certainly we can reduce the loss substantially." His action plan is simple: specialize and do it well. Change the mentality of customers. Let them know, for instance, that CN Express is moving chicks and flowers. Discourage what is termed as "small-small" business – that is, anything under fifty pounds – by raising charges.

But the big manoeuvre is to integrate operations with regional carriers. Perron conceived the idea of sending goods to thirty-five widely scattered terminals for trans-shipment, relying on local truckers to complete the contract while CN Express continued to retain responsibility for safe arrival. But this has entailed closing down about fifty terminals, with subsequent job losses. That, obviously, is where Perron's most delicate task lay. His initial approach was to establish labour-management committees across the country; he found that so long as he did not show favouritism or treat management-level people with preference, the unions accepted transfers, early retirement, and other measures. Even though the approach has been innovative and humane, it is still, in Perron's own words, "a cultural shock to the CN system; every employee is affected, directly or indirectly."

His is clearly the riskiest post in CN. Was it given to him as a "token" francophone? He rejects the notion that he is a mere symbol. Okay, then, has he been set up as a sacrificial goat in an unrewarding mission? He hesitates and admits that some of his friends did warn him precisely of that possibility. But he felt he could fulfil the assignment with a minimum of hardship for everyone because his style of management is different from that of predecessors who were rather authoritarian. A kind of built-in francophone sensitivity based on past adversity, he says, might be more acute than an anglo-phone's – and that means empathy. "If you haven't got it, you're not perceived to be helping people or encouraging them." He calls his "the Columbo approach," after the television detective who appears naive, fumbling, and never threatening. "If you frighten people, you fail. It's better to keep a low key." Moreover, he has learned in his variety of jobs to deal with a variety of people: conservatives in the world of textiles, radicals in the world of academics.

English only is spoken in Perron's office, but this does not bother him because he knows that times and attitudes have changed. He senses no hostility from anglophones who work under him, but admits that at first he had a tough time gaining acceptance from men ten years his senior. There is, in industry generally, still a gap, a shortage of francophones in middle management and up, but it is closing swiftly. At CN, an interesting group of francophones is coming along, but whoever moves into top levels must be "credible." Speaking of Montreal's future in general, Perron is, like virtually all his francophone peers, optimistic. What he sees as the greatest need primarily is "confidence based on the perception that things are moving. Many anglophones haven't yet the perception of a Montreal with a future."

In 1964, in researching a book on Canada, the writer met Claude Bachand, law student at the Université de Montréal. Bachand, like many nineteen-year-olds, was a separatist, though in those days he sought a relationship for Quebec called "associate state," rather than what later became described as "sovereignty-association." He wore his hair fashionably brushed forward, in addition to a wisp of a beard ringing his face. Today he has changed in physical appearance; the beard has been removed. He has added a J. before the Claude, and, at age thirty-six, is just as intense a person as he was eighteen years earlier. However, he is no longer a separatist, nor attracted to associate statehood or any similar disruption of Canada. "I think of broader issues today," he says. "Each idea has its own time. We've got the basic things in Quebec now, starting with Bill 101, and we can work together without fighting."

Bachand's transformation is not unlike that of many of his generation; nor is it much different from those who have followed. It began when he left the Université de Montréal and moved to London, Ontario, to take his MBA at the University of Western Ontario. After that followed a series of vocations and locations: a year and a half with an anglophone law firm in Montreal; three years in Paris as assistant to the president of a management consultant firm; then back home, in 1971, to join the Banque Nationale de Paris office in Montreal. There were thirty-five employees then, and a $50 million balance sheet. Today, 250 employees are spread across the country, and BNP Canada (the Paris bank's subsidiary), boasts a $1 billion balance sheet. Bachand is now senior vice-president whose travels have taken him to Bahrain, London, Zurich, and many other centres. He qualifies as a founder of the "élite panzer corps," persuaded that Montreal's destiny is a great one. He says: "In the 1960's the question was which city was more important – Montreal or Toronto? Toronto won the battle when it comes to being a money centre. But I compare the cities of Switzerland. You have Zurich, the money centre – and Geneva. If I had to choose it would be Geneva because it is more international and more interesting."

There is in Bachand, without question, self-confidence and self-esteem, and the explanation lies deeper than the simple one of a radical youth who grew into manhood, married, fathered a daughter, eleven, and a son, nine, and became a banker. He can say today of his peers and Quebecers generally: "We're much more aware that the world is not only Quebec or even Canada or North America – but a far bigger place." The clincher, however, erupts in his final statement. "In the 1960's we spoke of affirming and fulfilling ourselves through politics. Now we're doing it through the business world – through companies like Bombardier and Provigo. Now, instead of waving a Quebec flag, you buy up an Ontario company."

Another banker, Robert René de Cotret, is in an unusually good position to evaluate the "élite panzer corps," since, in his own words, he is a member of it but was not brought up with the other members. Born in Ottawa, he is a franco-Ontarian who lacks the intensity of the Quebecer. Moreover, a remarkable record, achieved before the age of thirty-five (an MBA from McGill University; graduate school in business economics at the University of Michigan; the economic board of advisers to President Lyndon Johnson; and then politics, first as Conservative member of Parliament for Ottawa Centre, and later as the appointed senator and minister of industry and trade and commerce under Prime Minister Joe Clark), gives him the kind of varied background and exposure that enables him to look on Montreal with some detachment. Thirty-eight now, and out of politics, he is senior vice-president and general manager of the Banque Nationale du Canada.

How does de Cotret think the young francophone executive will emerge from the present transition period? Will he be content to serve merely as a branch plant manager, or aspire to something more? De Cotret, a very serious man, chooses his words cautiously. "Maybe the foremost point is that the group today, compared with preceding generations, has no inferiority complex. In the past, being a plant manager was the ultimate ambition. Today that's not enough; we want to be head of the whole damn show. At least you *think* of running the whole show; you don't think of being just a plant manager. It's a positive thing to say, 'I want to be in control of my destiny.'" He doesn't reject the Claude Bachand challenge of taking over Ontario companies. But he doesn't let it go too far. "There is a certain amount of fighting the 'establishment,' but I wouldn't consider that the driving force. It's not a question of one-upmanship over the anglophone. It's more a question of 'That's where I want to go.' What's happening is that we're leaving behind a ghetto mentality. We're becoming much more citizens of the world. For someone like Pierre Lortie or me it doesn't matter whether you become president of a francophone firm or an anglophone firm. The point is that we don't feel limited. The fact that the Bank of Montreal is an anglophone institution is not going to inhibit me from wanting to become its president." Does he really believe that possibility is open to him? He nods in silent affirmation and repeats: "It's not just a question of age, it's an attitude."

One of the myths still common among many English Canadians is about the supposed backwardness of Quebec education. Yet as long ago as 1965, 88 per cent of Quebec youth between fourteen and seventeen was enrolled in schools – a higher percentage than in Ontario. In the fifteen year period between 1950 and 1965, university attendance rose sixfold, involving again a higher proportion of the population than in Ontario. But perhaps no illustration of the phenomenon of educational upheaval, and with it the rapid development of the French-Canadian managerial class, is more graphic than in colleges of business administration. While the Quebec managerial group in large industries was mostly anglophone until the

1960's, in recent years a half dozen French-language universities have established programs turning out many hundreds of MBA's each year. These institutions attract more business administration students than in any other province. Moreover, the average starting salary for an MBA in Montreal, particularly a bilingual, is higher by several thousand dollars than that of a counterpart anywhere else in the country.

Notable among such schools is L'Ecole des Hautes Etudes Commerciales (HEC), founded in 1907 but brought into the modern world, and international recognition, by Pierre Laurin, its director since 1975. Pierre, forty-two, is a younger brother of Camille Laurin, the Parti Québécois cabinet minister who created Bill 101 and with whom he has sharp political differences but shares strong family ties. Himself a graduate of HEC, Laurin went on to Harvard University where he won his PhD in business administration. That exposure stimulated him into accelerating a plan which had already been introduced by previous HEC directors – to induce outstanding graduates of HEC to go on to further training at Harvard, Stanford, Wharton, Yale, Columbia, Louvain, University of Paris, and London School of Economics. The investment was related to an awareness that Quebec was in need of francophone experts in marketing, and it has produced results. Of the four who went abroad in 1980, all returned to teach at HEC.

Indeed, of the institution's 120 faculty members, more than one third hold doctorates from Harvard, Stanford, and other great business centres. The size and quality of its library – 200,000 volumes and 5,000 periodicals from Canada, the US, and Europe – place it alongside Harvard. Admission standards at HEC are so demanding that three out of four applicants are rejected. Still, 1,700, including 100 from abroad, are enrolled, with 500 graduating each year; (HEC accommodates another 4,000 evening students). This in itself is a striking alteration of the old pattern of the Quebecer who headed for law, medicine, or the church. "Nowhere in Canada is business as popular with young people as right here," says Laurin. He also notes a positive outlook. "They have a new frontier spirit, but are much more serene than a few years ago. Aggressiveness against the English has disappeared. This is not surprising. Aggressiveness and submissiveness are the two sides of the same coin, related consciously or unconsciously to a sense of inferiority. This is the first generation without a feeling of inferiority. They want to work in French but they are not emotional now about using English as well."

Laurin calls the young "le pétrole du Québec" (the petroleum of Quebec), "the best natural resource we have." He has done much to introduce the generation into the realities and friendliness of the anglophone world. In 1981, some twenty companies across Canada – IBM, the Royal Bank, and The Bay among them – accepted twenty-six HEC students at the end of their second year for three to four months of summer work. The purpose was twofold: exposure of the francophones to a different culture, so that if they decided on graduation to work outside Quebec they would know what to expect; and introduction to anglophone firms of the capabilities of francophones. An obvious question occurs: why didn't anglophone companies in Montreal itself do this a generation ago? Laurin shrugs and simply says, "A lot of water went into the river." The results were so satisfactory that the plan for 1982 was to double the number of summer placements.

L'Ecole des Hautes Etudes Commerciales has a loose affiliation with the Université de Montréal, whose campus it shares. A couple of years ago, René Lévesque paid a visit to HEC students. But with no meeting hall big enough, Laurin borrowed one from the university, saying to Lévesque, "This is the only successful example of sovereignty-association you'll ever find." The remark, while made in good humour, was not entirely inappropriate. One finds among HEC undergraduates a preoccupation with obtaining profitable and interesting work, and little support for a political system that would hinder freedom of action or movement across Canada. The writer selected four students for conversation on the basis of their elected positions, influence on classmates, and representative opinions. They were: Michel Lavoie, twenty-two, president of the students' council and in his third and final year in accounting; René Morisette, twenty-one, editor of the fortnightly student paper *Lit-Poc-Hec*, in his third and final year of economics; Danielle Laferrière, twenty-two, vice-president of the students' council and liaison officer with McGill University students (a number of HEC programs are operated in conjunction with anglophone institutions), in her final year of marketing and financing; and Gilles Robillard, twenty-two, a veteran of summer jobs in a bank and therefore the most practical in experience, in his third and final year in accounting.

All were heading for their BA in administration, thinking it would get them far enough without the added time required for an

MBA. The emphasis on accounting is fairly typical of HEC, contrasted with McGill where a larger percentage aim at marketing. But accountants – in a society of intricate tax laws and an awareness of the needs for modern methods among new firms in Montreal – are in tremendous demand (95 per cent of students interviewed by recruiters were placed months before graduation). All those in discussion with the writer spoke good English. Lavoie learned his in a course at the University of Ottawa and in the summer of 1981 working for a Montreal group of accountants. Morisette acquired his at a CEGEP, a junior college, in Shawinigan. Laferrière picked up English in Sault Ste. Marie, Ontario, where her father, an engineer, was transferred by his Montreal company for a year. Robillard came by it naturally on the streets of Verdun and at home, where his father, a food broker, emphasized the two languages.

The remarkable feature about these students, in common with others at HEC, is that only three or four years ago they were in CEGEP's, caught up in radicalism and indoctrination by teachers and peers, hostile to anglophones and favourable to separatism. Now, in their embarkation on business careers, the only complaint about discrimination (and it was expressed by Danielle Laferrière), was that women were not given the same consideration as men in job interviews. Otherwise the hangups, the fears of the late 1970's, were non-existent. None would spurn a job offer in Toronto or Calgary, though the intention – each made this clear – would be to return ultimately to Montreal.

Just a few years ago, young francophones (these four included), ridiculed any notion of leaving Quebec. How do they regard the future for the anglophone community, the strength of Montreal? These questions were answered candidly. But first, why did they decide on choosing a life in business instead of the more traditional law or medicine? What follows is an abridged account:

LAVOIE: I've discovered more and more what business means, and it appeals to me. There are more and more places for francophones and the future is good. We can deal with everything. We have no complex now, and it doesn't matter whether we work with francophones or anglophones.

LAFERRIÈRE: When we came here, three years ago, Mr. Laurin told us, "You are the new natural resource of Quebec." In a way I believe it, too, but what I'm afraid of is that there is too much entrepreneurship, too many people may try to open their own businesses. For the first years I want to work for a big company. It doesn't matter whether I join a multinational or a Quebec company. But this is not a popular thing to say here. Some students still believe our future is to build small companies.

LAVOIE: I disagree with those students. I'm an accountant. We need big companies for practical experience; and after that, in three or four years, we can go our own way or stay with a big company. More and more managers are needed each day – just look at the ads in the newspapers.

ROBILLARD: The big problem is that, when you have security in a big firm, after a few years you are afraid to move into your own and be in competition. That's why a lot of small companies have problems recruiting.

MORISETTE: I'm a little skeptical of what Laurin said. There are more chances for economic growth in Quebec, but firms are getting bigger and bigger with higher technology. With the diplomas we get here we have the possibility to reach middle-management jobs. I don't mind working with English-speaking people, but the fact that we may not be the bosses would bother me.

LAVOIE: Before we came to HEC, no one at the CEGEP's talked to us the way Laurin has. Now we have professors from Harvard and Stanford and all over the place – without the narrow vision of CEGEP teachers. I remember one professor saying that when he attended HEC he was one of ten or fifteen in his graduating class. Now there are 400 or 500. The professor called it "the law of the big numbers," meaning that we have a greater chance in the world. Every couple of months we meet in conferences with leaders from the business world, many francophones – from SNC or Lavalin or Provigo – or anglophones from multinationals like Alcan, who tell us of their experiences and how to succeed in business.

ROBILLARD: Would I accept a job with Alcan if it meant moving from Montreal? It depends on what they would offer in Calgary or Toronto. If it gives me a chance to reach a higher level, there's no reason to refuse. You need jobs and you need guts. If you are asked to move, and you don't, someone else will.

LAFERRIÈRE: I think my progress will be limited by the fact that I'm a woman. There is still discrimination everywhere. You can see it by the way big companies do their recruiting. The important interviews by multinationals are with men. (A pause, and then the next sentence is said in a tone of apprehension.) I've known people who've gone to Calgary and they'll never come back.

(There is now a minor debate among them, and the overall conclusion is that ideally each would prefer a job with a francophone company but would not reject an attractive offer from an anglophone company, regardless of location. A time factor is emphasized. Two or three years away from Montreal would be the maximum, simply because they enjoy life in Montreal, rather than because of any particular interest in political activity here. On the contrary, the political philosophy of the Parti Québécois leaves them somewhat indifferent.)

ROBILLARD: When we went to CEGEP's we were influenced by people around us. But I never supported the Parti Québécois then and I don't know why I should start now.

MORISETTE: Students at CEGEP's are much quieter now than when I was there. They're not so influenced by small groups; they think for themselves now. They're going to the other extreme of caution, but what's worse is what is happening here, at HEC. Students are not revolutionary enough. They just think of business; they just want to look at their own problems. They don't think of social problems, such as pollution, and ask themselves, "If I am head of a company will I be influenced by the cost of pollution control and let pollution hit other people? Or will I try to avoid it even if it cuts profits?" Students are too passive today. They don't ask questions as students did in the past. What kind of leaders are we going to be? I write many columns in *Lit-Poc-Hec* about this indifference, but the results are limited...(Sadly) Maybe we have to be modest about changing the world. Sovereignty-association is not necessarily a solution for us. But I still vote Parti Québécois because on social issues they are more progressive than the Liberals.

ROBILLARD: The future of Montreal? That's a very good question. It all depends on what happens in the next few years – not politically, but rather what the big companies do. The referendum reassured a lot of companies, but I don't really know the answer to the big question about the future.

MORISETTE: I haven't a firm answer, either. But it's not only a question of head offices moving. You also have to consider that the centre of gravity is shifting from central Canada to the west.

LAFERRIÈRE: For a few years – four or five years – it will shift west. But in the long term Canada will learn that secondary industries are as important as natural resources such as oil, and we'll average out. Calgary, Toronto, and Montreal will be on the same level.

ROBILLARD: The anglophone community in Montreal? It's secure. People are starting to think and realize that the only problem is the language barrier. Before, they used to believe there were social and other problems. But now even the language barrier is dropping. I notice it at the bank where I work summers, a branch in Notre Dame de Grâce, when older anglophones try to use their French. They may not be good at it, but that is not important. They're trying. The trend is even more marked among the young. When I was interviewed a while ago by an anglophone company there were nine candidates – myself and eight from McGill. The McGill students all spoke French to me.

LAFERRIÈRE: All the political things that happened in Quebec woke up the English. The English community will grow. But the English will have to work more to get what they want. It won't be as easy as before. Now there'll be healthy competition.

MORISETTE: I don't think that English language is in danger. The main point is to keep the francophone community constant, because we all know that English is attractive to immigrants. The two communities are going to improve relations.

Thus one senses a deep conservatism among the HEC group. Any support for the Parti Québécois is not usually on ideological grounds but rather in the belief that it cares about such matters as environmental control and other factors affecting the public generally. Certainly the mood of radicalism that was prevalent even a few years ago has become subdued. One might argue that since these are business-minded young people, their stolid bent is predictable and inevitable. Yet even among other students the same trend towards conservatism is apparent. Three hundred feet of red-brick tunnel connect HEC with the social sciences building of Université de Montréal – where one would expect a different world. The radicals of the past were attracted by the atmosphere of social sciences. But today? There is undoubtedly support for the Parti Québécois, but mainly because of its program of social legislation rather than any doctrine of separatism. The noteworthy feature about this generation is not its concern for politics (a minimal concern), but rather its preoccupation with career and jobs.

Here are three elected members of the central council of the student federation of Université de Montréal: Michel Giguère, twenty, majoring in mathematics; Richard Proulx, twenty-six, who has his BA in translation (English-French), and is working for his master's degree in political science; and Nicole Robert, twenty-two, heading for an MA in geography. Robert prefers to speak French while the others are at ease in English. Her specialty of geography is motivated by an interest in ecology, and she wants to work for Environment Canada, in Montreal. Why not for Environment Quebec? Simple. It is not comparable in facilities or scope to Environment Canada, so she is prepared to work for a federal agency. But supposing Environment Canada hires her and wants to post her to Ottawa or Edmonton or somewhere else in Canada for a year or two? "I would feel like a stranger," she responds, after a lengthy pause.

But one suspects, since Robert still has a year or so to go in her studies, that this unease might not be so rigid. Certainly she admits that she is far more flexible and moderate than her brothers, older than her by only four years and two years. "When they were younger, they talked about 'independence,'" she explains. "I talk about 'sovereignty-association.'" What, precisely, does she mean by the phrase? "A contract between two parties – Quebec and Canada." But she does not pursue this in detail, content to say only: "We're trying to work progressively to make changes." Richard Proulx perhaps puts it into context more bluntly: "Right now everyone wants a job. That is the main thing. When you hear students in a living room speak of 'revolution' or 'change' it does not mean they'll take to the streets. There's a big difference between what we say and what we'll do." And that difference relates directly to the quest for meaningful employment. Proulx is aiming for work in the office of the secretary of state in Ottawa, because that is where he knows the best opportunity lies for a translator. He would, in theory, prefer Quebec, but he doesn't think its civil service offers as much variety as the federal.

Michel Giguère wants to teach mathematics, preferably in a CEGEP. But he would accept a job if offered one at McGill. Such a concession by a Université de Montréal social science student ten years ago, or even three years ago, would have been heresy. But with comfort about the use of French as the prime language, and the knowledge that the francophone has stepped into a world of opportunity, the old-style radicalism has been supplanted by realism – and that means, to the majority, the desire and need to find gainful occupation.

The Jewish Presence

It is commonly thought that the first Jew to arrive in Canada was Aaron Hart, commissary to General Amherst who was closing in on Montreal with a British army while Wolfe's guns were thundering at Quebec. Hart was a pioneer all right, but he was preceded by a little wisp of a thing, Esther Brandau, twenty-one years earlier. In those days, during the French régime, only Catholics were permitted to stay in New France, though a dozen or so Huguenots managed to obtain royal permission, provided they did not practise their religion. Esther Brandau, a French Jew, sought no approval. Twenty years old, inquisitive and imaginative, she disguised herself as a boy, slipped aboard a vessel, and sailed for Quebec in 1738. Detected, she was sent to jail, where, for a full year, day after day, priests and nuns tried to get her to renounce Judaism. Finally, frustrated, they shipped her back to France.

But Hart, London-born, did settle; and by 1768 there were enough Jews – many of them fellow army officers – to open a synagogue, the Shearith Israel, in a rented hall on Little St. James Street. It was the first non-Catholic place of worship in Quebec. Since a majority of members were descended from exiles from Spain, they adhered to the Sephardic rites of Spanish and Portuguese Jews. Interestingly, the most recent wave of Jewish immigrants to Montreal, French-speaking Moroccans of the 1950's, also observe Sephardic traditions. In between came the mass from Eastern Europe – Ashkenazim Jews – whose descendants make up the bulk of today's community of 100,000.

It is a lively and thriving community, and, with its mixture of culture, history, and language, the most distinctive in North America. It is also highly respected by francophones who relate to it in essential ways: a determination to retain an identity, and an ambition to prove themselves in business and professions. Antoine Turmel, of Provigo, likes to recount what his son, André, a sociologist who is now a professor at Université Laval, said ten years ago. The two groups who would succeed most in Quebec were French Canadians and Jews; neither had the recognition they deserved, in an environment dominated by "Wasps," and this made them aggressive and innovative. Much the same is repeated by young francophone executives who make a point of citing the good corporate citizenship and adaptability of Jews in the current transformation of Quebec. "The Jews have come through so many calamities in their history that the fittest have survived," says Pierre Robitaille, managing partner of Ernst & Whinney, the chartered accountants. "Many, many more adjust to language than anglophones generally. So they are going to emerge as part of a flexible society."

In 1789 Aaron Hart's nephew, Henry Joseph, arrived from England. There were so many later Henrys that a sixth generation descendant of the Harts and the Josephs, Annette R. Wolff, labels him Henry I. Miss Wolff, born in Montreal in 1911, lives in genteel retirement, an amateur historian who takes great pride in preserving family records. Her apartment is crowded with portraits and memorabilia, some of the most noteworthy being copies of a diary kept by her great-grandfather (Henry I's son, Abraham Joseph), from 1836 until 1866. In one entry in the 1840's he noted how sad it was that all his friends were going "home" – to England or Scotland – for the winter, because, with the St. Lawrence River frozen over, there was no major trade for anyone.

Abraham Joseph, a commission merchant and representative for shipping companies, divided his time between Montreal and Quebec City. Once he sadly observed: "I wish I had wings to get to Montreal for my sister's ball." But the most significant, and prescient, comments dealt with how important it was for the English to learn French. On April 3, 1840, he wrote in his diary: "Rose at 7. Took my first lesson in French." His teacher was a M. l'Espérance, and the lessons, lasting an hour, began at 7:30 A.M. and went on for two winters.

It is clear from the record that Abraham Joseph's friends included as many French as English, and the young ladies seemed to be particularly receptive. Mlle Panet, daughter of the "old gentleman, the seigneur," invited him to visit the seigniory. On another occasion he attended a wedding at the village of Cap Santé, including Mass at 7:00 A.M. After a call in Trois-Rivières on February 27, 1841, he described his cousins' store where he found "a number of Canadians (that is, French) smoking and drinking with Adolphus and Sam Hart – talking politics." Almost all of Abraham Joseph's business in the countryside was conducted in French, but there are notations of meetings in the city when a conversation would begin in English and someone would say that "for our French friends" he would interpret. There was no sense in those days of Two Solitudes. All mixed – English and French, Protestant and Catholic. No distinction was made between Jew and non-Jew. This equality, of course, was determined by social position, which in turn was dependent on economic standing.

Jacob Henry Joseph (1814-1907), qualified for membership in the Royal Montreal Golf Club because he was an investor in railways and shipping, which also enabled him to become a founder and director of the Montreal City and District Savings Bank as well as of the Montreal Street Railway. His brother, Jesse, who made his fortune importing Belgian glass and cement, was chairman of the Street Railway in 1892, when a progressive French-Canadian director, Louis J. Forget, moved to electrify it. "No self-respecting person," Jesse Joseph argued, "would ride in a horseless street car." He lost the battle. But, as Miss Wolff says sympathetically, Jesse Joseph was ninety years old at the time. He left ninety-nine heirs to his estate, most of them in England. A dozen or so descendants remain in Montreal, but with memories rather than wealth.

There were others of the old Jewish aristocracy, but they were few. In 1892 the entire Jewish community in Montreal numbered 2,460. By 1911 it reached 28,838, a result of the influx from Eastern Europe – the poor, the hungry, and the abused of Poland, Russia, and Romania. This was the origin of the Steinbergs and the Pascals and the Reitmans and others who, adding to the foundation of the Harts and the Josephs and the early pioneers, built up a Jewish presence. But it was different – bereft of the status and education, largely obtained in England, that had made predecessors acceptable.

Sir Mortimer Davis, head of the Imperial Tobacco Company, still managed in 1908 to obtain admission to the Mount Royal Club; but only because the son of Lord Shaughnessy, having worked for Sir Mortimer, slipped around to members individually and said that if there was a blackball, he would resign and turn his full attention to the rival Saint James's Club. Sir Mortimer Davis, after all, was still of the gentry, a definition determined not only by what money a person possessed but how he had obtained it. Later, Samuel Bronfman, the liquor baron, was not acceptable; only his son, Charles, in recent years made it. In the interval, however, great changes had occurred. McGill University no longer imposed a quota on Jews; and, after a span of several decades, Jews were once again named as bank directors.

Mitzi Dobrin is an example. In 1976, when she was in her mid-forties, she achieved the distinction of becoming the first woman appointed to the board of directors of the Royal Bank of Canada (two male Jews preceded her). Mrs. Dobrin, with drive and daring inherited from her father, Sam Steinberg – wizard of the supermarkets – has never lost sight of the values implanted by her grandmother, Ida Steinberg, who started it all with a tiny grocery on St. Lawrence Boulevard in 1917. If there was little education or polish in that generation, there was wisdom. Mitzi Dobrin recalls that her late father frequently said his mother was the greatest psychologist he had ever encountered. An illustration: One day a woman customer arrived who Sam knew was heavily in debt to Mrs. Steinberg for previous purchases. He watched while she selected a large order and departed, again paying nothing. Upset and puzzled, he demanded of his mother: "Why didn't you stop her?" "What," said Mrs. Steinberg, "and turn away a cash customer?" Obviously, one day the woman did pay up. Sam Steinberg, Mitzi says, built his business on classical lines learned from his mother.

There are matching stories from each inheritor of the Eastern European migration. The sons of Jacob Pascal, a glazier who founded what was to become the biggest hardware business in Canada, remembers how they tried to induce him to install a modern electronics system to detect shoplifters. Jacob Pascal rejected such a device, saying, "Who needs it – so long as they leave me a profit at the end of the year?" Describing contributions to the community, Jack Reitman, head of a chain of 538 ladies' apparel stores across the country, says: "My father had a philosophy. When an old charity collector – with black beard and little black valise – came into the shop, my father would give him ten dollars. My older brother, Louis, would say, 'Why do you give it to him? You know he'll keep eight dollars for himself.' My father always answered, 'How will the two dollars get to the poor people if I don't give him ten dollars?' "

Mitzi Dobrin, petite, with strawberry blonde hair, quiet charm, and a straightforward manner, runs the Miracle Mart part of the business. Her husband, Melvyn, is chairman of the board of the Steinberg network, which includes 224 supermarkets, thirty-two Miracle Marts in Quebec and Ontario, and 200 restaurants in those provinces and the west. It employs a force of 26,000 and amasses sales of $2.5 billion. In addition, in 1980, the company acquired the Smitty's group in Phoenix, Arizona: nineteen combination stores (food, hardware, clothing, drugs), with a staff of 5,000 and a volume of $375 million. Mrs. Dobrin calls Phoenix "the silver spoon area." How can invaders from Canada claim an edge over Americans experienced in their own home territory? Again she quotes from her father, who once was besieged by store managers screaming for Grade B eggs. Grade A were Mr. Sam's choice because they were the best. Though they were also more expensive than Grade B, he couldn't bring himself to sanction an inferior item. Finally, he submitted to the pressure, telling his managers: "Sell those Grade B eggs – but at Grade C prices." That concept influences the direction here and in the US. "We're innovators and pluggers," Mitzi says simply.

When Mrs. Dobrin, mother of three and a lawyer by profession, took over Miracle Mart in 1973 on her father's appeal, it was floundering – a hodge-podge of retail items badly displayed. Today it is a success, and Mrs. Dobrin, taking into account her impact on the whole Steinberg operation, is probably the most powerful female executive in the country. Why is the empire still based in Montreal, when headquarters could be in Toronto or anywhere else? Managing major portfolios, Mrs. Dobrin concedes, might be advantageous in Toronto, the financial centre. But merchandising in soft goods (that is, buying), is better in Montreal because it is the apparel centre. Yet even that doesn't matter, she admits, because Miracle Mart deals in hard goods, too, and this comes from all over the world. So the rationale can be argued either way, and again the answer comes down simply to: "We grew up in Montreal and we love it here." And if that isn't quite enough: "The climate, political and social, has improved. There's so much more confidence among francophones today."

Steinberg has played its part. It is the second biggest non-government employer in Quebec (Bell of Canada is first), and even in the worst moments of uncertainty it continued to expand. In the first four years of Parti Québécois government, the company added twenty new food stores throughout the province; when a saturation point was reached, with good locations difficult to find, it bought the Hypermarché chain. Long before French was legislated into use, Mr. Sam's policy was to make customers feel comfortable in either language. Having been brought up in the retail trade, he already possessed a knowledge of French. Nonetheless, in 1960 he registered, along with other executives, for an intensive summer course at the Université de Montréal. His brother, Nathan, didn't need it. Nathan's son, Arnold Steinberg, who is executive vice-president of the company, says of his childhood: "The great thrill was to get up at 2:00 A.M. and go to Bonsecours Market with my father to select fresh fruits and vegetables for the stores. Everything was in French." On Sundays he accompanied his father on social visits to the farmers with whom he had done business. To this day, Nathan, who is seventy-three and in semi-retirement, speaks patois French.

Arnold, forty-nine, also remembers how, as a student in Herbert Symonds School in Notre Dame de Grâce, he had to answer in a written French test the question: "Where does your mother buy her groceries?" He answered: "Steinberg's." The teacher marked it "incorrect." It was then that he learned there is no apostrophe "S" in French. It was dropped from Steinberg logos and store signs twenty years ago – long before Bill 101 – because "it made no sense." But the gesture was also symptomatic of the Steinberg family sensitivity to the public it served. The company entered heavily into the recruiting of French-Canadian university graduates as executives, and in 1965, twelve years ahead of Camille Laurin, made French the working language in Quebec. The response of francophone employees showed itself in a pioneering venture which started in the food division: a committee of non-Jewish workers runs the company's annual Israel bond drive.

With it all, there is humour. Mitzi Dobrin recalls meeting René Lévesque socially not long after his election in 1976. "Mrs. Dobrin," Lévesque told her, "you're one of the few anglophones who doesn't have a poisoned mind."

"Come on, Mr. Lévesque," she said. "There are many of us."

No, insisted the premier, and then he referred to the advertising slogan: Steinberg Is On Your Side. Steinberg, he said, "is on *our* side."

"Mr. Lévesque, please don't say that," said Mrs. Dobrin. "We've enough trouble as it is."

Herman Reitman, an emigrant from Romania, began life in the New World with a pushcart. Then, in 1909, he decided to open a little grocery store on Vitre Street. But tailoring was what the family did best – at least that was what his father and brother, who had preceded him to Montreal, argued. So Herman established a business with the resounding title, "American Ladies' Tailoring and Dressmaking Company," the three men sitting in the back of a store on St. Lawrence Boulevard making coats and suits. (*Everyone* began on St. Lawrence, or the Main, as it was called.) Herman also sold piece goods. Gradually it turned into a general women's apparel shop, and by 1926 Herman had moved into much more fashionable quarters on Ste. Catherine Street, opposite the old Princess Theatre. In four years he had five stores, by now known as Reitman's.

He also had four sons. Each family member, including Herman, managed a store. When the sons proposed opening a sixth, Herman said, "Who'll look after it?" He couldn't understand dealing with the public unless there was personal and constant family involvement. But the sons won their point, continuing to expand during the Depression when rents were cheap. In 1933 the company lost $500 and never lost again, the sons having learned their father's maxim: Buy on credit and sell for cash. In 1947 Reitman's went public; one share, listing then for $7, was worth $1,300 in 1981. Sales now reach $250 million. In 1978, feeling they had virtually saturated the market in Canada with more than 500 outlets, the two surviving brothers, Sam, chairman of the board, and Jack, the president, decided to stretch into the US. The company took over a St. Louis apparel chain, Worth's, which had remained static with forty stores. Reitman added twenty-six. "It takes a certain mentality to operate more than forty stores," says Jack Reitman, who is seventy-two.

Quebec accounts for only 20 per cent of the Reitman business, in volume and profits. Ontario is bigger, at 30 per cent. The company never ceased adding outlets in Quebec, even after the Parti Québécois came to power. But why continue to work from here? Why maintain a warehouse and head office employing 700 under cumbersome language rules and other restraints? Jack Reitman argues that most suppliers are in Montreal, but finally he admits that that is not a logical reason for staying. What motivates him? "We love Montreal." There is more. There is the kind of responsibility to the community imparted by Herman. A program of philanthropy for Jewish and non-Jewish causes is handled in a family circle which includes the late Louis' son-in-law, Gerald Smith; Sam's son Cyril; and Jack's sons Jeremy and Stephen – all officers of the company. Each has a favourite charity. Large contributions come up for discussion until a consensus is reached. "There is no global figure. We pay as we go," says Jack Reitman. "It is important that we instil in the younger members the same spirit we got from our father."

While Reitman and Steinberg stock is listed in the Montreal and Toronto exchanges, the Pascals keep their business entirely in their own hands. Four of Jacob's sons – Max, Hyman, Arthur, and Cecil – remain in charge. Even though they are in their late sixties or seventies, and several of their own sons and sons-in-law hold key positions, they still put in long hours. It is not quite the timetable established by Jacob, who kept his first hardware store (on St. Lawrence Boulevard, of course), open from 6:00 A.M. to 11:00 P.M.; but as Max, at eighty the eldest, recalls it, there was a need then. Painters and carpenters had to stop on their way to work to pick up supplies. Today they can plan ahead, or afford to invest in reserves.

Max, who is chairman, still manages most days to slip out of his office, atop the main store at the corner of Bleury and St. Antoine Streets, to relieve one of the clerks in the paint department at lunch time. "It helps me know what the public wants," he explains. But surely the computers do that? He does not answer – a silent commentary that you cannot keep an old warrior down, even if there are 3,400 other employees.

The title of chairman in itself means nothing. The brothers share responsibilities and have a simple way of operating through the power of veto. Or, in reverse, if one deeply desires to engage in a project – as Max did when he wanted to start a branch in Saint John, New Brunswick, to be near a summer home he owned at the time in St. Andrews – the others go along. Is that any way to run a business?

It must be, since the chain's sales in 1980 amounted to $180 million and in 1981 to $200 million.

Montreal still forms the core, with sixteen hardware and two furniture stores in the area. While the Pascals opened a new store in Quebec City in January 1980, three years after the Parti Québécois took office, they have been cautious about further expansion in the province. Arthur, who is seventy-two, explains it this way: "A hardware store is not like a grocery where you can have three to a block. People don't buy hammers every day." Moreover, some of the outlets in shopping centres range to 100,000 square feet, which means saturation is quickly attained. The fact is that the brothers have inaugurated four major stores in the Toronto area and one in Brampton, Ontario, since 1976, and are now exploring western Canada in what they call a normal growth procedure.

Still, their reputation among francophones is outstanding. Jacques Larivière, a director of the Chambre de Commerce, cites the Pascals as examples of loyal Quebecers. "They could easily have pulled out of here," he says. Arthur takes a modest view. "It's not so easy to pack up hardware." But couldn't they have sold out? Yes. Indeed, good offers over the past several years have been rejected. Then Arthur Pascal says: "I've taken a position – and it's a personal position – that we came here with very little, and this country and this province have been good to us. When things looked hard, and people were leaving under the Parti Québécois, I felt that we, as an important Jewish family, had a special responsibility to stay. We have money, we are mobile. But what about the little tailor in the corner store who isn't so mobile? What kind of example would we have been setting?"

Long ago, when one of the sons failed to collect a bill past due, Jacob decided to demonstrate how it was done. He left the store, and returned a half hour later with a shrug. "They were poor people," he said. "I gave them five dollars." The Pascals retain a deep sense of community obligation, and are among the largest contributors to charitable causes in Montreal. Five members of the family – Max, Arthur, Cecil, and sons-in-law Martin Levine and Sydney Glazer – have served as chairmen of the Combined Jewish Appeal, a record unmatched anywhere in Canada or the US.

If there is one person who, more than any other, has played the leading liaison role between Jew and francophone, it is Naim Kattan, author and literary critic. Born in Baghdad and educated in Paris, Kattan migrated to Montreal in 1954 at the age of twenty-six. His first stop for a job was at *La Presse* where an editor said: "My only advice to you is to go back to Paris. There is no place here for intellectuals." But the Canadian Jewish Congress, a comprehensive agency for the community, let him start up, on a part time basis, the *Bulletin du Cercle Juif*, designed to link Jewish and French quarters through information and meetings.

Kattan met groups such as the Richelieu Club, the first non-francophone to address them in their own language. There were, of course, many prominent French-speaking Jews in Montreal in those days – doctors, lawyers – but they didn't make appearances before French audiences. Partly it was because francophones themselves were only then beginning to emerge from the old shadow and dominance of the church, which discouraged such contact. But Kattan, a foreigner, was a curiosity and different.

For his part, Kattan was intrigued to discover that there was virtually no contact between English and French literary types, the ones who should have been the communicators between the two main bodies. He approached André Laurendeau, editor-publisher of *Le Devoir,* and asked bluntly, "How is it that there are no reviews of books by English-language authors?" Laurendeau said, "There is no interest, but if you want to try, go ahead." Thus it was Kattan who introduced *Le Devoir*, the most scholarly paper in Canada, to anglophone literature. Today he comments: "On both sides there was ignorance and indifference."

Kattan remembers a prominent French-Canadian, who, appearing before the Cercle Juif, said, "If you're not so noisy on tramways we'll like you better." In turn, Kattan told a conference of churchmen, "As Jews we have nothing to sell. We don't want French Canadians to be any less Catholic or any less French Canadian." Gradually he detected a change, a feeling of greater ease among French Canadians about Jews. Israel, not a decade old, served as a starting point for the new nationalism that was emerging. Jacques-Yvan Morin, later a Parti Québécois cabinet minister, promised the Cercle Juif: "Israel will be our example." To Kattan, as to others later, it was a revealing clue. Separatists felt Jews would understand any cry of independence, a misreading of Jewish loyalty to Canada and to Confederation.

But on reflection, Kattan says the signs of goodwill were there and have multiplied. Ironically, he is bothered by only one point today. In francophone eyes the Jewish community is legendary – seen as wealthy and strong and cohesive. The fact is that the diversity of the Jewish community and its fragmentation into so many sub-groups make it impossible for any faction to become dominant. If there is any struggle it is between the new and the old.

The Schouela family has carefully straddled the line between the old and the new with elegance and reserve and quiet wealth. Yet the Schouelas, shy and almost reclusive, are hardly known at all – except in the anglophone and francophone circles where it counts. They belong to international finance. All their holdings, and these now include shopping centres in Canada and the US, are in the family name. "The Schouela Group of Companies" occupies a large portion of one floor of Place du Canada, handsome offices as muted in decor as is the dark attire of the men in command. There are four brothers (and a sister), who have always been close, both now and when they were children in Damascus. They moved to Cairo in the early 1930's, twenty years before they immigrated here.

Ezekiel, the patriarch of the family, is seventy-two. Maurice, now sixty-three, was orphaned at the age of seven and raised by Ezekiel, as were the others: Edouard and Gamil. There was no university for any of them; nothing but humble upbringing. But for all there is such great culture, refinement, and learning – Maurice is an omnivorous reader – that one is tempted to think of the Harts and the Josephs. Yet a parallel with the Steinbergs and the Reitmans and the Pascals is also applicable. Maurice's first employment was as an unpaid apprentice to a jobber in textiles. When he was twenty-six he learned a lesson from a merchant who told him: "It is very easy to make money and very difficult to keep it."

It helps to explain the caution and conservatism that motivate the family. After 1949 and the first Arab-Israeli war, life for Jews in Cairo became uncertain. By then engaged in international finance, the brothers spread out to Milan and Hong Kong and New York. Ezekiel reunited the family in Montreal in 1953. There have been no regrets. The Schouela insight is based not only on experience in the unstable Middle East, but on what they see in the rest of the world. "Where else," asks Maurice, "can you find the security of Montreal? Certainly not in Italy or France. Or the absence of anti-Semitism?"

There is wisdom, too, born of background. "In the 1960's, when the political climate was changing, I used to say if separation is to take place I prefer to have it happen now because of all the uncertainty the talk is producing – politically, economically, and in the quality of life. We lost something because the question was not resolved until 1980. But the climate today is better than the year before, and the year before that."

Jewish life for the Schouelas is meaningful. They were absorbed into the general community almost from the start. Having French among their four languages gives them a common denominator with other Jews from North Africa. But the Moroccans arrived a little later – separated not only by time but by social and financial positions.

Four days after Ralph Lallouz landed from Casablanca he was hired by the Royal Bank of Canada. It was in the foreign exchange department, the same work he had done in Morocco, and the French Canadian at the desk next to him was named Melançon. Melançon had heard Jews speak French before, but usually it was uneven or primitive – certainly not with the perfect grammar and accent of Ralph Lallouz. Melançon was so puzzled and suspicious that he showed up one morning with his parish priest. After a quick conversation with Lallouz, the priest swung around and said, "Vous savez, Melançon, c'est un Juif Catholique." It was said in grim seriousness, and Lallouz, though amused, made no effort to point to the contradiction in the phrase, "a Catholic Jew."

Lallouz arrived in 1957, when he was twenty-seven, because Morocco, having just obtained independence from France, gave no guarantees of civil liberties. Of 300,000 Moroccan Jews, two thirds headed for Israel; 70,000, the most affluent, went to France; and the third largest group chose Montreal because of familiarity with the French language. Including some Algerians and Tunisians, there are now 20,000 French-speaking North African Jews in Montreal – one fifth of the entire community. Most, experienced as accountants or tellers or book-keepers, had little difficulty finding employment. They are in good middle-class positions.

Within three years Ralph, who had been accompanied by his wife and ten-month-old daughter, helped – with a seventy-five dollar weekly salary – to bring over his parents, sister, seven brothers, and assorted kinfolk totalling eighteen. One brother, a hairdresser, started what became the fashionable Charles of Westmount salon. Others entered construction or restaurant business and prospered. Ralph Lallouz is now senior representative for foreign investment at Montreal Trust in Place Ville Marie.

The Moroccans were well received by established organizations such as the Canadian Jewish Congress, of which Lallouz eventually became vice-chairman. Some, wishing to retain their Sephardic customs, different from those of Ashkenazim Jews of Eastern Europe, gravitated to their own community centre. But the younger generation – born here in the last twenty-five years and for whom French is still the mother tongue – mix in a broader world. One in four is married to a French Canadian. (The same ratio of intermarriage applies to other Jews, but almost invariably those with an anglophone background wed anglophones.)

The Melançons have vanished. After numerous documentaries on television, and social and business encounters, Quebecers have become aware of their fellow French-speaking citizens. However, some misconceptions prevail. During the referendum campaign of 1980, the Parti Québécois spread rumours that the Moroccans were going to support sovereignty-association. So community members made a quiet door-to-door canvas (most are home-owners in the Côte St. Luc and St. Laurent areas), and determined that virtually 100 per cent were voting *Non.*

Lallouz has a simple explanation: "Having left a country that underwent a troubled period of independence, we don't want a repeat experience. We're part of the mainstream of Quebec, but we're Canadians."

Is there a leader of Montreal's Jewish community? Asked in 1970 the question would have been easy to answer. Only one name would have sprung up: Samuel Bronfman, head of the biggest distillery empire and one of the greatest family fortunes in the world. Sam Bronfman needed merely to pick up the phone to call a few people and demand sizable contributions to worthwhile causes. It was not dissimilar to the autocratic method of men such as J.W. McConnell (flour, sugar, newspapers), who enjoyed awesome personal power. But that age ended with the deaths of the old-style tycoons. Charles Bronfman works in the same building, a miniature castle, that his father erected on Peel Street in 1928. But an immediate difference is visible. While Sam Bronfman's style was reflected in busts of Napoleon in his office, in Charles' office one notes the gentle tones of paintings by Canadian artists. A quiet and reserved man, Charles shrinks from any suggestion that he is *the* community leader.

Charles, who is fifty-one, might defer to Arthur Pascal, twenty years his senior and a highly respected figure. But Pascal, too, declines any such honour. The fact is there is no single chief. Yet Charles can – and does – use his power to raise money for charity. Oddly, it is a situation that came about only in fairly recent times. He had been president of the Allied Jewish Community Services; he had also visited Israel. But it was not until a few years after his father's death that he emerged as a distinctive personality. He says frankly: "If you live in the same town as a father who is so dominant, it takes time to work out your role. If you have to live your life being what other people expect of you, it's not your life."

People may have expected him automatically to pick up his father's crown, but, while he was prepared to do so jointly in business with his brother Edgar, he wasn't sure he wanted to go beyond that. If he has to select an arbitrary date, the turning point came in 1973 with the Yom Kippur war. Charles was asked to fly over to Israel to see for himself how grave the situation was (a secret Israeli leaders shared with few outsiders). Bronfman realized the country was in danger of collapse without prompt overseas support. From then on he made an emotional and financial commitment. He plunged actively into fund-raising for Israeli and Canadian causes.

Others have done the same. Jack Cummings discovered Israel belatedly but now averages four trips there a year as chairman of the board of governors of Tel Aviv University. One of three men – along with his father, Maxwell, and brother, Robert – who built a small real estate operation into a family-owned diversified company worth $100 million, he takes keenly as well to local voluntary work. The Cummings Gallery at the Montreal Museum of Fine Arts resulted from a family contribution of $500,000. The Cummings lecture series at McGill, endowed at $100,000, brings in one or two prominent international figures a year. There is no conflict between Jack Cummings' Montreal and Israeli interests. The combination results from the not uncommon experience of a man of his generation (he is fifty-nine), wondering about the function, identity, and purpose of a Jew. Where do one's loyalties lie? Cummings' summation is precise:

"I have a Canadian passport and a Jewish heart. I love both."

Today, for the first time, the Montreal Jewish community is smaller than that in Toronto, which numbers 115,000. But it is more generous in fund-raising campaigns. There is great wealth in Toronto, but a single grant from the Bronfmans can make the difference. More telling, however, is the combination at play in Montreal: the tradition of an older community, with one generation carrying on from another, and the atmosphere of political change which inspires even greater challenge. The people with big money did not leave Montreal. They are determined to keep the community alive and important.

While Toronto's ranks benefited by an influx of perhaps 5,000 Montreal Jews, curiously those who left were not refugees from another era, from Hitler's Europe. A survivor says: "To compare the situation in Quebec to Nazi Germany is to defile the memory of the Holocaust. It is also a slander on Quebec." Those who have gone are mostly in their twenties and thirties, at the start of careers. It means the population may be aging. (Apart from the fact that 20 per cent of Montreal Jews live below the poverty line, there are twice as many elderly as in society at large.) Yet the movement away has dwindled dramatically, with the young now saying the determinant will not be politics or language but availability of jobs. In a revealing indicator, the Shaar Hashomayim, an old and prestigious synagogue, reported in 1980 that the rate of its membership enrolment was once again at the pre-1976 level.

What is clear, in the present climate of Quebec, is that anti-Semitism is no longer an issue. Anyone old enough can recall with horror the machinations of Adrien Arcand, who, in the late 1930's and 1940's, led a fascist group that preached a Hitler line and boycotted Jewish shops. Neither the ultra-nationalist Société Saint-Jean-Baptiste nor the church did anything to discourage such virulence. McGill University, with its quota system, was relatively subtle. But all has changed, both among francophones and anglophones. As a student, Arnold Steinberg needed much higher grades than a Gentile to gain entry into McGill. Today he is on the board of governors, which was chaired by another Jew, Alan B. Gold, chief judge of the Quebec provincial court from January 1978 to July 1982. Arnold Steinberg is also on the board of the Mercantile Bank of Canada, while Charles Bronfman easily entered the boardroom of the Bank of Montreal, which his father had difficulty reaching.

Harry J. Stern, rabbi emeritus of the Temple Emanu-El, who did much to promote ecumenicity in Montreal, fears that anti-Semitism may still live in the guise of anti-Zionism. But if it does, according to Jack Kantrowitz, former executive director of the Quebec region of Canadian Jewish Congress, it is individual and not of an organized pattern. "If you look for institutionalized anti-Semitism, of the type that existed under Adrien Arcand, there is very little – far less than in Toronto," says Kantrowitz. He illustrates: During the entire referendum campaign of five weeks the Congress found only five cases of anti-Semitic graffiti, and four of these were in English. When Kantrowitz told a colleague in Toronto, the quiet response was: "We find five in a week." The Steinberg group, whose name is so highly regarded in Quebec that customers display decals on their cars, operates its supermarket chain in most of Ontario under the title of Miracle Food Mart, a decision made largely out of concern for anti-Jewish backlash.

Ralph Lallouz, of Moroccan origin, says: "Anti-Semitism? When you've worked and studied in France, as I have, you know what anti-Semitism is. There is none here." The remarkable point is that francophones, who have undergone a searing period of self-analysis and social and political revolution, have done so at a cost perhaps to the non-French community as a whole but not to the Jews in particular. In historic terms this is virtually unprecedented.

The New Culture...

How do you define a Quebecer? "Someone," says Yvon Deschamps, "who wants an independent Quebec in a strong Canada." He laughs, or rather giggles, much the same as when he first used this celebrated line on stage in 1977. Actually, it is not a bad summary of his kind of "separatism" – a belief that what the country needs now is to be divided into five regions held together by a collective system. You could call it sovereignty association, but at the moment Deschamps doesn't even dwell on the subject in public. That is over, done with. He is now professionally involved in the much more personal matter of human relations: how people cope with fatherhood, with friendship, with other everyday tests. This is the same Yvon Deschamps who earns $500,000 a year delivering monologues that border on genius; the same Yvon Deschamps who until a few years ago delved into social and political issues; the same Yvon Deschamps who refused to make appearances in English even though he speaks it flawlessly.

What makes the difference – a profound one – is that the climate has changed. There is no longer the need to feel preoccupied with nationalism; there is no longer the need to fight a war. French Canadians possess self-assurance and dignity, manifest in the dominance of their language. That is what counts. The only difference between Yvon Deschamps and his fellow artists, almost all of whom are *péquistes*, is in the mild debate about when the war stopped. There is no disagreement about when it began: 1960, with the Quiet Revolution. The only doubt for some is whether the second key date is 1976, when the Parti Québécois swept to power, answering all their dreams. For others 1980 is more significant, because it was then that the majority of Quebecers turned down the idea of sovereignty-

165

association, and it meant that the playwrights and the novelists could shrug their shoulders and get down to other subjects. One thing is agreed: the topic of nationalism and all its kindred offshoots was pursued for fifteen or sixteen or even twenty years and it was now a bore. It was a bore to the interpreters of it and to the audiences.

To Deschamps what counts is that the change to broader themes after 1976 was significant and important. "We got through in a few years what sometimes takes decades to evolve," he says. "I'm a Quebecer but I became tired of a certain smugness of Quebecers – that just to be called a Quebecer was enough. I felt you had to show achievement to deserve to be called a Quebecer. I knew you could go through a phase of being political. But I became aware that if a plumber or carpenter coming into my house didn't do a job properly he wasn't living up to his obligations." Yet he looks back on the 1960's with fondness, for that is when he emerged artistically. A lot of other young people – singers, writers, painters – were also achieving fame. "There was something in the air," he says. "I don't know what. It was political, of course, but why should that affect culture?"

He asks this with a shrug, a smile, a quest for an answer that by inference he admits he cannot find. He feels more at ease analyzing the present; for he believes that his generation, and the one following, can now call themselves "citoyens du monde" since their interests are universal. Deschamps sits in his home in Westmount (to say this suburb was once the enclave of *les Anglais* is tedious, if not irrelevant), to discuss the evolution, the transition. It is a very comfortable home, not ostentatious but with enough good French-Canadian paintings and flair in decor to suggest a quiet, moneyed approach. There are two young daughters and a wife, Judi, who, Toronto-born, spoke not a word of French until she met Yvon in 1971. Now she is fluent, and when she enters the living room to hear her husband in conversation in English, she says, "What is that strange language?" And maybe it is not said entirely facetiously, for Judi is an artiste, a composer-singer in her own name.

Yvon Deschamps is very gentle in manner. At forty-five he is slender and slight, with abundant grey hair and a most appealing, whimsical way of talking, often marked by a giggle. But he is troubled by the fact that he is by far the highest paid entertainer in Quebec. What right does a poor boy from St. Henri, who once almost went to reform school for stealing chocolate bars, have to make half a million dollars a year? It bothered him until 1979, when he and Judi decided to establish a foundation to help physically and mentally handicapped children. In its first year of operation it gave away $200,000, with not a penny of overhead. Deschamps used the office and secretary of his close friend, Gilles Vigneault, who also does one-man shows.

He is still perplexed, too, by comments he encountered in English Canada when he was on a cross-country tour in 1977, his fifth such journey. Reviewers wrote that he could not be a separatist because here he was, willing to work in English Canada. But letter writers to newspapers said nastily: "Here's someone who is making money from us while he wants to break up the country." So Deschamps announced he would not again perform for audiences outside Quebec – at least until after the referendum. It was partly a political gesture, but mainly, as he analyzes it now, an expression of wounded pride. But he'll be back in English Canada in 1983, "because I feel there has been a change among anglophones." He can't do it before then for a simple reason of strategy. In odd-numbered years he does his solo *tour de force*. The years that end in an even figure he devotes to writing or working with others in a movie.

The 1981 season for monologues was applied to the subject of security: emotional, financial, physical. The 1982 year of the film concentrates on one theme: "How will we ever be rich if we work all the time?" There is nothing political in it, any more than there was in the 1981 monology. Moreover, Deschamps hopes the movie will work out in English as well as in French, for this would contribute to his distinctive theory about travel. If a performer is on the road frequently he is tempted to stick to "old recipes." But this, to Deschamps, is disastrous artistically. "When you have to face the same audience repeatedly you're compelled to write new material. It's the only way to keep creative." Quebecers are prepared to wait two years to see their idol in person. But while the artist cannot, or should not, travel too much, a movie of him can be exposed over and over again.

The formula obviously works. Deschamps spurns offers in New York and Paris. There is no need to seek satisfaction or income elsewhere. He is booked solidly years ahead on Quebec projects alone, and 125,000 men and women reserve seats at Place des Arts. In the audiences are a fair number of anglophones because of the universality of his pathos and humour. "To some people," he says, "a Québécois skit seems like Jewish humour, with the same quality of guilt and innocence." If he finds that younger francophones "don't have the hangups we had ten years ago," something else pleases him as much: the English Montrealers who've stayed or come back. In characteristically biting yet affectionate style, he says, "They were Quebecers and they didn't know it."

But one should not exaggerate the significance of anglophone attendance at francophone performances. Yvon Deschamps, because of his unique qualities, enjoys a special appeal. French theatre in general draws far fewer anglophones than one might expect, given the fact that English playhouses are limited in number and that some French companies, such as Théâtre du Nouveau Monde (TNM), are of the highest quality. The outgoing artistic director of TNM, Jean-Louis Roux, says no precise figures are collated but he would guess his audience includes a maximum of 10 per cent anglophones, and "probably 5 to 8 per cent would be more realistic." Roux admits that TNM has never made any real effort to attract anglophones; the budget limits advertising to French-language newspapers. He is even more charitable in suggesting that it is one thing for an anglophone to employ French in his everyday work and something else to sit through a play peppered with idiom or difficult vocabulary.

Roux, co-founder with Jean Gascon of TNM in 1951, has long been a creative force of considerable importance to the cultural life of Montreal. At age fifty-nine he is one of the few federalists in an arena of mild revolutionaries, and this gives him, perhaps, an ability to appraise dispassionately what has taken place. "Ten years ago practically all the people working in theatre were writing on political issues, with a heavy nationalistic point of view. I'm not questioning that, of course. But after the Parti Québécois came to office, the balance wasn't the same. Artists feel ill at ease when they're in power. Artists are shaped to be in the opposition – to question society. It's their essential role. Otherwise they become 'patriotic' poets or propagandists, and that's bound to lead to bad art or theatre."

But the fact is there has been no continuation of the trend that began in the 1960's; nor has there been any wailing about what happened in the referendum. Roux guesses that maybe by 1983 or 1984 some playwrights will be raising the question of why a majority of people turned down sovereignty-association. In the meanwhile, the tendency today is to deal with social issues of broad dimensions. Before, if they weren't being political, Quebec writers were talking of social injustices, but in the confines of Quebec. Now they see problems of the wealthy nations needing to share their riches with the poor nations.

How long will this go on? Roux, who uses the base period of the immediate past as 1960 to 1980, figures the current cycle could bring us to the year 2000. "But who can say? Certainly one can anticipate that it will go on over the next several years." What is happening in Quebec is more or less in keeping with movements elsewhere. The plays Roux saw on his last trip to London dealt with subjects TNM has under consideration: the difficulties of youth within a society of high consumption, or the problems of older people managing in an impersonal, inflationary world. Overall, the universality of writing touches on the human condition. Roux is struck by the preoccupations of Montreal's feminist authors. Of the fifty to sixty plays he now receives a year, some deal with feminism in terms of male-female relations or women trying to live in an environment structured by men. But the majority are in the realm of mysticism or metaphysics. One such manuscript, reminiscent of Arthur Rimbaud, the nineteenth century poet who was an important forerunner of symbolism and in some respects surrealism, tells of a poetess who committed suicide at the age of seventeen; she was a lover of God in every sense, including a physical relationship.

"This," says Roux, "is definitely a healthy trend. I'm not trying to say that previously the plays were bad. We had to go through the phase of the 1960's and the 1970's. But now writers have to find new inspiration. They're no longer fighting against the old power." In actuality, the number of high quality plays of ten years ago may have been greater than today because of the motivation. But TNM can still find one or two a season – of the six productions a year – and this is an encouraging sign. Moreover, Roux is impressed by the language in use. He hesitates how to describe it, winding up almost apologetically by calling it "international French." It is not as original, maybe, as in the 1960's, when *joual* was "liberated." But *joual* was overdone then. No one in real life spoke it to the degree that playwrights embraced it, any more than Englishmen spoke like Shakespearean actors. To Roux this was a breakdown in a theatre's function of communicating. "We weren't even talking to five million Quebecers, because *joual* is an urban language, a Montreal language for only two million people. We should have gone outside as well, for the language of the Gaspé and other rural areas." But Roux recognizes its emphasis as symptomatic of the times. It served as a means of identification, national and personal, as well as a form of exorcism.

The man who started it all in the theatre, Michel Tremblay, is still employing *joual*, but much more carefully and in essentially dramatic terms. Tremblay hates the word because it is a malformation of "cheval" and therefore to him contemptuous, an attempt to place a bad meaning on a back street language. It does not originate in France and is not known there. Tremblay calls it, instead of *joual*, "Québécois," though he admits that perhaps he should refer to it as "Montréalais." All the "French" words that derive from English are strictly of Montreal breeding. An example of the distortion is what happened to the English verb "to call." It became in French "caller" – vous callez, nous callons, and so on. Tremblay explains it thus: "Our fathers were obliged to work in English and they brought English words home with them. These became mixed up with the French our mothers would use."

But an interesting evolution, as Jean-Louis Roux mentioned, has indeed taken place. Tremblay describes it as "extraordinary." His first play for TNM, in 1972, was followed by an open discussion with the audience. Tremblay was confronted by hostile questions demanding to know why he wrote *joual*. He recalls replying, "One day I'll do a play and no one will discuss the language." That is precisely what did happen with his last offering, *Bonjour la, bonjour* in 1981. In an open session, members of the audience discussed the story line in detail but not a single question was raised about the *joual*. What had been shocking a decade earlier was now taken for granted. "I always used to say," comments Tremblay, "that Quebec was the only place where language was a problem. This no longer applies." To him the nonchalance of the most recent audience was clearly related to the cultural battle which had been won with Bill 101; the comfort and ease people felt with their own language, no matter in what form it was presented. But the fact is that *joual*, as Roux points out, is now dressed up with more respectability and acceptance partly because it is subdued. In any event there is no doubt about the mark Tremblay – emulated by many other writers – has left on the theatre. Lawrence Sabbath, a wise and experienced critic, has called the 1970's "the decade of Michel Tremblay."

Tremblay, forty, is rather formidable in appearance, with a thick black beard and steel-rimmed glasses. His roots are working class; his first job was a Linotype operator and he never got near a university. But he is self-taught and enormously well read, and if not a fanatic about separatism has argued that if Montreal anglophones wanted to understand the French-Canadian mentality they had to pick up books or see plays in the original. Thus he rejected permission for his works to be performed in English in Montreal, even though he happily approved of their translated versions across Canada. His refusal in Montreal was not a political ploy but rather a cultural demand. "I felt anglophones should know us in our own milieu." He lifted the embargo in 1976, after the election of the Parti Québécois, because to him it represented a triumph for French-Canadian identity and respect from anglophones. "It was quite beautiful," he says, "to see people waking up and telling the world, 'Here we are. Love us or hate us, but here we are.' "

Ironically, though, he calls the referendum of 1980 "a lesson in humility" for writers and artists generally. "Before," he says, "we thought we could change the world, that we had a big influence on the public. People still see my plays and they buy my books, but they voted *Non*. It was a revelation to me, and tough to learn." The referendum was clearly a point of sharp demarcation and more important than the subsequent election results in 1981. "I'm not certain about the future," Tremblay says. "The danger is this: For the last twenty years some people put the well being of Quebec above their own personal well being. Now that new opportunities in work have opened for the young people it's possible they'll go after wealth and comfort. This will work against independence."

But even he has changed, he admits, at least in his writing style. He calls it "more tender." Really what he means is that he possesses two styles: one for theatre, the other for novels. In theatre, he explains, "you have to shout." But he is less strident in his books. *Thérèse et Pierrette à l'école des Saints-Anges* is about his own Fabre Street, a poor neighbourhood, during the Second World War. A reviewer called his language a delight. "Purists can learn from him." This was quite a distinction for someone condemned earlier for his *joual*. But Tremblay has never fit a simple category. He was never, for instance, a Roch Carrier who wrote testily about English Canadians. Tremblay, both in script and novel, has striven mainly to interpret the struggle for personal identity through inter-relationships among families, whether the wealthy of Outremont or the poor of east end Montreal.

But even Roch Carrier, who in the 1970's made a national impact with his book and play, *La guerre, yes sir*, has mellowed – and he is in the forefront of the movement away from social-political themes. *La guerre, yes sir*, which sold 100,000 copies in English alone, and in its stage version played not only Canada but Europe, was about the problems of communication between English and French, ending on the note that each looks on the other with suspicion and some hostility. At Ontario's Stratford Festival, some critics said it was anti-English or anti-French; to others it was anti-military or pro-military. But to Carrier it was universal because in France they called it a "French condition," in Belgium a "Belgian condition," and in Switzerland a "Swiss condition."

More to the point, his latest play, *La celeste bicyclette*, staged at Place des Arts in 1981, contains not a single word about anglophones or politics. An allegory, it depicts a man who tries to persuade his audience that he has made a trip to outer space – and it's up to the audience to decide whether or not it's true. What was Carrier's purpose? He ponders only briefly and says: "Now I am big enough to forget about small problems like politics and play with the world like a kid. It's an admission of freedom. I don't forget what's behind me but I think it's time to move on, to be less critical and more creative."

Carrier, who is forty-five, feels it is also an indication of a new maturity of the public. "Three or four years ago," he says, "it would have been unthinkable to do a play without at least some allusion to politics." But now he senses that both viewers and critics appreciate what he set out to do in *La celeste bicyclette*. He reflects on his earlier days and those of his contemporaries and says: "A young playwright or author finds it easier to speak about social or political problems than to deal with human relations. Remember that most artists in the period of the 1960's and 1970's were young. When an author knows his craft, and when he has lived a little more, he understands that realities are not good or bad; they're much more complex. Now what we see on stage is the work of authors who have learned their craft and have lived a little more. That's why theatre has become much more open."

Carrier has written fourteen books so far, with most of them, including his recent *Hockey Sweater and Other Stories*, translated into English. He admits he has learned a great deal from this exposure; translations have led to publicity tours and the discovery of a Canada outside Quebec. He says: "The more I've come to know it, the more I like Canada." When he returned from one tour he told friends: "We don't have to think we are alone." What stood out particularly was a visit to Regina where a guide, an old and knowledgeable resident, made a point of taking him to a cemetery and standing before various tombstones to describe those who had gone before: pioneers and homesteaders, victims of drought and depression and bad times. Carrier says now, on reflection: "I appreciated all the more what Canada meant. I realized that my guide's roots in the west were as deep as mine in Quebec." Does this make him any less a *péquiste*? He answers: "I don't like separatism. But ultimately we will have to come to a kind of agreement among maybe five provinces or regions. It seems more realistic to me to negotiate and have exchanges and take advantage of the richness, the balance that can be reached among all Canadians."

Carrier was born in a small village, St. Justin, on the south shore of the St. Lawrence River 100 kilometres from Quebec City. "Living so far away," he says drolly, "we were already separated." When he moved to Montreal in 1956, at the age of nineteen, there were only a couple of full-fledged theatres. Now there are at least ten (categorized as such by full time management teams and private premises) In addition, "le jeune théâtre" is strong. In at least a score of "Off Broadway" type theatres, professional or semi-professional, much experimental work of high standard goes on. Roland Lepage, whose *Le temps d'une vie* – the story of a woman's alienation and struggle in a change from rural to urban life – won a critics' award as the best Canadian play of the year when it was presented in Toronto in 1978, is a member of the advisory committee on theatre for the Canada Council. He sees many English-Canadian plays, and he quotes their producers as saying: "You in Quebec are so lucky. You do your own theatre. We feel too much of ours is British or American." Lepage replies that Quebecers found the solution more than a decade ago. "For us it was a desire to make it Québécois. For you it was an attempt to make it Canadian. But we achieved something, making Québécois theatre also of international interest." *Le temps d'une vie* toured France and Belgium in 1978 and was presented again in Belgium in 1981. Lepage is persuaded it is because of the universality of the subject.

He also sees as a heartening sign the increasing number of directors who visit from France every year to examine what Montreal is doing. "They are fascinated by the strong link between theatre and public." Nothing could be a more graphic illustration of this than the performances by a group of "le jeune théâtre" who meet in an amphitheatre at the Université du Québec à Montréal at 11:00 P.M. These are mostly professional actors who convene after their work is done at TNM and other theatres. They come together to improvise and have fun along with their audience. And the fun starts when they don hockey sweaters and form up as opposing teams, the stage even marked with blue lines. Members of the audience select from a list of prepared topics and, for example, shout out to the players: "You are worms in a garden." Each side must enact how it would fill such a role. The extemporization goes on for nine minutes, then a referee blows his whistle. The audience votes to decide which team has won, or done the more credible job. Meanwhile, if you dislike a performance you manifest it. A player emulates Christ in suffering; he is not very persuasive, so heave at him a rolled up newspaper or a shoe. But do something! After all, these actors must not be taken lightly; they are deliberately dressed as hockey players because of the game's special flavour and importance.

Even the major playhouses, such as Théâtre d'Aujourd'hui, can offer intimacy because of their size or shape. Théâtre d'Aujourd'hui is located on Papineau Avenue in a former machine shop which the audience enters through a fire-escape. Its mainstay as director-general, Jean-Claude Germain, is one of the most literate spokesmen for theatre today and without doubt its biggest man physically – a huge, corpulent figure, with a beard so straggly it looks almost ludicrous. He is a prolific and powerful playwright and even in private conversation he expounds in booming tones refreshing ideas about theatre and government.

"The fact that the Parti Québécois was elected was the big change. Up to that time theatre was a voice repeating old topics like, 'We are in a bad state.' It was a melodramatic voice, moaning, shedding tears in its beer. It was very Irish that way. The election closed the door on the past. The main character of plays had been some sort of underdog – in terms of theatre an underdog is always sympathetic. After the election there was no reason to use this underdog." Indeed, he adds, after Bill 101 "the other one," the anglophone, became the underdog. Germain says this with a heavy, but not mocking, laugh. In effect, what happened was this: "In theatre we passed from a melodramatic stage to drama – a more complex and sophisticated conception of reality. I found it curious that some artists complained that now they had nothing to say. It meant that, before, they were

174

only bearers of a national torch. Now we are facing a modern reality, not the image of an old forgotten Quebec. We have to cope with reality. We have to choose between modernity and the past."

In his case the contrast is sharply etched in *A Canadian Play/Une plaie canadienne* and *Les bretelles*. In the former, Germain postulated that French Canadians had had an emotional love affair with an English figure, Lord Durham (who was sent out to Canada to investigate the rebellion of 1837), and that it needed to be exorcised. Germain's message was that French Canadians had endured humiliation too long and they should not stumble now in their objective of sovereignty. *A Canadian Play/Une plaie canadienne* was written and performed in 1979, before the referendum. It is plain that since then Germain has moved on. After having tapped the Quebec soul for the previous two decades – he is forty-two, now – he takes as his theme in *Les bretelles* an actor who witnesses himself during three periods in life. The twenty-year-old says of the forty-year-old: "You're not a liberal." The forty-year-old hates the sixty-year-old – who wants to die on stage because he thinks we all must try to be heroic. Apart from the non-political subject matter, the play deals with sex and money. "I never talked about money before," says Germain. "I used to talk about ideas and dreams and images. Now I feel reality."

This reality translates itself into a candid look at audiences. For a period of several years he found it upsetting that playgoers did not permit the theatre to be critical of the Parti Québécois. Then, in November 1980, Théâtre d'Aujourd'hui was preparing to put on a play, written not by Germain but by another dramatist, in which there was a fleeting reference to Premier Lévesque. An offstage voice described him and the Parti Québécois as "underdogs" (this was six months after the referendum). It had no relationship to the main theme of the play and Germain, as director, debated with himself whether to chance it; he decided to go ahead. The audience at first chuckled, then broke into laughter. Germain recalls what he thought at the time: "It's back – the critical mind is back." What this suggests, of course, is self-confidence. With at least the battle of culture won, the francophone was at ease. Germain makes another point. "The Parti Québécois was an act of faith, and I don't think people should have faith in political parties. This doesn't make me any less an *indépendantiste*. But you don't do it with 'faith' or you'll wind up a bunch of holy rollers."

Germain's theatre does five plays a year – exclusively Canadian and virtually all Québécois. It is the only one of the "Big Ten" with this policy. Therefore he is perhaps more vociferous than other directors – though his view is widely shared – when he criticizes the present provincial government. Writers have graduated from their insular preoccupation with historic or political problems. But since 1976, Parti Québécois ministers have retrogressed to old cultural values – old furniture, old homes – known as "les patrimoines" (heritage). To Germain, this is "terrible" because it intrudes on creativity. Theatre in Montreal is subsidized from three main sources: the Canada Council, the Arts Council of the Montreal Urban Community, and the Quebec cultural ministry. Montreal put the Parti Québécois into power, but the men in it, striving for broader support, decided soon after to spread the wealth more widely. "Rarely," says Germain, "has a government been so anti-Montreal culturally. The ministry thinks everyone should do theatre in a backyard – in Chicoutimi or Trois-Rivières. This translates into less funding for Montreal. But Montreal is the heart of Quebec, the pump. There can be no living art in Chicoutimi unless blood is pumped into the fingers from the heart." In other words, Montreal must be the principal cultural centre, to which artists from Chicoutimi and Trois-Rivières would gravitate.

Even worse, adds Germain, is the personal attitude of Parti Québécois politicians who are products of the 1960's, when they attended universities and theatres. Theirs is a view based on classical education and literature, and it is not in keeping with the evolution of the 1970's and 1980's. However, since Parti Québécois ministers think they know more about culture than the men and women directly engaged in it, they rarely feel any need to consult the practitioners. It took L'Association des directeurs de théâtre, a professional group, two and a half years to get an appointment with Camille Laurin when he was cultural affairs minister. Ironically, says Germain, who remains an ardent *péquiste*, the Liberals under Premier Bourassa, not being dogmatic about the arts, took a simple pragmatic route, filling up holes with funds where needed – and this meant, in the main, Montreal.

Oddly, no complaint is registered by the leading figure in English theatre, Maurice Podbrey. Under the Liberals, the Centaur Theatre, of which he is artistic and executive director, was low in the pecking order of grants. But much to his surprise the cultural ministry under the Parti Québécois came through with a 25 per cent increase for the

1980-81 season (making it $97,500, compared with $210,000 from the Canada Council and $55,000 from the Montreal Arts Council). Equally ironic was the fact that Centaur's best years coincided with Parti Québécois ascendancy. This was due to English theatre's determination to prove it was creative and durable at a time when the anglophone community needed a psychological uplift. French theatre, after its long session of political preaching, embarked on what Podbrey calls "traditional, bourgeois entertainment." English theatre? Small in comparison, he considers nonetheless that it is displaying more originality and vitality than it has in many years – and this includes the Saidye Bronfman Centre (with its English-language and Yiddish offerings), and two or three commendable amateur groups.

Certainly the Centaur has progressed impressively since 1969 when Podbrey, a thirty-five-year-old South African actor who couldn't find enough employment in Montreal, decided to start his own theatre. He raised barely enough money to take over the former Stock Exchange on Rue St. François-Xavier in Old Montreal. That colourful and unusual setting has since expanded into the building next door, and the first season's production, *The Prime of Miss Jean Brodie*, grew to seven plays a year, of which at least three are Canadian. Centaur's most successful effort was David Fennario's *Balconville*, with two runs during the 1978-79 season and a repeat in 1980 at Place des Arts, where three solid weeks could have been extended to four months if the theatre had been available. Even so, 60,000 Montrealers saw it, in addition to audiences in Ottawa and Toronto.

Then *Balconville* reached its apogee, playing for a fortnight in April 1981 at London's Old Vic. The reviews ranged from medium to glowing. In Belfast, where residents could relate to cultural clashes, it was an enormous hit. Fennario, in depicting the deeper issues and humanity behind a language conflict, devotes about 30 per cent of the dialogue to French. Jean-Louis Roux thought that *La guerre, yes sir*, which also dealt with English-French relations, was more effective because it ended on a note of uncertainty. Podbrey challenges that judgement if only because Roux must have seen an early rendition of *Balconville*. The first time round, when a fire next door pulls together French and English tenement neighbours to fight it successfully, the street scene turns into a big fête. Fennario himself suggested the amended version – shown in revivals. *Balconville* concludes on a question. A francophone mother says, as the fire moves closer, "What are we going to do now?"

Fennario, who was brought up in Point St. Charles, a district of the poor, and who calls himself a Marxist, says he would have preferred seeing his francophone and anglophone characters – all of them from the working class – unite: "But artistically I felt I should leave it up to the audience to decide the outcome." His language, street jargon, is parallel to that of Michel Tremblay, but he considers himself more committed ideologically. At thirty-five, he comes by his conviction the hard way, having quit school in ninth grade to start working as a shipping clerk in a garment factory. *Balconville* played at Place des Arts when the ushers were on strike. Fennario hoisted a placard to join in picketing against his own play. "I was," he explains, "a Marxist before I was a writer."

By his definition, no country that claims it is Communist today – Albania and China included – qualifies. "I want direct control of industry by the workers themselves, not by people appointed over them," he says. Indirectly this concept comes out in his writing, though it is hard to detect in *Balconville* or his two earlier plays, *On the Job* and *Nothing to Lose*. But it manifests itself, he says, in the book on which he was working in 1981, the story of the struggles by his father and family during the Duplessis era. The title, *Black Rock*, stems from Point St. Charles, a dumping ground for Irish immigrants who fled the potato famine only to become victims of the cholera and typhus epidemics of the 1840's. Fennario, somewhat emaciated looking at five feet ten inches and 140 pounds, feels close to francophone writers who emerged from an impoverished background similar to his own. He is ill at ease with people of higher social levels, and nothing relaxes him more than to sit in a tavern over a couple of beers and warm conversation. He thinks it is healthy today that not only francophones, but a growing number of anglophones, consider themselves Quebecers.

Podbrey estimates that half of the Montrealers who have seen *Balconville* are francophones. This "crossing over" of audiences – that is, of people of different origins – gives theatre in Montreal a special force. What impresses him most is the acceptance by anglophones of the psychological and political changes in Quebec. "If they were on the run or worried about the future," says Podbrey, "they wouldn't be so eager to seek out the new and challenging in theatre." He is equally encouraged by the new confidence of francophones. "There is no longer a feeling of personal vendetta. Francophones respond to us warmly." This translates itself in the considerable co-operation between anglophone and francophone theatre groups, and in the way Centaur, Saidye Bronfman Centre, and other English-language productions are attentively reviewed in the French media. Even more tangibly, it is indicated in the form of private grants from corporations dominated by the new francophone managerial class.

One should not be misled. Centaur does not go in only for *Balconville* type stories. In its 1980-81 season it showed Tom Stoppard's *Night and Day*, a Briton's witty exploration of the hazards of war and the politics of journalism. But essentially its strength is in the presentation of subjects that once would have been regarded as too sensitive, and in their favourable reception by men and women who no longer question the pre-eminence of French language or culture.

... and the Old Plouffes

Not everyone goes to the theatre, but everyone watches television. How does this mass medium shape up in Montreal? It has its high points, but generally it is no better and no worse than in other major cities. What does make it different, however, is that it is mainly a home brew and that it boasts the biggest commercial success story in the world: CFTM on Channel 10. Nearly half of Montreal's two million francophones watch it consistently, in preference to a dozen other stations that are available – a viewing record that cannot be duplicated anywhere. Channel 10 and its affiliates in the province have changed the work habits of farmers with a participation show called *Les tannants* (*The Brats*). A studio audience cavorts in games and parties of the kind found in any big family in any big village. It is nostalgia for city people and a must for rural folk. Since the program runs every weekday evening from 5:00 P.M. to 6:00 P.M., a period when farmers are supposed to be winding up their chores, something had to yield. It was custom. Farmers now finish earlier so they can start supper at five while viewing *Les tannants*. The program was sneered at by rivals at Radio-Canada (CBC), until a Université Laval study determined it was regarded by Quebecers as a true reflection of their own lives.

Télé-Métropole, the parent company of Channel 10, was launched when a half dozen Radio-Canada producers became fed up with the way the corporation handled a strike in 1959. "We were six angry young men who wanted to fix the clock of CBC," says Jean-Paul Ladouceur. So, with financial backing from a film distributor and a bit of their own money (a total investment of $365,000), they inaugurated CFTM in 1960. Twenty years later it was worth $80 million and its annual revenue was $75 million; its complex on De Maisonneuve

180

Boulevard stretched a full block and housed eleven studios and 800 employees. The success has resulted from a simple formula rejected early on by CBC. Ladouceur, now sixty and vice-president of Télé-Métropole, recalls the battles he fought with junior producers working for him at Radio-Canada, where he was director of production. They were so highbrow, he says. He would tell them: "You are trying to judge the success of a program in inverse proportion to the number of viewers."

Channel 10, after market surveys, deliberately served a diet of what people wanted. "In every city," says Ladouceur, "there is a Nob Hill. Here – for French Canadians – it was Outremont. The rest of the city people hated people there; and Radio-Canada was catering to Outremont. Culture is not necessarily high-hat. Culture is a mirror of what you are." Channel 10 handles all the usual sitcoms, variety shows, panel discussions, and news reports. Oddly, it does not push heavily into sports, leaving the field more to CBC. Again the reason is surveys, which indicate that the majority of television viewers are women. So, while Radio-Canada is broadcasting National League hockey on Saturday night, Channel 10 puts on a light romantic movie. Yet, in paradox, it bid successfully against CBC for the *Holocaust* series. Fundamentally, though, Télé-Métropole, the mainstay for a network of independent television stations, produces seventy-two hours of original programs a week, of a total of 112 on the air.

This impressive record is matched by Radio-Canada which originates 65 per cent of its own shows. Combined, they make Montreal the fourth largest television production centre in the world, after Los Angeles, London, and New York. Quebecers, demanding their own culture, are not satisfied with programs from France or the US, and Channel 10 takes note of its record audiences, particularly in light of the huge assortment of channels available, either directly or on cable (including seven English or French-language Canadian stations, the three major US networks, and Public Broadcasting Service). Of francophone viewers, 89 per cent watch Channel 10 at some time during the week; 46 per cent watch it all the time. Its pull is such that a telethon for cerebral palsy in 1980 collected $3.8 million in twenty hours. Every year on its anniversary the channel offers prizes to viewers who write in to identify a tiny white sign on a corner of the screen; one year it was a four-leaf clover, another year a harp. In a four week period the station receives 2,000,000 letters.

Ladouceur, a federalist, is irritated by what he regards as a lack of English-Canadian recognition of Télé-Métropole's unique success story. "Here we are beating the daylights out of every private commercial station in the world," he says. "If we were in Toronto we'd be the talk of Canada. But since we're in Montreal..." The sentence is unfinished except for a shrug. But the overriding fact is that there is satisfaction in developing Québécois television. Télé-Métropole embraces its own world of stars, writers, and directors. It has branched into the film-making business and also rents space to producers from the US who are awed by the dimension of its studios and facilities. Ironically, while Channel 10 attracts an audience for twenty-four of the thirty most widely watched programs in Montreal, only one of American origin is on the list: *Little House on the Prairie*. Ladouceur's final word is about his old employer, CBC, which he claims has been attempting for the last five years to compete with Channel 10 on the latter's own terms. "They're crazy to try it."

Over at the Radio-Canada building on Dorchester Boulevard, Jean-Marie Dugas, the director of television and a former associate of Ladouceur, admits that while CBC's aim is still quality, "we have to dilute." An example is *Les beaux dimanches,* a Sunday night package that has run steadily since the mid-1970's. The objective is to lure people into culture. Thus the show is preceded at 6:30 P.M. by what is known in the trade as a "locomotive" program – something that hauls in an audience for the rest of the evening. In this instance it is *The World of Disney.* Once the youngsters are there, the chances are the parents will join in at 7:30 P.M. when *Les beaux dimanches* gets underway for three hours. It opens with a variety show, lasting an hour, that draws 1,250,000. At 8:30 P.M. a concert lures 1,000,000. The last portion, a documentary, will hold 800,000.

Radio-Canada knows of its losses, not only to Télé-Métropole but to the anglophone channels and US networks, but it regards as respectable any show that claims 200,000 viewers. It has always been strong on children's programs. "We were, and still are, the biggest original production centre for children's programs in the world," says Dugas. For the last twenty-five years one quarter of the schedule has been devoted to youngsters. At 4:00 P.M., the very young – of kindergarten age – still watch an actor, Bobino, who plays with a marionette named Bobinette. But now there is a problem with the older ones for whom, in the past, a play was put on between 4:30

P.M. and 5:30 P.M. *Les tannants*, on Channel 10, cut into that, so CBC has shuffled some new ideas for 1982. Another challenge involves teenagers. Radio-Canada tried to engage them at 6:30 P.M. with *Jeunesse oblige*, a magazine of quality and audience participation. "But," says Dugas ruefully, "we discovered that teenagers didn't exist as a group or weren't home when the show was on." What it really meant was that French-Canadian youth were no different from youth anywhere else. An adolescent's period of wonderment, of discovery – important as recently as a decade ago – had disappeared. So now CBC tries programs of more sophisticated content.

In broad terms, what Dugas says of Quebecers is this: "Up to now we've always claimed that the language barrier was a sort of protection. It helped us develop French-Canadian talent. Yvon Deschamps had his push on television. But in the last few years we've found that the more our people become citizens of the universe through television the more they become excited by outside events. It means we'll either be very good and hold our audience with quality – or lose them." Then, quietly, he adds, "We've been in limbo for years."

According to Dugas, CBC in Toronto has an even bigger problem. "At least in Montreal there is an awareness of cultural identity that has to be retained." Dugas illustrates what he means in a personal and telling way: "When I'm in Los Angeles or New York to see a screening with a Toronto colleague, he's at home. But I feel I'm in a foreign country. Simultaneously, when I go to Paris I love it – but I'm still in a foreign country." French Canadians, even if television is becoming more mass-oriented, can call it *their* television. They feel a closer relationship to it than English Canadians do to their television. There lies the difference."

Roger Lemelin, sixty-two, debonair, outspoken, and highly successful, fits into several categories: author, playwright, meat merchant, newspaper publisher – and millionaire. He comforts the perplexed questioner by saying, of his many hats, "I've always tried to be a Renaissance man." At the moment his acclaim is based on a family he created in a novel in the 1940's and brought to cinema life in the 1980's. The film, *Les Plouffe*, shot in Montreal and Quebec City at a cost of $5 million, received splendid reviews and hurrahs from audiences when it opened in April 1981. Its success indicates a hunger for popular entertainment that reflects the perpetually solid character of the Quebecer.

Lemelin, who was co-author of the screenplay, explains it thus: "What you see today is a triumph of people over the politicians, over the established order. It was important to say it again – the Plouffe family was last seen on television twenty years ago – because Quebec has tried to impose upon a good people a cultural revolution that was not at all pure. That is, it tried to impose the problems of the outside world, particularly those of France. You have a few intellectuals here who wanted to play a role that intellectuals played in France – a pseudo-Marxist role. But we are people with profoundly conservative roots. René Lévesque is a potpourri, a mixture of all kinds of things of a frustrated people. But you must not forget that a week after Lévesque was elected he was defeated, psychologically, by a majority of the people." What Lemelin means is that Quebecers, having chosen the Parti Québécois in 1976, made up their minds almost instantly that they would not permit extremism, such as separatism, to enter – even though they did not express this formally until three and a half years later.

Lemelin, a week before the May 1980 referendum, predicted the outcome by saying 60 per cent would vote *Non*. "Then there'll be trouble, violence," someone commented. Lemelin shook his head. "Why not?" he was asked. He said, "It's the baseball season." Such is the earthy reasoning Lemelin applies to all things Quebec, and it shows in the actions and thoughts of his Plouffe family. Indeed, he makes even this appraisal simple. "All the characters in the Plouffes are the expression of myself, because the human being is composed of many characters." An extension of this is his abiding interest in the past. "The best of the old traditions still survive. These are always the same for Quebec." So deep is this belief that Lemelin, with *Les Plouffe* hardly out of the way, began to make plans for a film based on *Maria Chapdelaine*, the celebrated account of rural Quebec life by an expatriate French novelist, Louis Hémon. Since the book, in its span of several decades, has sold 31,000,000 copies, Lemelin, being Lemelin, figures it merits treatment as a five hour epic.

Montreal possesses the facilities for such a mammoth undertaking, but, sadly, most of what emerged in the twenty feature films of 1981 – 60 per cent of Canada's output – was slickly commercial. It is particularly distressing because the foundation of the film industry was laid by the National Film Board (NFB), which moved to Montreal from Ottawa in 1956 and graduated a large number of creative people. *Mon oncle Antoine*, an NFB production by Claude Jutra, won eight awards in 1971. It was absorbing, and significant socially and politically, depicting the life of French Canadians in a small town dominated by English Canadians. But today most of the films made in Montreal are intended primarily for both American audiences and the producers who can take advantage of tax shelters and some government financing.

Yvon Deschamps laments: "In the 1960's when we decided to do a movie we just got a couple of dozen people together and made it. It didn't cost much. In Montreal today there are seven or eight crews who are among the best in the world, but they're so busy working for producers with a lot of money they command high prices." His current movie, he claims, would have been cheaper to make in New York or Los Angeles where pools of talent are trying to establish themselves in the fashion of Montrealers fifteen years ago.

In addition, the detectable trend in cinema today, as in theatre, is towards stories that are less profound or provocative than *Mon oncle Antoine*. To André Lamy, former chairman of the NFB and now head of the Canadian Film Development Corporation, this is not necessarily negative or a setback. "Films can be based on Quebec but attempt to reach out to the rest of the world," he argues. In this sense there is a unique opportunity to tell stories of the past. Italian film makers recently produced, in collaboration with the Chinese, a film about Marco Polo. "It's a world trend, taking people back to their roots," says Lamy; which means that once again Roger Lemelin – if his dream about *Maria Chapdelaine* is borne out – will be in the mainstream.

Lemelin, of course, embraces both the visual and the written story. But he is of an older generation, while the Michel Tremblays and the Roch Carriers fill the middle-aged level. A younger group has come along, represented by Pierre Turgeon who won the Governor General's 1980 award for French-language fiction with *La première personne*, published in English Canada and the US in 1981 under the title *L.A.* It is the tale of a man who leaves his family, job, and country for Los Angeles. There he changes his identity, works as a private investigator, and finds the freedom he wants – but it amounts to emptiness. Turgeon, thirty-three, has written four novels, all in the "American" genre, a break from the traditional style of France that has influenced Quebec authors. But Turgeon possesses more than a writer's skill; he is also a publisher, which gives him an insight into French-Canadian habits. He points out that not all readers or authors in Quebec went through the social-political cycle of the 1960's and 1970's. Some (he among them), thought, rather, that what counted, and still counts, is a work that has literary merit and does not try to appeal merely with a message. An interesting side effect is that in 1981 for the first time his firm of Quebec book publishers, Sogides Ltée, reversed an old pattern: they sold more books in France than competitive French houses were able to sell in Quebec.

But not everyone is impressed by such a statistic. Jean Ethier-Blais, professor of French-Canadian literature at McGill University, for many years wrote literary reviews for *Le Devoir*; now he conducts a weekly column about any subject that pleases him, and rarely does it include a book. "I'm bored, plain bored with the kind of stuff that's been coming out," he says. It is a cantankerous judgement and may be due to a sentimentality for authors of the style of Gabrielle Roy. Roy, seventy-two, herself admits to confusion and inability to understand some of the new books. This refers particularly to such feminist writers as Louky Bersianik and Nicole Brossard. Louky Bersianik (whose approach has been discussed in an earlier chapter), says of Nicole Brossard: "She is very intellectual, I am not."

Few will dispute Nicole Brossard's brilliance in both poetry and prose. The only question is whether she conveys successfully the thesis which so absorbs her: "The big challenge of the 1980's for women will be to produce not only what they want but to establish institutions – that is, traditions – that will speak for them." The trouble is that Nicole, a winsome brunette of thirty-nine, depends on allusions which can be rather obscure. She refers to the emergence of writers in South America who have created a literature in which torture is prevalent and imagination most important. "Women are also victims of a kind of torture in a male society," she says; but this calls on her, as a feminist, to utilize craftsmanship and unusual style to evoke imagination. Men become frustrated or angry when they cannot follow her subtle language. She tells them: "You will lose something and I will lose something if I start writing simply. I write to find new dimensions." Otherwise, she says, she could turn out magazine or newspaper articles. But mostly she does not bother to explain; it detracts from the energy she requires for her creativity.

Born in the east end of Montreal, but brought up in the Snowdon area, Nicole calls herself a creature of the city. She is fascinated by cities – whether Paris or New York, which she visits frequently to keep in touch with leading feminists – and says: "I fight symbolically in the streets because the city is part of my identity, even though cities are hard on women." One of her most successful books, *French Kiss*, is the musing of a woman who walks from one end of Sherbrooke Street to the other, imbibing the French atmosphere in the east and the English in the west. Sherbrooke is an artery in a figurative as well as literal sense. The book's only English words, incidentally, are those in the title. In common with some playwrights, Nicole refused, until Bill 101 reshaped the lives and attitudes of Montrealers generally, to employ any English, even though hers is near-perfect. But in a novel which she began in 1981, many English words appear. She has also changed in her estimate of Gabrielle Roy. She admits that as a youth she disdained the older author, deciding that Roy was not sufficiently involved in feminist causes. But later Nicole realized that Roy was the first to write about urban society and its problems. Now she says, "It's fun to be able to salute Gabrielle Roy."

The recipient of the accolade takes it with quiet calm. She always doubted that young feminists understood what she did, and from time to time still senses some satire of herself. "It's rather silly," she says. "It doesn't bother me." The simple truth is that as far back as 1946 with *The Tin Flute*, a novel of poverty in Montreal, Gabrielle Roy portrayed her women as hard-working, courageous, and individualistic. "I did not label it as such." So she does feel a rapport with today's feminist writers even if she is "put off a bit" by their style. "They have talent," she says, "but I'm afraid they're spoiling it, forgetting a story must be told." Roy's last major novel, *Children of My Heart*, about the youngsters she knew as a teacher, appeared in 1977. She is something of a recluse – "I'm a runner; the moment people know where I live, I run" – and she is also a very great lady. Her comments about authors such as Nicole Brossard are not intended in any sense to be critical. "It's just," she says, "that they could have a little more human warmth and feeling, because women are the civilizers. It's up to us to change things for the better by keeping in mind always the human quality."

Marie-Claire Blais, another great story weaver, considers that her approach falls somewhere between that of Gabrielle Roy and Nicole Brossard. She categorizes Nicole (and Louky Bersianik), as "avant-garde," while she herself is "much more of a novelist telling a story in the old traditional way." She admires their radical style but warns that feminist writing as such needs to be more universal; a step beyond feminism is to combat racism, and she wonders what the feminist writers here are doing for Indian women. At the moment, Marie-Claire Blais' preoccupation is with the plight of Vietnamese refugees, though this does not reflect itself in her work. Vietnam has marked significant departure points for her. She lived in the Boston area for many years but could not tolerate the violence and tensions attending the Vietnam war. Her "French blood" brought her back to Montreal in 1975, too late for any involvement in activist or political writing about Quebec. In any event, hers has been a literary scene of much wider dimension than Quebec alone.

As long ago as 1966 Edmund Wilson, the American critic extraordinaire, wrote that "French-Canadian literature, after producing a great deal of creditable work of merely local interest, is able to send out to the larger world original books of high quality." It was specifically the writing of Marie-Claire Blais that inspired the comment. She was young then – twenty-seven; and she remains youthful in appearance at the age of forty-two, her long hair forming a brown veil that almost covers her face. Occasional glimpses indicate its prettiness, innocent of any makeup. But she is a figure of stature, having received in 1980 the Governor General's Award for her novel *Le sourd dans la ville*. Published in English in 1981 under the title *Deaf to the City*, it relates the story of a woman who searches for refuge after abandonment by the husband she loved passionately. But not all of Marie-Claire's score of books have been translated, nor has she received the public recognition in English Canada of a Margaret Atwood. Yet she says her treatment now is "not so bad" – certainly much better than it was a decade ago. Partly she attributes this to the personal rapport established at conferences among publishers and English and French literary figures.

Roch Carrier, who has done very well with the translation of his books into English, is convinced there is not enough communicating between the two sides. He points out that many more French-Canadian books are turned into English than the other way around, "and we miss some good English books." A mystery to him is why Mordecai Richler, who chose to return to his native Montreal after many years abroad, does not appeal to francophone readers. Carrier went on a French television panel show to discuss Richler's *Joshua Then and Now*, and "what we talked about was the phenomenon of a great writer not known even to francophone authors, let alone the public." What is the reason? Carrier admits that he could come up with no answer on the program; even in private conversation it eludes him.

Richler does have an answer, or at least an explanation: "French-Canadian cultural society is almost totally self-absorbed." His first books, including *The Apprenticeship of Duddy Kravitz*, were published in French – but in Paris, not Montreal. Many years later *Duddy Kravitz* was re-issued in Montreal along with *The Street*, a collection of short stories. But all along the Paris press has carried many more critical essays on Richler's works than have Quebec periodicals. "There's a strange dichotomy here," he says, recalling how he was not even asked to attend a book fair in Montreal while, in 1978, the French government invited him, all expenses paid, to a book fair in Nice. The next year the Department of External Affairs sent him on a lecture tour of German universities, at the universities' request. One stop was in Trier. Richler discovered that Camille Laurin had preceded him, to donate to the library there a collection of books by Quebec authors. As a matter of curiosity, Richler checked to see whether any of his titles were included. The answer was negative. "I guess I was regarded as an anglophone author, not a Quebec author," Richler says with a characteristic little shrug. Did it bother him? "I find it incongruous and parochial but I don't brood about it."

Richler continues to write about what he knows best: Montreal and his own background. In 1981 he converted *Joshua Then and Now* into a screenplay. But Hugh MacLennan, who also remains a Montrealer, long ago departed from the local scene artistically. His most recent book, *Voices in Time*, deals with a world destroyed by nuclear holocaust. On a kind of global kick, MacLennan, seventy-three, worries about over-population, pollution, and kindred ecological subjects. He says that his *Two Solitudes*, which came out in 1945, would be "completely inappropriate" today. Essentially, the main characters in the book, French and English, could only conclude that a massive divide kept them apart. Now their creator says: "The referendum showed me the important thing. We've learned to like one another."

To some people Hugh MacLennan's use of the word "like" may be a trifle excessive, but few would disagree that francophones and anglophones have learned to *live* with one another. Nothing illustrates this better than the way an archaic cultural world – of symphony orchestra and art gallery – has collapsed. In the place of rival or monolithic organizations have come joint community efforts that point up the better features of Montreal's character. All this transpired in little more than the last decade.

The Montreal Orchestra, as it was called then, dates back to 1929, when Douglas Clarke was the conductor. It was trained by Clarke and financed largely by the English establishment. But a clash occurred in the committee between strong personalities about who was to have a bigger say. Leading the French side, Mme Athanese David, wife of a prominent and wealthy senator, broke off in 1934 and established another orchestra that put on Les Concerts Symphoniques at Plateau Hall. The same musicians played in both orchestras, but while one had a permanent conductor, Clarke, the other engaged guest conductors such as Wilfrid Pelletier. The David venture was made possible by private contributions and grants from the Duplessis government. But for virtually six years Montreal had to support two orchestras when it could barely afford one.

The conflict ended officially in 1939, when Pierre Béique, member of a prominent family, said he would take on the task of unification on condition that programs would be completely bilingual. Béique's efforts were rewarding, but even he conceded that anglophones supported the new Montreal Symphony Orchestra far out of proportion to numbers. As recently as 1970 more than half of the season subscriptions were from members of the English community. From the French point of view, this resulted partly from a sense of alienation. Francophones regarded Place des Arts, the cultural complex which opened in 1962, as an English domain, even though it was a francophone mayor, Jean Drapeau, who had pushed for its creation. In truth, the massive campaign to raise money for its construction was headed by an anglophone whose committee was more than half English. And apart from government aid, it was anglophone society that put up the major share of the financing.

Nonetheless, Place des Arts gradually became home to French and English alike, with corresponding support for the Montreal Symphony Orchestra. Eric McLean, who draws on a background of thirty years as a distinguished music critic, thinks the "purifying fire" that pulled both elements together was the October 1970 crisis, when the communities realized they had to make peace. In any event, a much stronger sense of collaboration took place among committee members and showed up in audience figures. Today the orchestra is a healthy unifying force and one needs only to hear the preponderance of French spoken in intermissions or to glance down the list of subscribers to catch the polyglot mix. Names include Beauchamp, Prud'homme, Scott, Webster, Cohen, Papachristidis, Lomez. The orchestra has also overcome some previous bad patches caused by conflict between musicians and management. Today McLean ranks it with "the dozen best orchestras on this continent."

The history of the Montreal Museum of Fine Arts is even more extreme. In 1913, when the present building was erected on Sherbrooke Street, it was little more than a private club for a small group of collectors, almost all English. Even as recently as 1959 there were only two francophone trustees on a board of twenty-seven. Today the composition is more in keeping with the population. Moreover, the eighteen francophones on the board include such disparate types as Pierre Bourgault, arch-separatist, and Maurice Sauvé, arch-federalist. What happened to change the museum so radically? For one thing, an energetic, imaginative cosmopolite, Doctor Sean B. Murphy, became president in 1969. A good diplomat, he brought together representatives of the two communities. Born in London, of an American father and a Montreal mother who were both professional artists, Murphy grew up fluently bilingual. He took his medical degree at McGill University (where he is now professor and chairman of the department of ophthalmology), but never lost his interest in art. Just as 1970 was significant for the Montreal Symphony Orchestra, so it turned out to be a landmark date for the museum. For the first time the provincial government agreed to help funding in substantial amounts. No longer was the museum dependent chiefly on private benefactors. And no longer could it classify itself, or be so categorized, as "anglophone," for a condition of the agreement was that Quebec would appoint a dozen of the trustees. The first grant, from a Liberal government, was $200,000. The most recent, from the

Parti Québécois government, was an annual $3 million, covering two thirds of the budget.

What was once a formidable neo-classic building, intimidating visitors from the east end of Montreal, turned into a common meeting ground for English and French alike. One exhibition, depicting the adventures of a popular fictional Belgian reporter named Tintin, attracted 144,000 visitors in two summer months of 1980. The Tintin offerings may not have been as lofty as paintings from the Hermitage which were displayed in 1976. But Tintin outdrew the masters. Museum officials, answering phone inquiries (many of which wanted to know where the Montreal Museum of Fine Arts was located), judged the majority to be francophone. What impressed the museum's director, Jean Trudel, was the success of his strategy: exposure for the first time of many Montrealers to an art gallery. Trudel, forty-two, and appointed in 1977, is not only a francophone but the first Canadian in that post; two of his predecessors were Americans, two were British. "What we're aiming at," he says, "is to make the museum of interest to everyone." He feels this is being achieved, that "culturally today it is a microcosm of Montreal society." Doctor Murphy, who left the presidency in 1979 to become chairman of the National Museums of Canada, still keeps a close watch. "It's very exciting to see what's happening," he says. "It shows the evolution of an important institution. Once the spark starts, the flame grows, and the community takes note of a priceless resource."

Apart from the Museum of Fine Arts, Montreal can claim several good public galleries. Commercial galleries are not as plentiful or rich as in Toronto, yet three *vernissages* a week are not uncommon. It may be difficult to find innovative painters of the class of a Borduas or a Riopelle, but the amount of talent on the Montreal scene is comparable to any North American city with the exception of New York. Revealing, and a sign of dissolving barriers, is what happened to John Little, an anglophone artist. Little's paintings fetched, until a few years ago, perhaps $50 or $100. Today francophones pay up to $20,000 for one of his canvases because he is a chronicler of the Montreal street scene which they love so much. It is a cliché to say that art is an international language. But the cliché did not apply to Montreal earlier. It does now.

192

Mayor Drapeau's Town

It is his town, all of it – from the waterfront to the north end housing development that rises from former swampland. And as he sits behind the wheel of his black Lincoln Continental and guides his guest, Mayor Jean Drapeau explains why he loves it so much. "It's my domain. I was born in Montreal, my parents were born in Montreal, two of my grandparents were born in Montreal." Later – two hours later, still at the wheel and expounding exuberantly on everything he sees – he adds a point. "My father had a car, and I remember once when he wanted to take my grandmother, his mother, for a drive in the countryside, she said, 'I was born in the countryside. I know the countryside. Why don't you show me downtown?'" Is this the clue, why he, Jean Drapeau, is such a city boy? "Maybe, maybe." But he is not content with that, for he says, "The city is terrific, simply terrific." And it is more. It is a "world metropolis." One must never forget this. Montreal is not merely another big city. Never mind that it cannot even call itself the biggest in Canada, Toronto having slipped in along the way. It is, and to Jean Drapeau it always will be, a "world city," or, making it still clearer, "*the* city of the future."

The man is irrepressible. Ignore what the critics say – that he overspends, that he engages in wild schemes. He is the city: imaginative, colourful, exciting. Camillien Houde, a predecessor in office, was known as "Mr. Montreal." But that was different. That was in the days when Montreal was a sin town, when tourists habitually asked for directions to 312 Ontario Street, the address of an internationally famous brothel situated across the road from a police station. Drapeau helped to close down all the 312's in Montreal, so his city, while hardly a Puritan's haven, is not the flamboyant place of a generation ago. Nor does he even remotely resemble the other Mr. Montreal, in appearance or manner. Houde was enormous in size, gargantuan in appetite, with the most public of private lives. Drapeau weighs a neat 160 pounds (he is five feet eight inches); enjoys gracious dining, but not overindulgence; and refuses to serve at any pre-dinner reception the hard liquor that will mutilate the taste buds. Wine only. That is his style: quality, elegance, and the most private of private lives.

It is in public that the image is so arresting, for no one quite knows what he will come up with next. Another Expo 67? Another métro? Another Olympics? Not quite. At the moment it is a huge office and housing complex at the rear of city hall – if the provincial government will accommodate by selling the property it controls. What is a reality is the quarter in which he is now driving: Old Montreal, restored to the style of centuries ago, cobblestone streets and simulated gas-illuminated lamp posts. Drapeau slows down the Lincoln to explain in great detail to his passenger that the work that is now progressing alongside the waterfront – an expanse of several blocks, from McGill Street to Berri Street – will form a linear park that will enable Montrealers and visitors to wander near the ships and savour the city as Drapeau thinks it should be enjoyed. "Why shouldn't it be inviting for people to come and walk along the waterfront?" he asks.

Ottawa is paying the bill (the harbour is federal property), but Drapeau doesn't mind taking some credit, having urged the project for many years. The facing buildings on Rue de la Commune, many of them abandoned or neglected, are undergoing restoration to convert them into offices and residences. The work is being done with a combination of federal, provincial, and municipal financing, and a large measure of private enterprise. "Within five years you will not recognize the street," he says. Convincingly. But not defensively, for even when faultfinders over the years said he was neglecting the poor by not promoting enough low-cost housing, he held out for his concept of urban renewal. He always maintained that by moving people from old slum areas into their own isolated dwellings, whether low, medium, or high rise, you simply created new slum areas.

Drapeau explains: "I always favoured housing development, but not necessarily *public* housing. You see, I always thought of the boys and girls living there. Eventually they go to school, and then maybe to university. A girl meets a boy and they fall in love, or they like each other, and if the girl lives in public housing she will be reluctant to give her address. I always thought public housing was not humanistic." Thus, though some experts are dubious about his motives, Drapeau held out for a system in which government induced private developers to put up, with the aid of subsidies, reasonably priced dwellings built in the midst of higher priced homes and commercial establishments, so the mix would prevent segregation of poor people into what he calls ghettos. It is a concept of urban renewal that actually was ahead of its time and has caught on in many parts of North America.

So here, along Rue St. Paul, is one of these public-private projects, and, near the restored Bonsecours Market, another. The latter, Drapeau says, is intended for the elderly. He knows everything, this mayor, or at least appears to recognize each new or renovated structure in town; and one suspects he must personally approve any building permit of significance. Now, after he points out the obelisk at La Pointe à Callières, where Maisonneuve landed in 1642, he identifies the old Rasco's Hotel – five storeys of characteristic Montreal limestone – where Charles Dickens stayed in 1842 and which the city has just sold to a private developer in "a good financial deal" for both. He cites the condominiums in Old Montreal by name, knows the better boutiques, and singles out the good restaurants.

Ah, that is something, the restaurants, for the conversation inevitably swings to his own experience as a restaurateur. Would he perhaps become one again on retirement? His mind, as he ponders an answer, must go back to those days in the 1960's when he, as mayor of a "world metropolis," operated his own establishment, Le Vaisseau d'Or, in the Windsor Hotel. (While you were dining, you couldn't talk. Instead, Jean Drapeau decreed that you should listen to the opera singers who were there to provide culture. Imagine, the man who greeted you and warned you was actually the mayor of Montreal!) Only a Jean Drapeau, with his special touch and imperviousness to raised eyebrows, could get away with the incongruity of a post as mayor-cum-maître-d'hôtel. But it didn't last long, that fantasy. There were creditors and what he calls "terrorists." On the infamous night of October 7, 1969, when striking police remained off the streets, vandals stormed into Le Vaisseau d'Or and pushed it into sharp decline. But now, in his car, Drapeau arrives at a response about whether he would do it again, and says, "I never make predictions. When I retire I will decide, depending on the circumstances."

He takes a left turn and heads towards Olympic Stadium.

The people love him. Jacques Léveillée, professor of political science at the Université du Québec à Montréal, has a neat way of describing the affair: "If there is any criticism of extravagance or overspending, they say he is guilty only of a 'crime passionnel.'" The fact is they have elected and re-elected the same mayor seven times since 1954, because in Drapeau a Montrealer sees a little of what he wants in himself – imagination, daring, and romance with a city. But there are dissenters; some sharp ones such as Michael Fainstat, fifty-nine, one of two members of the opposition in City Council. All the other fifty-two seats belong to Drapeau's Civic Party.

Fainstat speaks, in awe and anger, of Drapeau's political acumen. "He is a master at being able to arrange his formulation in such a way as to make his point of view the logical one, seemingly – even if it means distortion of fact." Drapeau, with his lawyer's background, is a superb debater who knows how to manipulate legalities. Fainstat, whose background is in mechanical engineering, says, "He keeps referring to how City Council operates on a parliamentary, democratic line, knowing all the time it's nowhere near it." For example, not long ago Drapeau decided to change the procedure for hiring senior staff in the offices of the mayor and chairman of the Executive Committee. In the past, these people, as other civil servants, were required to go through the municipal civil service commission and pass standard tests, so a mayor could not reward political hacks. (Drapeau, apart from sweeping away brothels, had cleared city hall of much of the abuse left by the Houde administration.) But now the chairman's office found a loophole to bypass the commission and appoint five persons, at $30 an hour, as "special assistants." The subservient City Council automatically approved.

Fainstat called it "political chicanery." Drapeau calmly replied that it was in line with what other parliaments did. This riled Fainstat even more, because in Ottawa and Quebec City, members of the opposition are entitled to a staff and budget; but at city hall, Fainstat lacks not only a private office or secretary, but even a locker. And his point about the "special assistants" was that they were placed on a city payroll primarily to do political work – to prepare the Civic Party for the next election, in November 1982.

Drapeau's reaction to any charge of this type is to deny it and say "we follow the law," a favourite expression of his. In a bigger sense, what irks Fainstat is the autocratic manner in which the mayor, who claims the Executive Committee is the only one required, refuses to operate with standing committees. Toronto works under a series of standing committees – finance, public security, parks and recreation – with meetings open to the public. What Montreal has are "advisory" committees, which consist exclusively of Civic Party members who meet privately with functionaries. Neither the public nor the press is present. Fainstat says he has sought in vain to find out what each committee's mandate is, or even the names of the various chairmen. All information about their operations or recommendations is screened by the Executive Committee, with Drapeau's approval, before it is released to the media. Does Drapeau realize how autocratic he is? "He knows exactly how autocratic he is," says Fainstat.

Fainstat does not question the mayor's personal honesty. "Drapeau gets his kicks out of running the city single-handedly, being the only boss. He doesn't issue routine building permits, but in anything that isn't routine he makes all the decisions." To Drapeau, consultation takes place on election day. And that, to him, is democracy. Once every four years Montrealers vote "yes" or "no," and between these dates the city hall is the producer and the citizens are the consumers – isolated from the process of government. This enables Drapeau to arrive at important decisions without public debate. For instance, there was the question of a water filtration plant. It wasn't so much the expenditure of $200 million; rather, it was whether it should be a single massive plant or a series of small ones, insurance in case of accident or sabotage. In Calgary or Vancouver or Toronto a decision of this importance would have been reached only after public hearings. But Drapeau felt a single plant was the answer – and that was that.

Yet what else, one might ask, can you expect of a man who brought considerable activity to Montreal through precisely the same dogmatic tactics? The decision or initiative to start the subway, the métro, after talk spanning a half century, was Drapeau's; the decision or initiative to get the Olympics for 1976 was his. Expo 67 was pushed for and inspired by Drapeau, even if the federal and provincial governments moved in for the planning and control of costs; and the decision or initiative to revive Expo as Man and His World, an annual exhibition, was his. Again, the decision or initiative to start Grand Prix racing in 1978 belonged to him.

Fainstat is not necessarily opposed to the Grand Prix scheme. But he questions the selection of Île Notre Dame as the site for the event. (That was the same man-made island which Drapeau created for Expo 67, much to the bewilderment of Prime Minister Lester Pearson, who later admitted it took a certain kind of genius to think of and sell the idea of *making* land in the St. Lawrence River when there was so much *real* land available elsewhere.) Fainstat contends there should be a review whether Île Notre Dame would better serve as the location for low-income housing rather than racing. Montreal, he points out, is the only major city with a Grand Prix contest within its boundaries; elsewhere they're run on roads outside town. About the only notable thing Drapeau pushed for and didn't succeed in was to have the discarded liner *Île de France* tied up in port in Montreal as a permanent gambling casino. The provincial government refused.

With it all, Fainstat still finds Montreal a highly attractive city. He and his wife, Ruth, pick a different district each weekend and ride their bicycles through it, discovering new wonders all the time. What distresses him is that "city hall is such a great big enigma. It should be close to the people, because everything it does touches on their daily lives. But Drapeau has created élitism. People feel more distant from their city councillor than they do their federal MP or provincial assembly deputy." Fainstat's final word is that of a man caught in the dilemma of recognizing unusual attributes while challenging them: "Drapeau's technique doesn't take away from the special character of Montreal. We'd have an even more exciting place if there were more public debate."

The Lincoln swings onto Sherbrooke Street and there looms the great Olympic complex, a mammoth crane lurking over the stadium as a distressing reminder that it still awaits a roof. What does it matter if a project that was supposed to cost $400 million came in at a price closer to $1.4 billion? What does it matter if an inquiry, conducted by Judge Albert Malouf of the Superior Court, focussed on massive extravagance and waste? What stands out is the unwitting tribute paid to Drapeau when the inquiry cited as the greatest single cause his "personality" and "extraordinary power," based on the fashion in which he controlled every detail, just as he had done in the three decades of overseeing Montreal's evolution. Drapeau, as he clings to the wheel, and slows down slightly, asks his passenger, "Have you ever read about what happened when they built the Parliament building in Ottawa? It started in 1859, but the cost became so high they had to stop for a royal commission, and then they decided to continue. It was still an incredible cost – ten times what it was supposed to be. And they had no strikes or inflation in those days, as we had for the Olympics." So, again, Drapeau emerges with a rebuttal or answer to any contentious issue (even if there *is* slight distortion; the cost of the original Parliament building actually amounted to only threefold the initial estimate of $300,000).

In any event, the $25 million a year that Montreal taxpayers still contribute to pay off the 1976 games (of a total municipal budget of $1 billion), is "a small price" for the benefits. "People in a few years will not believe there was ever a period of criticism," Drapeau says; and then lists the advantages "that without any doubt will be confirmed more and more from year to year." To begin with: "Psychologically, in a world metropolis, it is a must to have a big stadium. In New York there used to be two – one for the Giants and the other for the Yankees. When the people heard the Giants were leaving, there was an uproar. But it was too late. The deal had been made." It is that emphasis on "the people" that also delineates the Drapeau approach. And it is quite genuine. He talks of the pleasure "the people" derive from football or soccer or baseball in the stadium, or living in Olympic Village. The Village was derided at the time of construction because of excessive expenditures. Drapeau, with a deadline rapidly approaching, and no suitable plan on hand, finally decided when a developer showed him a photo in a magazine, *Paris Match*, of a pyramid-like apartment block in the south of France. Olympic Village was a copy, and today, operated by the Quebec government and occupied by nearly 1,000 tenants (with a couple of hundred in low-rental units but others paying as much as $900 a month), it shows a profit of some $2 million a year. "No one," comments Drapeau, "now condemns the Village. It's a success."

He directs the car northward, about six miles from the city centre, to a project that he feels also answers the carpers on the question of housing – a development that is part of a program to create 10,000 new units by 1984. The concept is innovative: to sell city-owned land to builders at well below the market price, provided they construct dwellings – houses, duplexes, triplexes, condominiums – that conform to specific standards. In addition, the buyer of each residence receives a cash grant of $2,000. The purpose is to draw back to the city suburbanites, who would then pay taxes to Montreal. The man in charge of the program is Pierre Shooner, commissioner general of the Montreal Economic and Development Commission. Shooner recalls that when he worked for the Chambre de Commerce, back in 1964, he was appalled that the city lacked any department designed to encourage Montreal's growth. Drapeau was uninterested. Fifteen years later, when the commission was set up, Shooner asked Drapeau, "Why do you want it now?" "Because," the mayor replied, "the people want it." There – that phrase again; tying in with Drapeau's artful claim that he really follows, rather than leads.

Now Drapeau is highly pleased with the progress of the housing operation. In the first year and a half 3,000 units have gone up, and as he surveys the site in the north end the mayor notes that it was once swampland which the Houde administration bought from a religious order for six cents a square foot. "We're not losing money," he says, chuckling over the thought that it now goes for a minimum of $5 a square foot. What about the criticism by Michael Fainstat that the program doesn't help low-income people but rather those in a comfortable bracket? As always, Drapeau has a quick response. "If a dwelling is $300 a month, of course the poor cannot go there. But someone living in a $150 dwelling will go there, and this will open up a place for the poor." One may shake one's head in a kind of puzzlement, but before the issue is pursued, Drapeau mentions that the mayor of Toronto, Arthur Eggleton, was here a while ago and remarked that he was impressed. There was a shortage of rental housing in Toronto and he would take the Montreal idea back with him, though the city of Toronto had no land of its own to sell.

Drapeau turns the Lincoln down Park Avenue and talks of another project underway: to convert seventeen important streets, including stretches of Ste. Catherine, Sherbrooke, and St. Denis, into modern shopping areas, complete with soft lighting and parking lots. It is part of urban renewal, "to keep our own people here so they won't drive to the suburbs to buy what they need; and to attract people from the outside to shop here." And that applies to tourists as well, for "tourism should not be just a folklore affair but put to commercial use." The passenger comments that other changes are noteworthy; for instance, that Montreal has become a "French city." Drapeau prefers to call it a "European city," observing, as the car proceeds along Park Avenue, the number of Greek shops and restaurants. "We have sixty ethnic groups here," he says, "and they have not been melted down in a pot, as in the US." He goes into mild raptures about the variety of foodstuffs available in the stores along St. Lawrence Boulevard. He is somewhat more subdued when he talks about the mélange of municipalities that comprise "Montreal." In actuality, Drapeau's "domain" numbers only one million inhabitants. It is only one of the twenty-nine municipalities on the Island of Montreal, members of the Montreal Urban Community with a combined population of 1.8 million. Greater Montreal, which embraces independent suburbs such as St. Lambert and Laval, numbers 2.8 million. When one speaks of "Montreal" it is usually with the thought of all the people – the 2.8 million – who work or study or play in the city itself or are directly affected by its decrees and manoeuvres.

In that sense, Drapeau's domain is very large; and it is even bigger if one takes into account his impact on Quebec as a whole. In the past, particularly in a speech in London in the late 1960's, he referred to Montreal as a "city-state," but it is a subject he prefers now to speak of softly because of his dependence on the provincial government for financing in housing and other areas. Yet he does concede that "there are characteristics of a state" in Montreal. It goes back not only to the early days of Maisonneuve. In modern times, Montreal has developed spectacular politicians because of its unique position as the only major industrial centre in the province. The government in Quebec City lacks the kind of specialists available to Montreal, and usually loses in any contest involving such items as land use or transportation.

Thus, all along, there has been a wariness of the power held by just one city, especially when its leaders have been men like Houde and Drapeau. Implicitly it is something Drapeau recognizes, for he points to the example of Paris (Paris is a favourite of his, and he often makes comparisons between it and Montreal), which has had a mayor only in recent years because the central government, with its recollection of revolutions that began in the French capital, feared too powerful a figure as its head. "So," says Drapeau, speaking of the suspicions of the politicians in Quebec City, "I understand their mentality." Then a turn of the wheel and another sentence. "Nevertheless, they cannot prevent the development of a metropolis." But deals, obviously, can be made. While Drapeau's notion was that one island should be one city – that is, *his* city – the provincial government, always cautious, wanted Montreal to possess merely one voice among twenty-nine. The compromise was the Montreal Urban Community – with the integration of disparate police departments being its only achievement worthy of record. Drapeau, however, still retained leverage, for the Public Security Council – in charge of police – was under his control. Changes proposed by Quebec in 1982 were again opposed by the mayor.

Nick Auf der Maur, columnist and broadcaster, is the other member of the opposition in City Council. He does not get along with Fainstat, whom he considers too dour and extreme in denouncing Drapeau. Auf der Maur is also a critic, but he prefers a milder approach which includes jollying the mayor. This may or may not be appropriate for a junior who was only twelve years old when Jean Drapeau was first elected. But it is consistent with Auf der Maur's admiration – or at least respect – for Drapeau the man, and it makes for livelier times in the council chamber. Drapeau shares Auf der Maur's sense of ironic humour, and written notes frequently pass between the two of them. In one exchange, when there was speculation that Drapeau might become leader of the provincial Union Nationale party, Auf der Maur sent him a message suggesting that he, Nick, could offer the support of the Democratic Alliance (his own one-man party). Drapeau scribbled back: "I'll accept, if you shave your moustache."

In more serious moments, Auf der Maur confronts Drapeau over what he regards as autocratic methods and wrong kinds of priorities. The Dozois Plan of the 1950's (named for an opposition councillor, Paul Dozois), called for the construction of high-rise housing for low-income people. Drapeau fought it. It turned out that Drapeau was right in his disapproval, but as Auf der Maur sees it, it was "for the wrong reasons." Drapeau thought such developments would lead to sin, that residents would gravitate from floor to floor, fornicating. Drapeau was far-sighted in his concept of urban renewal – that high-rises are not the answer for a city interested in retaining a quality of life and avoiding new slums – but he should have said so in the 1950's instead of the 1970's or 1980's. Yet Auf der Maur's appreciation of Drapeau includes an awareness that the mayor possesses a feel for the unheralded individual that is lacking in other politicians. His appeal is to blue collar or working-class people, to whom the city's spending on such grandiose schemes as the Olympics means employment. (The fact is that in the 1978 election, two years after the Olympics, Drapeau took 61 per cent of the vote, compared with his nearest rival's 26 per cent.) "He is not stupid," says Auf der Maur. "He understands his supporters." Auf der Maur keeps in mind a favourite expression of Drapeau's: "Don't measure projects with a one foot ruler."

Today Auf der Maur admits the errors of his own ways. At one point he resisted, as an unnecessary expenditure, the continuation of Expo 67 in the form of Man and His World, until, in 1975 – a year after he became a city councillor – he visited the grounds and chatted with people there. Many of them were pensioners or men and women of modest means who could not even dream of taking a trip to exotic places; yet there they were, surrounded by pavilions of foreign countries and by masses of lovely flowers. On the basis of that experience, Auf der Maur decided that Drapeau was right and from then on supported the continuation of Man and His World.

Drapeau parks the Lincoln on an incline of Atwater Avenue, in order to show his guest what lies below: construction of a condominium on land a developer bought from the Sulpicians, the religious order identified with the earliest days of Montreal. The property, a large expanse on which a seminary still stands, embraces Montreal's oldest existing landmarks, two stone towers dating to 1694. Neither the seminary nor the towers are touched by the development, and Drapeau says, "The land was of no use, but people put up a stupid fight saying it had historic value." That is strong language – "a stupid fight" – especially when one takes into account that a leader of the fight was Mrs. Phyllis Lambert, daughter of the late Samuel Bronfman, the liquor magnate, a distinguished architect in her own right and president of Heritage Montreal, a foundation that has conducted a campaign for the preservation of old places, not from an antiquarian view but for the broader sake of a decent atmosphere for everyone to live in.

Mrs. Lambert strongly condemns the city's approval of the building of Le Fort de la Montagne, the condominium, as "privileged housing for privileged people." Her main objection is that it was the site of "a great historic place, a beautiful piece of land that everyone should be allowed to enjoy." As for Drapeau himself, Mrs. Lambert says bluntly that it is a myth to believe he was a pioneer in urban renewal. He started to think of conservation only *after* it was an established trend in North America. "He was not an instigator, he was a follower." Moreover, it was the province, not the city, that began to designate that certain buildings must be preserved, after the public outcry that followed the clandestine demolition of the mansion once occupied by Sir William Van Horne, a builder of the Canadian Pacific Railway.

Drapeau is impervious to Mrs. Lambert's reproof, and, as he surveys the condominium site below, he repeats that the land has no historic value, "none whatever." But it is of commercial value because it is bringing in people who will spend $185,000 to $300,000 per apartment, and pay taxes in Montreal. "The more they pay," the mayor says, "the less the load will be on the poor." The tour continues, on to Jeanne Mance Street where one of his achievements – Place des Arts, the cultural centre – stands. He reminisces about how he sold prominent anglophones on the location, among them J.W. McConnell, the newspaper proprietor and industrialist, who, in turn, persuaded his great ally, Premier Maurice Duplessis, to contribute to the financing. Now the district is thriving with such relatively new structures as Complexe Desjardins, and, under construction, Complexe Guy-Favreau, and just below it, due for completion in 1983, a convention centre. The cranes rise, and Drapeau is already thinking ahead, to what may well happen one street to the west.

That is a stretch on Bleury Street that consists of dilapidated stores and the ancient Wilder Building, occupied by generations of garment manufacturers. But soon it will all come down, if Drapeau's planners can complete a deal with a developer. It calls for a combination of office buildings and apartments, at a cost of at least $75 million. "We must co-operate and facilitate the work," Drapeau says, "but we cannot provide all the money." Again his emphasis is on private enterprise. And again his concept is of a blend between dwellings and offices to keep the heart of a city pumping all the time. Place Ville Marie was a great accomplishment in collaboration with his friend William Zeckendorf, the American builder, but now, in retrospect a quarter of a century later, it lacks a dimension. "People work there, but why should they leave Place Ville Marie and go far off to home?" he asks. "At night it is dull. There must be life." That is why he has insisted on the inclusion of housing if the Bleury Street development is to succeed.

To reiterate his philosophy he drives east several blocks until he comes to the corner of Ontario Street and St. Lawrence Boulevard, where he can point to an old tobacco factory whose structure is still sturdy, allowing for the interior's conversion into apartments for the elderly. The financing is by Quebec; but the urging, Drapeau makes clear, was by the city in its effort to bring more and more residents to the downtown area. It is quite incredible how Drapeau appears to know of every new building, every development under way or even in the most preliminary of stages. But then one remembers that on many days he works from 7:00 A.M. until midnight and this is his domain; or, as he again expresses it: "The city is terrific, simply terrific." He appears to know his people equally well, for frequently he repeats that they want only "the best," the finest in quality, whether it is in a subway station or a baseball team.

His judgement, his evaluation of the people – even to their political leanings – can be quite impressive. His passenger remembers an earlier conversation, just before the 1981 provincial election, when Drapeau was asked how he thought he would be able to get along with Claude Ryan if the Liberal leader became premier. "Wait, wait," said the mayor, "it's too early to know how the election will go." He was one of the few men at the time who did not cling to a belief that the Liberals would defeat the Parti Québécois. "All right," his questioner had persisted, "assuming theoretically that the Liberals win, how do you think you'll get along with someone who once called you a 'megalomaniac'?" Drapeau, as always, had his answer. He counted off the names of the premiers whose regimes he had survived – a total of eight! His approach, he said, was always the same; he simply told each, "You are the boss." That was a beautiful bit of Drapeauism, for all, with the possible exception of Duplessis, found themselves up against a man who could not be outmanoeuvred. ("Yeah, he can come up with things like that," says René Lévesque. "He's an old fox.") Interestingly, Ryan, who, as editor-publisher of *Le Devoir*, wrote extensively and unflatteringly about Drapeau, now, as politician, acknowledges that the mayor reflects the spirit of the city. "Drapeau personifies that very well," he says. "Despite my grievances with him, I have to recognize that he went beyond his own roots – into a city of international and multicultural dimensions."

Drapeau's conviction about a global view from Montreal persuades him that "separation is impossible." The people would never support such a move. Moreover, he is convinced that Premier René Lévesque and Claude Morin, the former minister of intergovernmental affairs, think exactly as he does. "They have both told me so. They are working with their minds as well as their hearts, while some others work only with their hearts." Not long ago, before an audience in Chicago, Drapeau predicted that Quebec would no more become an independent state than Illinois would leave the US union. Montrealers, with their own determination, will make sure of that. This is underscored now as Drapeau steers the Lincoln down St. Dominique Street, towards city hall, for he is on to a favourite topic: a future – like the past – based on the constant factor of Montreal's geography. He goes into a lengthy recital about how Maisonneuve, when he had a mandate to establish a city, turned down a suggestion from the governor of New France to create it on Île d'Orleans, which was close to Quebec City, and which would have enabled the two communities to help one another. But no; Maisonneuve said his "duty" pulled him towards Ville Marie. (The crafty founder, wanting to keep as far as possible from other authorities, had an autonomous city in mind.) The St. Lawrence River was the "autoroute" then; and the next great artery will be Mirabel Airport. Oh, yes, says Drapeau with utter confidence, that is clear. Mirabel is the only airport in the world capable of operating twenty-four hours a day without disturbing masses of people. It boasts the potential for handling 60 million passengers a year, and 100 million tons of freight. "It will be the first super airport in the world," he says flatly.

The statistics roll off quickly and easily; and so do quotations from a lengthy report prepared by the Canadian Institute of Guided Ground Transport at Queen's University. "Do you know," he says, "that Mirabel could become Toronto's international airport?" High-speed trains would link Toronto, which faces a shortage of its own airport space, with Mirabel – in one hour and thirty-six minutes. And New York? That would take only three hours and would be faster than the delays encountered in the congested approaches to Kennedy Airport and the roads leading into Manhattan. Such high-speed trains operate even now in France, and, with the coming of the age of hydrogen fuel, will be practical here within a few years. "High-speed trains will play the same role the port of Montreal did in making this a world metropolis," Drapeau declares. "This is how I see the future."

One does not quibble over such a pronouncement. How can you, with a visionary who created an artificial island for Expo 67? But just in case his image of Mirabel proves faulty, Drapeau has begun looking into the development of a revolutionary type sailing vessel, faster and steadier than any predecessor and eliminating the use of oil. Tom Paskal, an editorialist on the now defunct *Montreal Star*, remembers writing an optimistic comment in 1979 under the heading: "The Bounding Main." The next day he was tracked down by a Drapeau aide who said the mayor would appreciate receiving all available information. Paskal sent over his file. Later he received a note from the aide apologizing for any trouble the mayor's curiosity may have created. Paskal replied, "Trouble? Hell, it pleased me that my mayor, the mayor of Montreal, is so aggressive and forward-looking."

What, one asks Drapeau, does he regard as his greatest accomplishment? Expo 67? The Olympics? The métro? There is no hesitation. The métro, "because it is used by all the people, all the time." He knows every station by heart, for each has its own character, shunning the uniformity and blandness of most subway systems. At the Berri-de-Montigny station the mural and glasswork pay homage to Maisonneuve, Jeanne Mance, and other figures of history. At the Lionel Groulx station the profiles of members of the family of man are carved in an old walnut tree trunk. The Cremazie station is distinctive for its large ceramic zodiac signs and the faces of poets – and so on, down the line. Montreal is the only city in the world, states his worship, where tours for VIP's include a run through the métro "I've taken General de Gaulle, I've taken Prince Rainier..." And he lists them – royalty and statesmen. But then his listener raises a technicality: what about the Moscow subway, which also attracts important visitors? "Yes," says Drapeau, conceding that Moscow's underground sculptures are of interest. "But on this continent, we are the only city."

One simply does not win against this indefatigable spirit, for he is as much a zealot as was Maisonneuve. "Montreal," he says, "was built for history." Now, arriving at city hall, he drives the car into the garage and escorts his guest up the elevator to his office and the terrace adjacent to it, for the pilgrimage is not yet over. One is obliged to stand there and look northward beyond Champs de Mars, the old military parade ground, to an open stretch alongside the Ville Marie expressway. For six blocks on that site, from St. Lawrence Boulevard to St. Denis Street, Drapeau visualizes a linear park bordered by a variety of buildings designed for work and living. The property is owned by the province, but Drapeau, with his usual confidence, anticipates no problem in striking a deal in which the municipality will purchase it and then sell it to a developer who will put up exactly what the mayor has in mind. For use by "the people."

Does he possess a simple definition of a Montrealer? Is the Montrealer like a Berliner or a Parisian or a New Yorker? Well, no. "We are at a different level," he says, "but our people are proud. The pride may be in the conviction they have about the potential of Montreal. It will never be killed, it will never be empty."

A final word. Right after the Olympics, Councillor Nick Auf der Maur wrote a forceful book attacking Drapeau for his overspending. Now Auf der Maur, in frank admiration, says: "If I were elected mayor of Montreal tomorrow, I would rename it 'The Jean Drapeau Stadium.'"

Anglophones Who Stayed

Frank R. Scott, the great poet, constitutional law expert, and civil libertarian, was the son of an outstanding man, Canon Frederick Scott, who spent four years as a chaplain in the trenches of the First World War and returned to Montreal to receive the acclaim and affection of an admiring public. Frank Scott, now in his eighties, recalls that when he was in his thirties, and deep in the pacifist mood of the post-war times, he said to his father, "I am afraid that if they give you a military funeral I shall be unable to attend." Without hesitation, Canon Scott replied, "That's all right, Frank. As long as I am there, it will be a success."

Obviously, something special emanated from that kind of home climate of tolerance and human understanding. But also with it came a mixture of attitudes, on Frank Scott's part, that one can only attribute to changing times. Apart from his pacifism, he was also an early supporter of the Co-operative Commonwealth Federation (CCF), which in those days marked him as a "radical." But mainly his concern was for the individual and the individual's rights, and this is best illustrated by his recollection of what happened in the early 1950's when Premier Maurice Duplessis' government enacted legislation which dictated that all stores must close for Catholic religious holidays. The major English department stores (Eaton's, Morgan's, Simpson's), decided in concert to defy that law and remained open. Police arrived, and fine after fine was imposed, but they fought the case to the Supreme Court – much to Scott's pride – and won it, on the grounds that religious holidays were not statutory holidays. Yet today there is a kind of ambivalence in his attitude. He approves of the departure of the Sun Life, saying company officers opposed what he regarded as unconstitutional measures by "voting with their feet." Conversely, he deplores the way numbers of anglophones have abnegated responsibilities by migrating from Montreal, and he quotes an old French expression: "Les absentes ont toujour tort" – the absent are always wrong.

It is difficult to know precisely where Frank Scott stands, because of these contradictions in his views. However, without citing him, one can perceive a sad reflection of anglophone attitudes in the behaviour of the Montreal business community during the St. Léonard episode of little more than a dozen years ago. Companies, including the big department stores, refused even to support financially the battle against educational discrimination that was, in its own way, equivalent to the Duplessis act of the 1950's. Much is now different. The most dramatic change in Montreal's anglophone community ("dramatic" may be too strong a word, perhaps "significant" would be more appropriate), is in the *spontaneous* outpouring of defence mechanisms against real or perceived francophone threats to English-Canadian identity.

A mere century ago – indeed, even as recently as the Duplessis era – there was no question about who ruled the business or social interests of Quebec. It was the established order of the English and the Scots, of course; and it controlled the full range of political affairs, even if it was by indifferently allowing premiers of the province or mayors of the city to operate autonomously until they offended the minority – that is, the non-French. There are still in industry such men as David Culver, of Alcan, and Eric Molson, of the Brewery, but theirs is not the approach of the tough-fisted barons of generations ago. It is, rather, the gentle acceptance that life has changed, that roles have tumbled, that the businessman's position must be one of willingness to accept the will of the majority. It is not submission. It is, rather, suppleness, and for that reason much more fascinating than the behaviour of the old-style tycoons.

Simultaneously, a new breed of anglophones has emerged to defend the English community's rights. These are men and women of much humbler backgrounds – economically, socially, ethnically – than the old squires of the Square Mile. They include teachers, lawyers, homemakers, and students. Theirs is a grass-roots movement, with only the vaguest co-ordination and without the leadership of any dominant individuals. Because of this, it draws on the strength of persuading many francophones that there is indeed a changed attitude on the part of anglophones who have elected to remain in

Montreal and to immerse themselves in the overall community, even while they cry out for preservation of the identity of the smaller community.

A representative story is that of Joan Dougherty, a spirited and attractive woman in her early fifties who has managed to engage in the delicate task of remaining in Montreal while her husband was obliged to join his head office move to Toronto – because she believes anglophones must learn to adjust to new realities. "As an individual," she says, "I've resisted the image of protector of English rights. I don't feel that. I much prefer to be thought of as bringing the English into the mainstream of the province. The new Quebec anglophone is going to be different from the old." Simultaneously, she is resolved to show that the anglophone instinct for survival is great, and so is the determination to keep it that way.

Much of this she demonstrated in a vital sector, perhaps the most vital – the education of children. As chairman of the Protestant School Board of Greater Montreal, Mrs. Dougherty found herself having to answer a question that other advanced educators and community leaders have faced: at what stage should society accept a common school board instead of the anachronistic system that still prevails, of separate Catholic and Protestant boards? She concedes that one day, maybe not too far off, this will be inevitable and desirable: "But the time is not yet right psychologically. When the English community sees its *institutions* going down the drain it sees itself going down the drain. Until mentalities on both sides evolve, and we're all comfortable, we'll need to keep the present institutions."

Part of this stubbornness now is her conviction that the Parti Québécois is out to destroy the anglophone presence. The technique, as she assesses it, is both blunt and subtle. Bill 101 was an arbitrary measure, and several years later it is still not clear to some families whether or not their children are eligible for English schooling. That is blatant Parti Québécois ingenuity. Meanwhile, the Protestant School Board has created a dozen centres where buildings are shared by both French and English pupils. But a subtle campaign has been underway (through francophone media commentators and Parti Québécois members of the National Assembly), to end the sharing and move children studying French into the Catholic French school system. Under the British North America Act, the provincial government cannot force a Protestant child into a Catholic school. But some immigrant youngsters are now enrolled in the dual centres, coming under the influence of both French and English-speaking peers – and these are the government's concern. The propaganda campaign is essentially predicated on the argument that there is something intrinsically wrong, illegitimate, about Protestants developing a French "alternative." To put it in Mrs. Dougherty's words: "What they're saying is, 'Hey, that's not what we intended.' " They really intended, she is persuaded, that anglophones should leave Quebec altogether; not stay and adapt, as she and others are doing. Are the anglophones going to survive? "You're damn right," she says adamantly. "By getting with it, by refusing to be put down. We'll be smaller, but we'll be here."

In her mind, the big villain in all this is René Lévesque himself, whom she considers intellectually dishonest – posing as a defender of minorities but in actuality having no use for anglophones. "He still thinks that we're all of the same stripe, that all anglophones are demons determined to destroy French culture and identity. It's to his advantage to maintain the stereotype because polarization of English and French keeps alive his movement. We have to prove, by our actions and deeds, that we're not the demons." Mrs. Dougherty's own contribution was to allow her family life to be altered. Her husband, Donald, senior vice-president of Simmons Limited, the furniture manufacturers, has lived in Toronto since the firm decided to move its headquarters from Montreal in 1976 – a month before the Parti Québécois victory. He commutes weekends to their home in the Town of Mount Royal, accepting his wife's belief that it is her responsibility as a native Montrealer, educated at McGill University, to remain a member of the community.

Maybe, if one wanted to be cynical, it could be argued that Joan Dougherty had another personal need: the need to be part of an active scene. She had worked on many local citizens' committees and generally enjoyed a full and stimulating life in community affairs, the kind that might be difficult to pick up again in a new city. But that is peripheral. Overriding everything else is what she calls "a gut feeling." She says, "Canada will be made or lost in Montreal. The degree to which we – anglophones and francophones – can learn to live together in Montreal will determine what can be done in the country at large. If we can make it work it will prove to people everywhere that a bicultural society is not restricting but enlarging." Her five children, ranging in age from twenty to thirty and in occupations from physical instructor to physician, share this view, and continue to live in Montreal despite the departure of many of their friends.

Mrs. Dougherty's latest involvement was to run in the provincial election of April 13, 1981. It was an auspicious introduction to politics. Her riding, Jacques-Cartier, which embraces much of the Lakeshore area of western Lachine, Dorval, and Pointe Claire, with two thirds of the residents anglophone, gave her the biggest Liberal vote in the province: 24,900 versus her Parti Québécois rival's 4,800. Apart from a desire to battle Lévesque in parliamentary style, her inspiration for the new career was the belief that government has taken over too many of the functions that citizens once handled at a local level. People have become "dehumanized," having lost the ability and power to make sensible decisions. "You see a terrible transformation in school boards. Men and women have become form-fillers instead of teachers."

Mrs. Dougherty recognizes that overbureaucracy (usually justified by rulers in the interest of economy), is a universal phenomenon. Moreover, in a touch of irony, much of the process of government manipulation and centralization took place in the 1960's during the tutelage of her own Liberal party, headed then by Jean Lesage. But she feels it has now gone too far in Quebec, and here is where Lévesque re-enters the scene, again as a knave. "Mystical collectivity that must override individuality is a *péquiste* device. It is used by Lévesque to put down individualism, especially anglophone, and is nothing less than degradation of individual dignity." She hopes to combat from the benches of the National Assembly the kind of creeping bureaucracy she was unable to deal with as an outsider – and to teach members of the Parti Québécois that diversity can be an asset. "They see it as a problem," she says, "but I want to prove that the kind of society we have here is a source of richness rather than something to get rid of."

The individual touch, the work at the community base, is not quite lost, despite Joan Dougherty's misgivings. Evidence to the contrary is provided by another lively woman, Anne Usher, who at one time even took on the Protestant School Board. That was because Mrs. Usher believed – with reason – that the level of French education was abysmal. This awareness was reinforced when she found that her daughters were being taught in the same futile half hour a day from the same text books she had used twenty years earlier. She and her husband, Robert, a pediatrician, had decided as long ago as the 1960's that they were going to remain in Montreal regardless of the emergence of francophone power. Indeed, it was that emergence, and the realization of her own inadequacy in French, that turned her into an activist on the street committee level.

Mrs. Usher, a nurse, worked as a volunteer at the Clinique St. Jacques in a low-income French neighbourhood, and was struck by how much could be done effectively by all kinds of people – not only doctors and nurses but plumbers and carpenters – who contributed their time and skills to provide services to a needy public. To become even more sensitive to this new world, having been a product of the middle-class, mostly English-speaking area of Snowdon, she took an intensive course in French at McGill University – and made the discovery that many other anglophones were also appalled by the low quality of French teaching provided by the Protestant School Board. Living then, as she does now, on Melrose Avenue in the mixed district of Notre Dame de Grâce, she joined with neighbours to attend school meetings. "We had one purpose in mind," she recalls, "and that was to push for a better product out of the school system. But the school board was putting out a different message – that the system was good enough for any English-speaking child." She categorizes the officials she met in the Protestant School Board at that time (and one needs to note that it was in the 1960's, long before there was a Parti Québécois or a Bill 101), as not only "all-powerful" but "racist-purists" in their determination to protect the entrenched dominance of English Montrealers.

A tall, striking blonde, with a strong streak of Irish obstinacy (her immigrant mother's side), Anne Usher decided in 1973 to run in school board elections. She was defeated. Her opponent, she says, told people: "Vote for Usher and English schools will be French within five years." Oddly, she determined that it was older, retired men and women who bought this line and turned out in the thousands to reject her. Her peers – she is now in her mid-forties – wanted to see, as much as she did, the entry of anglophones into modern times. "It was a painful experience," she admits. "It showed me there were large numbers of people who had not been caught up in a positive way by the Quiet Revolution and still held anti-French prejudices." But she didn't quit in the drive for better French education within the English system. (The Protestant School Board of

Greater Montreal has made "tremendous" advances, she concedes. "Today, a middle-class child has a reasonable chance of coming out of the system with the necessary tools to start a decent contact with francophones.") Nor did she lessen her involvement in other community affairs.

In 1980 (after serving five years on the Quebec Council on the Status of Women), Mrs. Usher was elected president of the Community Council of Notre Dame de Grâce, a collection of fifty youth and adult groups funded provincially and federally. Notre Dame de Grâce is a polyglot ward of 73,000 people of low to middle incomes, of whom 40 per cent are francophones. The rest, apart from older anglophone residents, include Italian and Portuguese immigrants and a large number of blacks from the Caribbean. The mélange is interesting and stimulating. (Yvon Deschamps, the monologist, was once a neighbour of the Ushers, whose children by now had learned "good" French in school; he taught them "street" French.) While council meetings are conducted in both main languages, Mrs. Usher finds a curious hangover from the days of parish lines that suggests a different style between anglophones and francophones in how they go about achieving objectives. While "parish" no longer carries the religious definition or designation that it once did, some French Canadians are inclined to refer to "parish members" when they say "we need something." They mean that the parish itself, represented by lay people with maybe a priest or two, will somehow get it done. Anglophones believe more in citizen power, of spreading out and recruiting everyone in the neighbourhood, whether or not they are spiritually members of the "parish."

But it is changing. To francophones it is becoming increasingly plain that they are not members of a parish but of a neighbourhood called Notre Dame de Grâce. Citizen action, therefore, bypasses boundaries – linguistic, religious, or cultural – especially when youngsters are involved. Residents of Beaconsfield Avenue, a blend of anglophones and francophones concerned about the safety of their children, united in the spring of 1980 to put up their own signs warning motorists of the 30 KPH speed limit when city action proved sluggish. Mme Annette Duhamel, a mother in her mid-thirties who works with Anne Usher on the council, wanted the city to buy an unused gasoline service station at the corner of Monkland and Girouard Avenues, and convert it into a mini-park (children nearby had no playground); the official response was negative. Anglophones such as Mrs. Usher could draw from hard experience in attracting media attention and planning petitions. They pulled behind Mme Duhamel in a concerted campaign and obtained the mini-park. In 1981, Mme Duhamel set off another citizens' movement to improve traffic safety when a new métro station was due to open, along with a greater number of connecting bus routes, in an area frequented by students from three schools.

What has Anne Usher learned since she and her husband made their decision to stay some twenty years ago? To begin with, there have obviously been no regrets. She feels their three daughters – Heather, nineteen, Susan, seventeen, and Kathleen, fourteen – are better, more rounded young women for having shared the Montreal experience. But an even broader lesson emerges: "What we've learned is that if you can focus on the human condition, people will identify with issues they're concerned about, ignoring whether it's an 'anglophone' or 'francophone' matter. To an older person interested in developing local services – meals-on-wheels or home-nursing care – the need is for allies, regardless of whether they're English or French. The same applies all along the line, with the young as well, and that's where our future lies."

The informality of the Anne Usher effort may have limitations, but it is complemented by the more highly organized approach of Alex K. Paterson, a prominent lawyer. What he shares with Anne Usher and Joan Dougherty is the belief that anglophones should find their way onto school boards, government commissions – indeed any agency where possible on the local, provincial, or federal level – so they can have a direct involvement in decisions that affect everyone. Only then will the anglophone community be able to claim its share in the future of Quebec. Paterson arrived at these conclusions over a period of time, but initially "something quite personal" struck him after the Parti Québécois victory. Born in Montreal in 1932, he had never really thought of his ancestry. But, taking inventory after November 15, 1976, he realized that his forbears went back several generations and had made a contribution to Quebec. The basic question was whether to leave, as others were doing, or to remain and engage in constructive activities.

"Quebec needs a pluralistic society," he decided. "If we cop out now it will be an end to the English presence completely. Rather than be the cause of this turnabout, let's be the interpreters of Quebec to anglophones in Quebec and outside the province." Thus the Positive Action Committee came into formation, with Paterson as a founding member and co-chairman. Meetings included representatives of business, professional, and academic groups, each with his own idea of how to deal with the Parti Québécois. But the common objectives were to persuade English Montrealers to accept the premise that the French Fact was indeed a fact, and to offset the francophone feeling that anglophones automatically were obstructionists – to make them realize that there were moderates with whom they could deal. This did not go unnoticed in the French media when Positive Action contested portions of Bill 101, so that a prestigious newspaper like *Le Devoir* gave the committee appropriate respect.

The name, Positive Action, was well chosen, for it did take steps when it felt abuse from any level – something of a throwback to the Montrealer with a city-state mentality, who always stood up against what he felt was an injustice. "We raised hell," is the way Paterson describes one incident involving the federal government, which, in 1978, decided it was going to move a fisheries laboratory from Ste. Anne de Bellevue, outside Montreal, to Ottawa. Positive Action, whose members, happily for the organization and the community, include Montrealers influential in politics, argued that here was an operation that employed not only francophones but anglophones who had come from all parts of the country – an important mixture for a Liberal government trying to promote the cause of bilingualism and biculturalism. Paterson suspects that the initial declaration from the department was inspired by two or three anglophones who didn't like living in the province. But their machinations would have affected forty to fifty others and eroded the federal presence in Quebec. The department reversed itself.

Later, under the Conservative government, the Department of Transport announced it intended to transfer one of its divisions from Montreal. Paterson and others in Positive Action feared that if this took place it might give Canadian National and Air Canada an excuse to pull out, so a telegram was sent to Dan Mazankowski, the transport minister: "If the government of Canada cannot hack it before the referendum, how can we argue with Sun Life and others who say they are going to move?" Mazankowski replied that the

217

announcement was due to an error committed by the previous government, and on re-examination the planned move was now dropped. Paterson does not claim that Positive Action is entitled to all the credit. Mayor Jean Drapeau and the Chambre de Commerce had been among other protesters.

Indeed, Paterson is objective enough to say, "As far as corporations go, I am convinced that we haven't changed the minds of anyone who had already decided to move." Then he adds the key point: "But if we hadn't said anything when they did move, others might have followed." Positive Action took a sharp line against Sun Life, going on radio and television to proclaim that the insurance company's decision to leave Montreal was "absolutely unacceptable" to many anglophones. Paterson is persuaded that Sun Life directors had never anticipated that their own friends would turn on them; and it was this kind of condemnation that may have made them re-think positions of other companies on whose boards they sat. There is little doubt that Positive Action's publicly proclaimed views, so far-sighted and untypical of the old establishment's dogma, encouraged some francophones to vote against sovereignty-association in the referendum.

Like others, Positive Action takes exception to the extremism of some Parti Québécois measures, such as unilingual signs, and what many anglophones regard as meanness or pettiness. But Paterson recounts a telling episode. He and a few other members of Positive Action invited, in 1979, five prominent *péquistes* to dinner at the McGill faculty club. He describes the atmosphere as "progressively strained," so that by the time dessert arrived hardly a word was spoken. But one of the *péquistes*, a gentle and sensitive man, said he thought he should say something appropriate, knowing what was on the minds of the anglophones. "It's like a horse that has been in the stable all winter, with the door bolted," he explained. "At last it's spring and you open the door and the horse dashes out, kicking whoever is in the way. He doesn't mean to do it deliberately, but he's been cooped up so long he can't help it." There was a pause and the speaker implored, "Don't blame him."

Paterson understands the francophone mood and is optimistic about the future. "We've got everything going for us," he says. "The challenge is to keep the young people from moving out. If we don't turn this around, we, the anglophones, are in trouble. But if it has indeed turned around, we're okay."

The reality is that, after an initial outflow, young people are staying so long as jobs are available. This is the conclusion reached in a survey published in 1981 by the Allied Jewish Community Services. Of the 500 men and women between the ages of eighteen and thirty-five who were questioned, a majority, 59 per cent, planned to remain in Montreal assuming employment prospects were good. Another significant group, 30 per cent, though undecided at the moment, said their answer would be affirmative if work opportunities presented themselves. This single factor far outweighed language or politics. Yet, curiously, these young people were not arriving at an entirely drastic decision. Even from the earliest notice of a shift away from Quebec, much more was made of the shift than of the point that many anglophones, young included, had chosen to keep faith with the province. A good example is Robert Raich, who graduated in law from McGill University in 1976 and was sworn into the bar the day after the Parti Québécois took over the government. Most of his classmates left for positions elsewhere. He stayed. "I love French Canadians," he says. "They don't take themselves too seriously. They know how to relax." But his fundamental reason was more practical. He was interested in tax law; and the field was wide open. Now, barely thirty, he is one of the leading experts in Montreal and further ahead, financially, than his contemporaries who settled in Toronto. His confidence in the future is such that on April 14, 1981, the day after the Parti Québécois was returned to office, he bought a duplex.

Sarah Scott of Westmount, twenty-four, took her BA at Queen's University and a master's degree in journalism at the University of Illinois. She worked for a year and a half in Washington on the *National Journal*, a weekly specializing in government affairs, and decided in 1981 to return to Montreal, even though, apart from occasional visits, she had not really lived there since the age of twelve; (her father, an investment broker, was located for several years in Vancouver). "Originally I'd planned on Toronto," she says, "but then realized I didn't want to be second fiddle to the US. Toronto or Lethbridge or any other place in Canada is so immersed in American culture, I might just as well be in the US. After sampling Washington, I knew that was not what I wanted. It was a conscious decision to come back to Quebec. I wanted to live in a French environment. Here I have my own identity."

Barbara Bourke, who is more than double Sarah Scott's age, chose to remain in Montreal even though her two sons – Steven, thirty-one, and Michael, twenty-nine – live in Toronto and Vancouver; and her daughter Julia, twenty-three, is an architecture student at Princeton University. As a divorcée, and theoretically mobile, why has she stayed? "I've asked myself many times," she replies without attempting to provide a simple answer. She was born in Montreal, into an upper middle-class family, and education included fashionable Trafalgar School and McGill University – thus there were roots. But these alone were not the motivating elements. Ironically, too, she calls herself "the token anglophone" in a francophone office. This is an oddity, for she works for Canadian International Paper, a subsidiary of Canadian Pacific Enterprises Limited. But a technicality backs up her claim, for she is the only anglophone among eight members of the public relations department. Then, again, why stay on? There is sensitive thoughtfulness. While, earlier, she had a sense of the "rightness" of the francophone cause, she confesses now to "a certain resentment" over the way "the pendulum has swung" in petty matters of language. "But it hasn't gone far enough, at least yet, to drive me away. Friends who've moved to Toronto say, when I visit there, that Montreal is a dead city. If anything, it's more alive than ever – but I don't even try to argue. They don't want to hear."

For the Scotts and the Bourkes, or any Montrealers who might require moral bolstering, there are several informal groups they can turn to, the most representative of them being Participation Quebec. Betty Palik, a freelance journalist, and her husband, Michael Prupas, a lawyer, were in their late twenties when the Parti Québécois election sweep stunned the anglophone community and set off fresh departures. At that point there was no language legislation to disturb the couple, no heavy talk of a referendum. So their attitude was not one of hostility towards the Parti Québécois; instead, concern was directed at the negativism of the anglophones. Accordingly, they invited a score of friends to their home – a modest but charming house on Chesterfield Avenue in Westmount – with the intention, as Betty recalls it, "to allay panic by saying the anglophone community could adapt." After three or four such casual sessions the group decided to hire a hall, and that was how Participation Quebec (which drew 250 members, mostly in the age bracket nineteen to thirty-five and from the professions of medicine, law, and education, with some businessmen), came into existence.

Later, when the white paper on Bill 101 was published, they took the view that freedom of school choice should be open to all Canadians but that immigrants should be directed to the French sector. That was an unpopular stand with the anglophone press which rejected any restrictions. As Betty Palik, who is president of Participation Quebec, explains it: "We knew the political realities. We felt we would have no credibility with the francophone community if we demanded complete freedom of choice." But they did fight portions of the bill. The point was that Participation Quebec, like the Paterson group and other moderates, put up opposition where required, while taking a basic stand that anglophones must learn flexibility. French-language newspapers such as *La Presse* and *Le Devoir* were impressed, and gave extensive coverage to Participation Quebec, with the general editorial comment that it was a young group trying to be Quebecers. But an important function for these campaigners was to provide what Betty Palik describes as "soulmates" for English Montrealers who wanted to stay but were pulled in other directions by fears or uncertainty about the future.

In a sense, Participation Quebec became like Alcoholics Anonymous. "We would ask ourselves," says Betty, " 'God, why are we staying?' We had supportive answers from each other. Now we look back on those as 'the old days' and reminisce about the bewildering time when you either quit or tried to take part in a constructive thought process. We never recruited. It was all word of mouth." Now, too, the tone has changed. The originals who gathered on Chesterfield Avenue, people who have almost without exception become successful in their business or professional careers, no longer feel a sense of urgency. They have indeed adjusted to the reality of the bigger French community around them. They no longer need the moral support of five years ago, or engage in the soul-searching that went on then, or over-react to every government move. Today they talk about their children, their vacation plans, their expanding opportunities.

Some established members of the community can credit Participation Quebec with at least providing a footing when it was required. Robert J. Doyle, thirty, who is with one of Montreal's most distinguished law firms, says that he attended meetings partly for social reasons, but largely to be reassured by serious discussions. Whether or not these talks actually swayed him in his decision to remain in

Montreal, he is not sure. But the sum is that he did remain, and he adds up his experience with Participation Quebec this way: "It was helpful to all of us. It took our minds off newspaper headlines and put us in the position of thinking things out for ourselves."

With the relative calm of the last couple of years, the group drew fewer people to its meetings; but in 1981 it enjoyed a revival through an infusion of younger participants. A common component that unites the younger with the older members is awareness of the importance of French as a language. Those who enjoy a good knowledge of it, feel comfortable in Montreal; those who are less proficient demand greater reassurance about their future. Eileen Wong, twenty, in the McGill arts class of 1983, took 40 per cent of her high school subjects in French but says, "It still doesn't give me anything like fluency. I'm barely functional." Nonetheless, she has no intention of quitting Montreal when she graduates. "My parents are Chinese. They migrated here in the early 1950's, and I've never experienced any prejudice. I want to make it here." So confident is Eileen on the future that she voted for the Parti Québécois in the 1981 election because of what she regarded as a social program superior to that of the Liberals; she says she would not have supported the Parti Québécois if she thought that separation was even a possibility.

Neil Saxe, twenty-one, McGill class of 1982, says: "What I've discovered is that older people take the attitude that youth either want to stay or to leave. What they don't realize is that there's a great big grey area in between." It was to reach that undecided area that Eileen and Neil volunteered to meet with CEGEP students, bring along university professors, and discuss the pros and cons of remaining in Quebec. Many students, they found, would say, "What do I know about it – whether or not to stay? It'll depend." And that, in turn, relates largely to the attitude of parents. Have these younger agents of Participation Quebec made converts? "We aren't trying to," says Neil. "We just want to get them thinking."

The process of "thinking" individually begins roughly after the age of twenty-two; in general, young people in the twenty to twenty-two age group have rarely encountered any unpleasant experiences themselves with francophones, but usually tell of an incident "that supposedly happened to someone else." The authority for this statement is Eric M. Maldoff, who has followed studies and surveys closely. He concludes: "You cannot overestimate the influence parents have had, just sitting around the dinner table, talking about situations that may or may not have occurred." Maldoff, like Robert Raich, was admitted to the bar the day after the Parti Québécois formed a majority in the National Assembly. As he was being sworn in, he wondered, "Is this the beginning of the shortest legal career in the history of Quebec?" He decided not only to stay on but to do something about establishing better communication and contact between Montreal's anglophones and francophones. (One notes with interest that while there was some departure of law graduates, a disproportionate number of lawyers, including the Alex Patersons, have immersed themselves in community activities.)

Maldoff was one of the founders of Participation Quebec. A few years later he was founding president of Alliance Quebec. Basically composed of members of Participation Quebec and Positive Action, the alliance provides an umbrella for dozens of ethnic organizations plus a variety of professional associations (teachers, nurses), to present a wide representative consensus. One purpose is to counteract the old notion that the political process involves only francophones, not anglophones. Another is to let the government know, in Maldoff's words, "that there are people out there watching." But primarily the alliance's aim is to attack the government's effort to dismiss non-francophones as disparate "ethnic" groups, to prove that the common and forceful link is the English language.

"We have learned, and we want others to learn, that members of the anglophone community are members of a linguistic community, not of different ethnic communities," says Maldoff. "They share an attachment to the English language." But even before the formation of the alliance, its predecessor, the Council of Quebec Minorities, of which Maldoff was head, did valuable work. Being able to draw on the expertise of its associates, (lawyers, for example), gave the council a strong weapon in contesting language regulations. For instance, Bill 101 stipulates that new entrants in any of thirty-eight designated professions – law, medicine, nursing, and accounting among them – must, after a specified period, pass tests to show proficiency in French. The council contended that the way in which the tests were given was unfair. For one thing, these were broken into two main parts: oral and written. If an applicant failed one, but passed the other, he or she received no credit, and therefore was unable to concentrate on the defective area for the next time around. Moreover, marks stated only a combined pass or fail, with no indication of where the weakness lay. The council succeeded in getting the regulations amended.

But some battles are virtually lost from the start. Article 20 of Bill 101 says that an individual who applies for a job in the public sector – the provincial civil services or Hydro-Québec – must possess a knowledge of French "appropriate" to the position (with no definition of "appropriate"). This includes the most menial of tasks, even the digging of a hole for a power pole. An Italian immigrant must pass a test to see if he can match a francophone competitor linguistically. "Who do you think will get the job?" Maldoff asks rhetorically. His objection here is that there is a difference between "francization" and "francophonization." When discrimination is involved, Maldoff, who generally empathizes with the French-Canadian cause, will fight back. His philosophy is this: "We're not giving yards, but we're also prepared to see the other point of view. Bill 101 was at first perceived as vindictive – it still may be – but when you relate it to francophone fears about continuity of culture, the challenge becomes: 'Let us understand why a certain measure has been introduced, so we can bring about changes that will help both main groups in Quebec society.' We've learned that this process of understanding is important."

Maldoff has thus calculated: "I feel I was right in staying. If level heads can prevail, Quebec can look to a very positive future. Those of us who stayed, and have become competent in French, enjoy an ideal situation. The demand for our skills and services is just going to grow. I feel annoyed at times, but I don't feel threatened – as I did in 1976. I didn't understand then what was happening. What I have found is that hostility towards me was not the principal objective. The objective was the pursuit of a French-Canadian national goal."

More recently he has also found a greater willingness on the part of members of the francophone media to look at the deep worries of the anglophone community rather than settle for superficialities. Soon after the emergence of Alliance Quebec, Maldoff, in February 1982, was interviewed by a Radio-Canada television journalist, André Bedard. In a taped session, Bedard asked only routine questions, such as how the alliance was funded. The interview over, Maldoff said, "If you have a moment, let's talk about other things." Bedard had a moment, and Maldoff went on: "We're not concerned about technicalities. We're concerned about the most fundamental issue –

Quebec society. The government is trying to tell Quebecers that Quebec is composed of ethnic groups, and the English are just an ethnic group. This is the basic cause of the anxiety of the English-speaking community, because English-speaking Quebecers see themselves as members of a *linguistic* community composed of all sorts of different backgrounds, origins, and religions. The social contract of Quebec has always recognized the legitimacy of two linguistic communities. When the government denies that reality, and unilaterally tries to change the contract, people will reach the conclusion that if reason doesn't work, the only alternative will be radicalism. The government is therefore promoting radicalism by discrediting reason and moderation, and it will have to bear full responsibility."

Several days later Bedard called Maldoff to say he had just seen the tape of the interview and it could not compare in interest and impact with what the Alliance Quebec leader had said afterwards. The interview was repeated and Maldoff's frank words went out to an audience of hundreds of thousands. "A year or two earlier, I wouldn't have been this blunt," Maldoff says. "Anglophones didn't know how to articulate, and the francophones were not listening. Therefore we were dismissed out of hand. But finally the message is beginning to be heard."

Among business firms, some who stayed – and met challenges – found unexpected dividends. Monty Berger, prominent in both community affairs (he is a past president of the Canadian Club), and public relations for more than thirty years, faced a substantial loss when clients began to move to other cities. He decided that the way to keep them was to stay with them. Thus he opened new offices. His company spread to encompass not only Montreal but Ottawa, Toronto, Calgary, Edmonton, and Vancouver – making him one of the leading practitioners in Canada. New clients have been added to old.

Perhaps no single vignette better illustrates the positive attitude found among anglophones than the case of Campbell Gordon. Lean in face, tall and slender, Campbell is an intense, appealing man of twenty-six. His French is flawless, the result of the advantage of constant contact with a French-Canadian nanny during his up-bringing, and of later education abroad, including Paris. None of this might be noteworthy, other than it recalls a vestige of the fading

Old Montreal aristocracy. But Campbell's tale has more to it than that. His father, the late Donald Gordon, who was president of Canadian National, was hanged in effigy by students from the Université de Montréal for remarking that no French Canadian was a vice-president of the publicly-owned railway because he had never met one with the proper professional qualifications.

Campbell Gordon was five at the time, and, of course, has no recollection of the incident or the furore it caused. But he is well aware that it remains alive in the minds of French Canadians. When he returned to Montreal after an absence of ten years, he was astonished at first to discover how people recalled it; even people of his own age who could also have had no first-hand memory of an event dating back to 1961. But the Donald Gordon gaffe has entered nationalist lore as a classic symbol of an anglophone mentality that was impossible to live with. It keeps recurring today in snippets in the press and on television. "It's one of the things nationalists can hang their hats on," says Campbell, with both insight and a trace of sadness. What is so touching to him – and Campbell talks freely of it because of an obvious great affection for his father – is that Donald Gordon loved Montreal. He was never anti-French, but his comment was seized upon and lifted out of context; (he had also said he would not hire an Indian or anyone else who wasn't qualified). Donald Gordon, according to Campbell, was very upset by the reaction and regretted having made what he himself conceded to be an insensitive remark.

In any event, what gives the son's story substance is that Campbell – after taking history and law at Trinity College, Cambridge, then obtaining his LL.D at Dalhousie University, Halifax, and working summers for Gerald Regan, the Liberal leader and former premier of Nova Scotia – was tempted by two choices: to make a life in the UK, a place he liked, or accept a job offer when Regan went to Ottawa to become a Trudeau cabinet minister in 1980. He chose another alternative: Montreal. "I'd always had back of my mind that I'd like to work for a francophone company," he explains.

There was, in a way, strangeness in Montreal. He had lost touch with an entire generation; almost all his former classmates from Selwyn House, a private school in the old establishment tradition, had departed for Toronto, Calgary, and other points. And when he encountered francophones, some expressed frank astonishment that the son of the notorious Donald Gordon was still around. He also met Robert Gratton, president of Crédit Foncier, who offered him a position as his assistant – which he accepted. Crédit Foncier, an old trust company, has grown into one of Canada's largest mortgage lenders with branches in eighteen cities, from St. John's to Victoria. So, from young Gordon's point of view, the business challenge was wide open. But most appealing was the opportunity to be thrust into the francophone milieu.

Gratton himself, at thirty-seven, was representative of "the élite panzer corps" – a graduate in law from the Université de Montréal, then Harvard Business School and London School of Economics, followed by a period as executive assistant to Paul Gérin-Lajoie, who was minister of education in the Lesage government. Ironically, as a U de M student, Gratton was said to have been one of the planners of the effigy execution of Donald Gordon, though he claims he was in New York during the actual incident. But Campbell feels comfortable. "Even francophone nationalism, despite its negative aspects, is exciting," he says. "Montreal is a city with an immense tradition of conversation – in a European sense. There is debate and dialogue in and between the communities. It's not the pretentious or hard and competitive conversation that you find in Toronto. Montreal is more intellectual."

But why did he really come back? Did he choose to work for a francophone company, maybe unconsciously, to make amends for his father's blunder? He admits that he did give great thought to this, and "perhaps in a way, even slightly consciously," he elected deliberately to return to Montreal to knock out the old image of Donald Gordon. This much out of the way, however, he does not feel confined to Crédit Foncier. He might be willing to go somewhere else in Canada for a short while. But always, he says, his intention is to return to Montreal. He agrees there is a gap – a large group of missing Montrealers of his generation – but he is also aware that increasing numbers like himself have come back to augment the ranks of those who continued to stay on. He regards the next five to ten years as crucial to Montreal's economic future; and this hangs on the willingness of governments and of people to get together. If they do, "there'll be a real turnabout; if not, there will be failure, caused by failure of will."

This is a strong young man, Campbell Gordon. Donald Gordon surely would have liked what he has done.

The Future

Robert Bandeen, as president and chief executive officer of Canadian National Railways, could hardly have been hanged in effigy. He commanded a modern and positive view of Montreal and the province, open to no misunderstanding. As he expresses it: "The new francophone generation wants to be treated just like any other new generation; that is the change compared to the old French-Canadian generation. There is a similar break in the anglophone community; the new generation doesn't think it has a God-given right to run things." This he says after pointing out how it struck him (when attending a recent cocktail party given by Donald Gordon's widow, Norma), that the Old Guard, French as well as English, stuck together: "And suddenly I realized they were of another age."

Bandeen, a tall, cheery, expansive man of fifty-one, is a native of Rodney, Ontario, and a graduate in economics and political science from the University of Western Ontario and Duke University, North Carolina. He is gifted with an astute and sensitive ability to translate broad ideas into simple, understandable examples. For instance...as a member of the Saint James's Club, he had noted how it tried to offset financial difficulties by conducting "Italian" or "Greek" or other ethnic nights in which the menus were designed to lure patronage. He assumed that the same principle was in operation at the Mount Royal Club (to which he also belongs), when, after a lengthy absence, he went there for dinner. He thought it was "French" night. All around him he heard French spoken. Soon, however, he realized that the diners were francophones, now members of what, not long ago, was virtually an anglophone enclave. They had risen high enough in the economic scale to qualify for membership.

That was one touch. Another irony was that most of the old waiters spoke no French. The francophones gave their orders for drinks and food in English. It was a nice twist of the departed image of French Canadians as retainers. Does it presage the fate of the anglophones who have stayed: a future as a tiny minority in menial tasks? Some of the Old Guard voice such a fear; but francophones like Michel Bélanger of the Banque Nationale du Canada warn instead that the future of Montreal depends on a strong anglophone presence. The facts indicate that while Montreal has become a "French" city, the position for the anglophones who can adapt and contribute remains robust. Roger Lemelin, the author-publisher, characteristically translates any uncertainty into an earthy hypothesis. "Suppose," he says, "you take all the English from Montreal and move them to Toronto. Do you know where the revolt would come from? The French Canadians from the east end, because they cannot live – physically or psychologically – without the English Canadians."

How does Bandeen regard the future of Montreal? "Montreal has never lost its role as a transportation centre," he says. "This will build up even more." He cites as "fortunate" that the two major railroads, Canadian Pacific (CP), as well as Canadian National (CN), both based in Montreal, tie in with expanding world needs. Like CP, CN sends its experts abroad, building or operating railways in Pakistan, Korea, and other countries. By being there, they indirectly encourage people in these places to look to Canada for other forms of technical guidance and products. More directly, however, Bandeen anticipates a bright tomorrow for the merchant marine. Very few vessels are registered in Canada (the whole of the CP fleet comes under the UK), because of regulations which demand payment of corporate taxes on all earnings, even if ships never touch ports here. An attempt is being made by CN to persuade the government to tax only those earnings made in Canadian waters. If that happens, many foreign owners who don't like Liberia or Panama might well move to Montreal. Ottawa understands this, but is afraid of a precedent, that multinational corporations would demand the same tax treatment.

Bandeen is hopeful that the CN argument, going on for several years, will prevail, especially since there is now added strength to it: with the decline in value of the Canadian dollar, foreign shippers would find it attractive to pay their crews here. So, for that matter, would Canadian-owned companies such as the Cast Group, which operates the biggest fleet of container ships between Europe and Canada. Cast, in which CN holds an 18 per cent interest, works out of landlocked Switzerland. Its logical base would be Montreal. (In a flashback to that historical period when Quebec City lost out to Montreal as a principal port, CP moved the terminal facilities of its container ships from Quebec City to Montreal in 1979, to take advantage of the closer rail link with the US midwest.)

"If we get the merchant marine to come to Montreal, and we build on the railways, we've a bright life ahead," says Bandeen, who then pauses and adds: "But I should say outright that I like Montreal." And that is a clue he is eager to provide, his contribution to the evidence that personal reasons, rather than corporate, often motivate chief executive officers. In many cases the anglophone who could not adjust to the changed climate of the province, especially to the dominance of French language, pulled out and took his firm with him. As a Crown company, CN is protected by the federal languages act which calls for bilingualism. Moreover, by law, it must be located in Canada. Thus in any breakaway by Quebec it would shift from Montreal. Yet even without separation the railway could have taken other measures. "Headquarters," for political reasons, could still have been claimed in Montreal even if only the chairman and a secretary stayed on, while the rest of the corporation moved away. The positive factor is that the board of directors, which functions independently from Ottawa, takes into account the reality that Montreal is still the transportation hub of the country. Unlike CP with its many divisions (among them hotels, airlines, mining), spread across Canada, CN continues to operate virtually all its empire from Montreal, with the principal exceptions of trucking and telecommunications, which are located in Toronto.

Any major move would be disastrous for Montreal. The maintenance shops alone employ between 4,000 and 5,000 men and women. Expansion, rather than contraction, is projected, with something like $5 billion to be spent in capital additions and equipment by 1985, much of it in the Montreal area through purchases such as more locomotives from Bombardier. Bandeen turns to the constructive example of Alcan allocating $500 million for a new smelter in Quebec and says, "a certain amount of faith is needed in big business." Essentially, he concludes, people from the outside who come to Montreal either love it or hate it. "I've found no one on a middle ground." He himself happens to be one of those who love it, and so do his wife and four sons. He left the CN presidency in March 1982, in keeping with his belief that no one should stay in such a post more than eight years.

Patrick J.J. Rich is another transplanted devoté of Montreal. A senior officer of Alcan, the fifty-year-old native of Strasbourg emerges as a remarkably unorthodox type, with a fertile, imaginative approach to life, plus some extraordinary talents unrelated to the production of aluminum. A graduate of the University of Strasbourg and Harvard, Rich had barely started to work for Alcan when he was called up by the French army and fought as a paratroop captain in Algeria. A brilliant musician, he played piano nights at the old Berkeley Hotel in Montreal – an unwittingly far-sighted and appropriate choice for, renovated, the hotel is to form part of Alcan's new international headquarters scheduled for completion in 1983.

Rich sports a short, neatly cropped beard and a quick, lively voice. As a Frenchman and internationalist (he speaks six languages), he can scrutinize the Quebec scene dispassionately. "The Lévesque government," he says, "will go down in history as the government that removed an inferiority complex. At the same time, the whole legislative apparatus of Bill 101 basically put the anglophone community, especially the younger members, in a position confronted by hard facts which say, 'Let's adjust.' You don't adjust to a situation unless there's an obstacle. It's like throwing a big rock in a stream; the water will find a way around it. The anglophones are discovering that another culture can be an exhilarating experience. And more francophones are now prepared to look at both sides. It has to add up to something positive. No city in the world can match Montreal's present opportunities, because people now are much more economically close to one another. In New York the Hispanics are so far below the general economic level that there are tensions. If there is a poverty line in Montreal it is not confined to French Canadians. Montreal will be the laboratory in which a social consensus will emerge."

Rich's wife is Québécoise. Each of his three children was born in a different country: Jean-Luc, nineteen, in Guinea; Eric, sixteen, in England; Natalie, fourteen, in Argentina. Because of them he developed an awareness of problems that many nationals do not encounter. "Children of international managers," he says, "are far from being privileged. They are deprived children. They encounter emotional insecurity, going through changes of friends and environment. The basic challenge for a child is to cope with the straitjacket of education, and when you keep changing it every two or three years it becomes an even greater burden." Thus Rich, who moved to Geneva in 1982 to head Alcan's European operations, found himself recruiting support from the Chambre de Commerce and the Board of Trade to establish schools in Montreal that would conform to an international curriculum and offer consistency to the families of men whose organizations keep transferring them from country to country. Its universality would attract not only multinationals with offices in Montreal, but such agencies as the United Nation's International Civil Aviation Organization which are located here. In 1981, the Department of Education approved the concept, with the first students to be enrolled by the autumn of 1982 in the pursuit of an international baccalaureate. The province subsidizes these institutions, in addition to its support for private as well as public schools in two languages and three religions (Catholic, Protestant, Jewish). This special flavour to Quebec education was often forgotten in the controversy that accompanied Bill 101.

The Frenchmen in Montreal bring special credentials in making comparison, since language works in their favour while heritage – that is, a bond with French Canadians – may be a handicap. But even the latter factor does not bother Louis Jalabert. He sees only the affirmative side of life in Montreal. Jalabert, who was born in Marseille in 1924, is a stocky man with shaven head and forthright manner, president and general manager of BNP Canada Incorporated, the offshoot of the Banque Nationale de Paris, one of the biggest financial institutions in the world. Jalabert thinks big, too. The new BNP head office for Canada, at the corner of De Maisonneuve Boulevard and McGill College Avenue, will become much more than that if he has his way. It will serve as BNP headquarters for all North America. The bank, with an attitude that dictates that Paris is the centre of the world, supervises its branches in New York and Chicago from Paris. To Jalabert the simpler answer is to regard Montreal, because of geography and duality of tongues, as the nucleus for the whole continent. He expects to be able to sell this idea to his chairman.

Part of his case is based on a passionate belief that Montreal is just at the start of a ten year growth period. He comes by the figure with a banker's mathematical precision. His first contact with Montreal was in 1961 when he became his bank's chief representative here. That work went on for ten years, during a prosperous era, and then he was assigned to Australia for another decade. Now he regards "the miserable years," the sluggishness of Montreal's economy that coincided with his absence, as perhaps necessary, for it meant that anglophones and francophones were busy discovering one another. In a simple illustration he, like Robert Bandeen, notes that in the 1960's the Mount Royal Club was almost exclusively a Wasp establishment, and he was unacceptable. This time round, when he returned in 1980, he encountered no difficulty in joining. Equally, he remembers that when a French Canadian met a Parisian in an elevator in Montreal he spoke English to him; the francophone was sensitive about his accent and afraid the Frenchman would mock him. But that's all finished. "There are no more complexes between the French and French Canadians, because the world is too small. Thousands of French Canadians visit Paris, and many French come here. It's completely different."

On a more profound level, Jalabert anticipates that the outlook for Montreal is bright because of the strength of its light industry and service sector, while Toronto is vulnerable to the illnesses suffered by heavy industry in southern Ontario. Toronto's power as a financial centre? Jalabert thinks it is a mistake for money institutions to flock to the same place. "When the ships all go together I prefer to stay on my mountain." Interestingly, BNP located itself in Montreal because it is easier to attract medium and upper executives, thanks to the French fact – a reverse of the Toronto syndrome that induced some anglophone firms to pull away. In summation, Jalabert says, "In 1961 I was frustrated – by the anglophones and also the francophones. But today I feel comfortable. That's why I'm so optimistic." To this he adds, "Toronto is at the end of its growth period. Calgary is limited. But Montreal has a new start."

Americans, especially those in banking, express a similar tone of confidence. Robert L. Davidson, fifty-two, a Californian who became a Canadian citizen in 1982, sits astride not only two countries but much of Asia and the rest of the world, having worked most of his career for the giant Citibank of New York. He is now chairman, president, and chief executive officer of the Mercantile Bank of Canada, in which Citibank holds 25 per cent of the shares. The Mercantile, the seventh largest bank in Canada, keeps not only its head office but its *entire* head office operation in Montreal, unlike the Royal Bank of Canada and the Bank of Montreal which have transferred substantial functions to other cities while still calling Montreal headquarters.

The Mercantile story is one of good corporate citizenship – and it is also the story of how a business might be conducted on the basis of wisdom and experience acquired the hard way in other parts of the world. Davidson arrived in Montreal in April 1977, five months after the Parti Québécois victory, and was asked by the board of directors to study whether this was the proper place to retain the bank's head office. Davidson analyzed the usual elements for and against, but always kept uppermost a lesson Citibank learned in the Second World War. With the Japanese already in Burma, and a fear that they would soon invade India, the bank closed down its branch in Calcutta. The Japanese never did reach India. Davidson was posted there in 1970 and found people still saying, "Why did you leave?" As the smoke from his pipe drifts up to blend with his grey fringe of hair, he quietly observes that "the ill-feeling had persisted more than a quarter of a century."

Davidson examined the list of Mercantile's customers in Montreal – among them Alcan, Hydro-Québec, the City of Montreal – and remembered the maxim learned by Citibank: Never leave a trouble spot voluntarily; wait until you are thrown out. "Governments come and go," he says, "but Alcan and others will stay on. There would have been bad relations for generations if we had left." In retrospect he also says that staying on was easy to decide, because "with any experience in international business you cannot get too excited about politics in Quebec. The situation here is benign compared with Chile or Central America." Mercantile employs 200 in its Montreal office, of whom twenty are vice-presidents and other executives. There has been no problem in bringing people from other cities. But in fact, Mercantile was able to benefit from the transfer of the bigger banks of some of their departments. It recruited from among the executives, computer experts, and others who did not want to leave Montreal.

Davidson regards with skepticism the switch to Toronto of money operations by other banks. In his judgement there are many considerations other than the actual place of work of traders. His staff, located in Montreal, can maintain instant contact on direct lines with New York, London, Zurich, and other centres. The governor of the Bank of Canada works in Ottawa, along with the minister of finance, and Montreal is closer to Ottawa than is Toronto. Davidson also likes the idea that Alcan – which has divisions in thirty-five countries and which follows the money market – is located close to Mercantile in Montreal. "But the big impact on the money market, whether we like it or not, is in New York or Chicago," he argues. "It is not in Toronto." Another major point he introduces is this: "I think it's important to keep all your team players together. If they're spread out, they lose contact."

In any event, Davidson looks beyond the label of whether one city is bigger in one way than another. Raised near San Francisco, he remembers how it was the dominant city in California until after the Second World War, when Los Angeles became the industrial centre. Yet the quality of life still makes San Francisco the more attractive city. His advice to Montrealers: "Don't try to be Number One in finance. Work on what you've got – quality of life."

Though there is hardly any doubt that, taking into account the stock exchange and other ingredients, Toronto is the financial capital of Canada, there is some question about whether it is the *banking* centre. Rowland C. Frazee, chairman and chief executive officer of the Royal Bank, the largest in the country, submits the question himself. While conceding that the Royal's own corporate banking is focussed on Toronto, he also emphasizes that such major functions as international banking are still concentrated in Montreal. More importantly, the key decision making remains in Montreal, and while many of the bank's executives live in Toronto, "they don't call us to Toronto; we call them." Even in terms of business generally, he feels it is almost impossible to work out the relative positions of Toronto and Montreal – which is Number One and which is Number Two. On what basis, he asks, do you determine comparison? On the number of employees in a company? On assets? On volume of trade?

Montreal, he believes, puts up a respectable performance when it comes to the big head offices: the Royal Bank, Alcan, Seagram, Power Corporation, the railways. In multinationals, with overseas as well as domestic operations, Montreal is ahead.

In 1977, when he became the bank's president, knowing he would be named chairman and chief executive officer in 1980, Frazee initiated a study into the economic prospects for Canada in the 1980's. The bank's specialists and economists identified several areas in which Canada's prospects would develop: for example, energy. Shortly afterward the Royal Bank expanded its energy department in Calgary. But first on the economists' list was trade, consistent with Canada's position as a major trading nation, and forgotten by many Canadians in the preoccupation with energy. "I see this international outlook as something to which Montreal should be directing its attention," says Frazee. "I don't know yet in what form – perhaps a free port. But I do believe that, given our geographic position, the future could be built around export and service. The two major railways are here. Alcan is here, and so are SNC and others – all in the export mould. That is why I have a lot of confidence in Montreal's future." Thus, once again, there is a reminder that history, related to geography, might well repeat itself.

William Mulholland, chairman and chief executive officer of the third largest bank in Canada, the Bank of Montreal, concurs with Frazee. Speaking of the head offices that have quit Montreal, he says, "It's nonsense to think of this as the end of the world." He is bothered by the possible effect on peripheral establishments, such as the legal profession and advertising firms, but in sum he says, "Montreal is not down and out. It's changing." So, too, is the Bank of Montreal. Off the sepulchral lobby in the St. James Street head office is a tiny museum, with memorabilia recalling that this was the first bank established in Canada, in 1817. But using the slogan First Canadian Bank has created some confusion. One of the buildings in First Canadian Place, the Toronto complex, is called First Bank Tower. But Mulholland is careful to point out that the bank merely rents space, it owns no part of it. He also recounts how he was showing a visitor through the executive suite in Montreal, and he warned him to be careful, to watch out for the construction material lying about. "We've just built a new boardroom," Mulholland explained. The visitor, a businessman from out of town, went on for a step or two, and then, in a movie-style double take, halted and said, "What?" He had thought the boardroom and head office were in Toronto.

Even though much of the bank's operation is indeed conducted in Toronto, and a new high-rise in Calgary serves as regional headquarters, Mulholland is emphatic in explaining that the head office remains in Montreal. His sensitivity may be based partly on the fact that he is American-born (Albany, NY, in 1926), and therefore feels entrusted with a special responsibility to keep the bank in the city of its name. Yet he is hardly a softy. He has a record as an infantry company commander in the US army in the Philippines in the Second World War, plus a reputation for stern managerial style. A bit stocky, he is athletic and powerful in appearance, and he can be slightly forbidding when an interviewer remarks that the Bank of Montreal is probably the most decentralized bank in Canada. "That," says Mulholland, who lifted the one-time ailing institution into a thriving position, "is your description." Then he relaxes, grins, and says that at least he has no intention of moving. "I don't think I could move. I've got two houses, nine children, six horses – and one wife."

This is not entirely a facetious rationale, for Mulholland agrees that decisions to move head offices are made more often on personal than on business grounds. Plainly he likes Montreal ("I'm not staying here to punish myself"), and the quality of life that enables him to switch from his city home to his farm, in the Eastern Townships, in an hour. Into this affection enters a distinct sense not only of community but of national responsibility. Though he has stood up to the Parti Québécois on issues affecting industry, Mulholland would need to be hard pushed to pull out. "It would be harmful to the country," he says. "It would be divisive, pouring gasoline on a fire. The bigger you are the more sensitive you have to be towards community and country."

One of the most optimistic notes about the future comes from the head of one of Quebec's biggest financial institutions, Alfred Rouleau, president of Le Mouvement Desjardins, the credit union association with $15 billion in assets. "There's a new mentality in Montreal," he says of the anglophones and francophones. "When we speak together we understand each other better than when we stayed apart." Equally, the mentality of rural Quebec towards the big city has changed. Where non-city dwellers in the past were suspicious of the moguls in Montreal, there is now a perception of trust and confidence. Complexe Desjardins, the handsome cluster of hotel and offices in four towers which opened in 1976 at a cost of $206 million, obtained nearly half its financing from credit unions outside the city.

In recent years the changes in Montreal, and in the habits of its residents, have ranged from the superficial to the profound. Among the lighter observations, one can record the swing away from Geneva gin, "le gros gin," which derives its characterization from a distinctively hardy taste and smell. Quebecers trace their proclivity to the liquor to the arrival of the first shipment from Holland in the 1790's. Later, the De Kuyper distillery in Montreal could count on Quebec for 90 per cent of its annual sales of $7 million; ("De Kuyper" is virtually part of the French language). But in 1979 it was impelled to introduce London gin, such was the impact of the trend towards the more sophisticated dry martini ("avec un twist"). It may or may not have been coincidence, but around the same transition period francophone radio and television stations began to broadcast Dow Jones and Toronto Stock Exchange indexes; previously they had considered that there was little interest in such vulgar commercial matters.

As far back as 1967, when the Chambre de Commerce and the Board of Trade decided to move into the same new building on Beaver Hall Hill, members of the rival organizations thought it might be appropriate to engage in a symbolic gesture. So a twin-trunked tree, representing comradeship, was hoisted at the topping-off ceremony. But each continued to go in its own direction, as it had for a century; until – in the late 1970's and early 1980's, under the leadership of Pierre Lortie and Arthur P. Earle – the two combined in some notable joint ventures. They showed that, finally, the anglophone and francophone business communities shared common interests.

Leo Kolber, the astute head of CEMP, the agency that oversees Bronfman family investments, recalls an incident that occurred in 1968 when he was chairman of Grey Cup weekend in Montreal. He held a meeting with members of the Chambre de Commerce and Board of Trade to discuss festivities, and it began with a demand by the Chambre that the conversations should be conducted in French only. A long argument followed, and finally Kolber said that since his English was far better than his French, why not allow each participant to speak his own language? That's the way it was done, but it still lingers with him that here was a chance for Montreal to shine in an important national event – and the two principal arms of business were at odds over language priority. No longer does this happen. At combined sessions of the Chambre de Commerce and Board of Trade both languages are automatically used, as it suits the individual, in a refreshing spirit of co-operation and a foretaste that before long people might switch back and forth from one tongue to the other in comfort. Since French is now an established fact, francophones realize they have ownership of themselves by saying, in effect, "I'm me, and I'm proud of it." It is an encouraging sign of the times, just as is the experience of an anglophone businessman who, after moving to Toronto, decided eighteen months later that he wanted to live again in Montreal. He bought back his old home for $100,000 more than the $250,000 he had been paid, shrugging his shoulders and saying stoically, "I know the house. I like it. I built it."

Among the other reassuring trends is the distinct shift of emphasis in newspaper headlines. Only a few years ago, Quebecers, along with other Canadians, were reading a dismal litany of Montreal's troubles; in 1981, articles dwelt on the positive. "Good news," announced the *Financial Times* over an editorial. "In 1976 the economic crêpehangers said a Lévesque government would ruin the Quebec economy. In fact, Quebec's economy has grown by 14.5 per cent – in real terms not counting inflation – since 1976. This is almost twice as much as the 7.7 per cent growth in Ontario, the most comparable provincial economy." In a special section on Quebec *The Globe and Mail* declared: "Dramatic change in PQ-business climate." *The Gazette*, in a series pointing out that the hard knocks of the 1970's had ended, said: "Montreal's economy making a comeback." *The Toronto Star*, describing the paradise of dining, boldly decided: "Montreal still top city." *The New York Times* headed a report: "Building Activity Gains in Montreal." And *The Journal of Commerce* had no hesitation in deciding: "Separatism Behind it, Montreal Booms."

The Journal of Commerce connection with Montreal is noteworthy. The distinguished paper, published in New York since 1827, specializes in news about shipping and transportation. Because Montreal in recent years has returned to a position it occupied a century and a half ago, when it was perceived as a challenge to the port of New York, the *Journal*, for the first time in its history, opened a bureau in Canada in 1981. Its chief, forty-five year old Leo Ryan, is based in Montreal. For seventeen years he was a correspondent in Europe. "The port of Montreal is the jewel of the Montreal economy," says Ryan, and this is reflected in his reports on how it is winning traffic not only from New York but from Baltimore and Boston. The latest contest involves coal. Hampton Roads, Virginia, a major port close to Virginia and Pennsylvania mines, had enjoyed brisk trade in shipping coal to Europe. But because of long delays (up to six weeks), in clearing dock facilities there, the Cast Group was able to persuade US producers and European users that it could guarantee speedier and cheaper service, despite the transfer of several hundred miles by rail to Montreal. This denotes the rediscovery of the St. Lawrence River as one of the world's great transportation corridors.

Arthur Earle, a burly man who exudes confidence both in his Board of Trade capacity and in his position as senior vice-president of Dominion Textile, likes to cite how a gallon of fuel will move 600 tons of cargo one mile by water. "The same gallon of fuel will ship less than half the distance by rail, one tenth by truck, and one hundredth by air. The port must and will expand, and the accelerating world price of fuel will keep it full for many years to come." But that goal requires thinking and planning, and one of the remarkable features of life in Montreal today is the fashion in which not only the Board of Trade and Chambre de Commerce function in unison, but businessmen, trade unionists, academics, and government officials are able for the first time to sit at a common conference table. This was demonstrated in a two day session in March 1981, when the subject was the expansion of the port and business facilities in Montreal generally. Premier Lévesque admitted that the city had been neglected in the province's quest to establish industry in smaller towns. But now he said the emphasis would shift to Montreal.

One of the participants, Louis Laberge, president of the Quebec Federation of Labour, observed that there wasn't "one derogatory comment" during the entire conference. In terms of the traditional rivalry between labour and management, this to him was meaningful. Even more startling, however, is the way Laberge, leader of the biggest trade union federation in Quebec, talks today. He spent eight months in jail in 1972 for urging hospital workers, on strike, to defy a court injunction to return to work. But now, at the age of fifty-seven, he says, "If I had to go the same route again, my eyes would be more open." Does this imply that he would not advocate defiance?

"Well…" There is hesitation in the response, but one has a clear impression that Laberge would be cautious. The fact is that a degree of mellowness has replaced the militancy of a federation that not so long ago contributed to the image of a province swept by labour disputes.

Laberge, a short, rotund man who is colourful and expressive, talks about Montreal as "one of the great cities of the world." He adds: "There have been problems between anglophones and franco-phones, but nothing like the problems you see in other parts of the world. Toronto, with its racism, is a lot worse. In Montreal there is tolerance – no, that is a bad word, acceptance would be better – that everyone can be at home here. Things have changed." And this is when he delivers a philosophy that would have been unmentionable a few years ago. He wants labour to become involved with government and industry in the development of port facilities. "*Financially*," he emphasizes, "and not with just a token but with substantial participation."

This attitude is not inconsistent with a forecast by Joseph Smucker, chairman of the Department of Sociology and Anthropology at Concordia University and author of an important text book, *Industrialization in Canada*. Born in Ohio and educated in the US, he says that, from a sociologist's point of view, Montreal is an ideal place to examine. "Labour will play," he says, "a much stronger role in Quebec than in English Canada or the US. It is far more articulate than elsewhere, and leadership has a better feel for political issues and realities such as the social-political consciousness of the people. The level of debate will be more sophisticated and sensitive, with far greater involvement in management's style and general planning. This may not eliminate conflict, and management may scream in the short run, but in the long run – that is, over the next ten to twenty years – the future looks bright."

There are some sad elements in the transition of Montreal. At one time, not long ago, one could cherish the unique kind of bilingualism that prevailed in billboards or signs. Where else in the world, for instance, could you have found "Notre Dame de Grâce Kosher Meat Market"? Now it is a graceless "Marché NDG Ltée." However, a majority of francophones, as well as anglophones, feel that the language law should be more flexible, especially on the question of store designations. That kind of attitude, reported in a survey published by *Le Devoir* four years after the introduction of Bill 101, represents the new self-confidence of francophones. It may be regarded as a good omen for future easing of onerous restraints on anglophone activity. Meanwhile, more and more prominent French-Canadian leaders share the opinion of Michel Bélanger, president and chief executive officer of Banque Nationale du Canada. He says to anglophones in Montreal: "Be very careful to remain an English-speaking community. Communicate in French, if possible. But keep English traditions and institutions such as universities, newspapers, hospitals – with an emphasis on quality. Don't submerge to the point where you'll be represented by elevator operators who speak only English. It is important to the future of Montreal that the English community remains vital and energetic, even if it is not big. As a French-only city, Montreal would have to go outside and find experts on how the English part of the world operates and thinks. This would be costly, both in morale and money."

Obviously, the lines are going to become fuzzy. One may predict that there will be no more Square Mile, no more distinct solitude. The borders of both anglophones and francophones are merging. To take one example: McGill University has ceased to be a finishing school for Westmount Wasps. Not many years ago, the late Sam Steinberg, the supermarket master, appealed to department heads of the Jewish General Hospital, of which he was president, to affiliate themselves with Université de Montréal rather than with McGill University. He perceived, not inappropriately, that francophones and Jews felt a rapport for one another while the Wasps lived in a cocoon of their own. He was turned down by the Jewish General physicians and surgeons, and, as time progressed, McGill became a university for all Montreal. Only 60 per cent of students are categorized as "anglophones," among them many Jews. Twenty per cent are francophones. (In addition to its English editions, the student newspaper, *The McGill Daily*, publishes once a week in French as *Le McGill Daily*.) The rest, from other parts of Canada, the US, and overseas, originate in a variety of ethnic backgrounds.

Two phenomena are observable simultaneously. French Canadians feel that at least they have attained the objective set out by Quebec governments since 1960: they have become masters in their own house. At the same time, after some flight in the 1970's, the majority of anglophones regard Montreal as their present and future home.

Certainly there is no real threat to the English language or to English-Canadian culture. Meanwhile, Montreal remains one of the most attractive cities in the world. In less than one hour, city-dwellers can drive into the lovely Laurentian mountains. Within ten-minute walking distance, residents of the central core, without fear, can find Argentina, Morocco, Vietnam, France, Italy, Japan, China – if their taste in food draws them to these countries – or to a score of other ethnic restaurants. Culture abounds in a variety of fine concerts; and there is theatre in two languages. At little or no cost, the individual can choose from the vast parkland of Mount Royal, the setting of Man and His World, the Olympic complex, and many other recreational and sports facilities. But these relatively superficial attributes are pushed aside in the bigger realization of what makes Montreal such an appealing city. It is the growing acceptance of two cultures working, not alongside, but with one another. It is participation in the real world where revolutionary change is commonplace, a not insignificant consideration in bringing up children. There is excitement and stimulation. And in Montreal, one can be part of that revolution without endangering oneself, without even getting one's feet wet.